SOCIOLOGY
OF HOME

SOCIOLOGY OF HOME

Belonging, Community, and Place in
the Canadian Context

Edited by Gillian Anderson,
Joseph G. Moore, and Laura Suski

Canadian Scholars' Press
Toronto

Sociology of Home: Belonging, Community, and Place in the Canadian Context
Edited by Gillian Anderson, Joseph G. Moore, and Laura Suski

First published in 2016 by
Canadian Scholars' Press Inc.
425 Adelaide Street West, Suite 200
Toronto, Ontario
M5V 3C1

www.cspi.org

Library and Archives Canada Cataloguing in Publication

Sociology of home : belonging, community, and place in
the Canadian context / edited by Joseph G. Moore, Gillian
Anderson, and Laura Suski.

Includes bibliographical references.
Issued in print and electronic formats.
ISBN 978-1-55130-939-2 (paperback).—ISBN 978-1-55130-940-8
(pdf).—ISBN 978-1-55130-941-5 (epub)

    1. Dwellings--Social aspects—Canada. 2. Canada--Social conditions. I. Anderson, Gillian, 1972-, editor II. Suski, Laura, 1968-, editor III. Moore, Joseph G., 1966-, author, editor

GT228.S62 2016   392.3'60971   C2016-905630-9
                                              C2016-905631-7

Text design and layout by Aldo Fierro
Cover design by Jennifer Stimson
Cover image by Rudmer Zwerver/Shutterstock.com

16   17   18   19   20   5   4   3   2   1

Printed and bound in Canada by Webcom

Canada

MIX
Paper from
responsible sources
FSC® C004071

TABLE OF CONTENTS

Acknowledgements

Initially conceived as a colloquium broadly centred on the theme of "home" hosted by the Department of Sociology at Vancouver Island University, our shared interest in the sociology of home has since led us to the creation of this collection. As a collaborative project, a number of individuals and organizations have supported and contributed to the success of this work and we wish to extend our personal thanks to all those who helped bring it to life.

We would like to acknowledge Vancouver Island University (VIU) and in particular the Vancouver Island University Research and Scholarly Activity Committee (VIURAC) for their generous research grant in support of our work.

Thank you also to all our authors for their research and scholarship and for offering readers a variety of experiences and analyses of home. It has been a pleasure to work together and we value the breadth of your contributions, which serve to enhance and strengthen the collection.

Natalie Garriga, developmental editor at Canadian Scholars' Press/Women's Press, we appreciate your patience and guidance in helping us navigate the process of manuscript preparation. In addition, we recognize the assistance of Laura Godsoe and the CSPI/Women's Press production and marketing teams.

We would like to thank the anonymous reviewers for providing positive feedback and constructive comments, and Meg Luxton for her encouraging words upon reading an early draft of our manuscript proposal.

A number of sociology of home sessions were held as part of the annual meetings of the Canadian Sociological Association, and we are thankful to the association for inclusion in their conference programs.

Thank you also to our two VIU student research assistants, Roseanna Sowten and Ryan Butler.

Given these collective efforts, it is our hope that this collection not only inspires thoughtful reflection on lived experiences of home and homemaking practices, but also furthers the development of a sociology of home in Canada.

INTRODUCTION

For a Sociology of Home in Canada

This collection began with a colloquium, the goal of which was to provide undergraduate students a taste of the diverse research and teaching interests of the three editors. What struck us afterwards was how the sociology of home not only captured a broad range of sociological practice but also wove together often disparate strands of this practice. The sociology of home gave us a vocabulary to explore the intersection of our teaching and research and a platform for collaboration. It allowed us see our work and our discipline through a new lens.

But it cannot yet be said that a sociology of home exists. What can be said is that much sociology is about home, that over the last few years home has become an organizing concept in the social sciences, and that sociologists are important contributors to this literature. Literature reviews, conferences, and journals have brought together geographers, anthropologists, and interdisciplinary feminist scholars, using home as a meeting place of diverse academic and political engagements. While inspired by this outburst of work and by the possibility of home to speak to a breadth of theoretical, methodological, and political perspectives, this collection takes a modest, disciplinary approach.

A SOCIOLOGY OF HOME AND A HOME FOR SOCIOLOGY

First, this is a collection of *sociological* readings, the majority of which are written by sociologists. This is a strategic intervention. Most directly we hope to nurture and encourage the sociological study of home. We believe that the sociological gaze has much to offer here and that Canadian sociology is particularly well positioned. The study of family, of urban and rural communities, of migration and immigration have rich sociological traditions to be drawn upon. The range of methodology and theory, which has often sparked intense debate within our discipline, becomes an asset for the study of a

1

phenomenon that is multiscalar, intensely personal, steeped in interpretation, and so evidently shaped by economic and political forces.

However, if sociology offers much to the study of home, the study of home might bring even more to the discipline of sociology. We believe that the sociology of home might provide an anchor of sorts for sociologists whose work, and often careers, are in the main conducted in interdisciplinary or simply other disciplinary spaces—in geography journals, in anthropology conferences, in women's studies departments. This is not a defensive manoeuvre, a circling of the wagons, as we would expect that a renewed sociological interest in the sociology of home might encourage a reversal of this flow of ideas, where the tribes of geographers, anthropologists, economists, and others will then find a space under sociological banners to study home.

A sociology of home might also help knit together areas of sociology that recently have developed rather independently. To speak of home, one must speak of the private and the public, of the emotional and the material, of the individual and the collective, of history, present, and future. A developed sociology of home would necessitate, and encourage, areas such as the sociology of emotion and sociology of space, which have received relatively scant attention in the discipline, and it would encourage the dialogue between materialist and interactionist/interpretive approaches.

Despite all of this promise, we must admit that there are significant impediments that must be overcome if the sociology of home is to become more central to the burgeoning interdisciplinary study of home, or indeed to the discipline of sociology itself.

We have just alluded to one of these obstacles: contemporary sociology has shied away from questions of natural or built environments, ceding this ground to geographers, anthropologists, and social historians. The reasons for this are multiple and beyond the scope of this introduction; however, we tend to agree with Murphy (1995) that the spectres of social Darwinism and biological determinism, and pragmatic attempts to carve out disciplinary specialization, have played their part. Of equal import, however, is the way that the study of home demands attention to questions of emotion, nostalgia, and intimacy, areas of study that the positivist bent of sociology has neglected. Also, the study of home takes us into difficult political territory. Post-911 homeland security in the United States and anti-immigrant rhetoric in much of Europe have imparted home with a reactionary flavour and equated the study of home with questions of nationhood. Closer to home, the pro-family rhetoric of conservative politicians and the role of private home ownership in neoliberal accumulation strategies may have pulled progressive sociologists away from direct consideration of homemaking strategies and more nuanced home politics. However central home may be to those individuals and societies that sociologists study, this terrain of walls and water, love and longing is uncomfortable for the discipline.

In spite of all this, there does exist a nascent sociology of home. Rooted in urban, rural, and environmental sociology, feminist political economy, and the critical sociological engagement with issues of social attachment and belonging, this sociology of home draws upon sociological tradition, crafts connections between established fields, and moves into new territory. Our goal here is to nurture this momentum, and we do so with an acknowledgement that our editorial decisions also shape this momentum. A few words on these choices are in order.

HOMES AS SPACES AND PLACES, IN CANADA, THROUGH A HUMANIST LENS

The chapters in this collection each, in some significant way, address home as constructed in both the material and the cultural sense. They speak of homes as structures, homes with walls, homes built upon, over, and under real earth. This is not to say that home as a cultural, and culturally contested, phenomenon gets lost along the way—indeed such matters are often the overwhelming focus. However, what does mark each of these chapters is a material mindfulness, the understanding that our constructions of home are in meaningful ways linked to actual physical constructions. The chapters both accept and question the distinction often made between space (material) and place (constructed). Mostly these authors speak of space as a necessary but insufficient condition of home. Individuals, families, and communities must provision spaces to make home places, and such provisioning remakes space (Fine, 2010). Here, spaces are inhabited, the physical limitations of space are negotiated and reworked, physically *and* culturally, rather than being overcome. This is true for both homemaking in intimate spaces, such as homes and apartments, and homemaking in public on street corners, pubs, and parks. Each of the chapters follows Gieryn's (2000) prescription for nonreductionist place-sensitive sociology as they each consider home as location, material form, and meaningfulness—in one bundled package.

This is also a Canadian collection. Here we buck an important trend, according to which anthologies on such interdisciplinary topics are increasingly international collections. Indeed, the only collection on the sociology of home that we know of is such an international survey (Kusenbach & Paulsen, 2013). There are of course important reasons for this. We live at a time when economic and political systems, cultural phenomena, and interpersonal networks are increasingly global. Though perhaps not sufficiently, sociology itself has globalized, and our teaching increasingly, and more accurately, reflects global contexts. And the topic of home, which is arguably an inevitable part of what it means to be human (Ingold, 2012), lends itself nicely to comparative study. Our choice to create a Canadian collection is not to deny any of this. Canadian experiences of home, from the time of Canada's settlement

4 Sociology of Home

by Europeans onward, have—often tragically—been shaped by international politics, global markets, world wars, imperialist struggle, and flows of immigration and emigration. Many of the chapters in this collection speak to this global context and its influence on Canadian experiences of home.

There are, however, compelling reasons for such a Canadian collection. Not the least of these is the fact that there is a spectacularly diverse set of cultural, political, built, and natural landscapes that ground Canadian experiences of home. The range of chapters that follow address this diversity, exploring multicultural, multinational, coastal, urban and rural, elite and working-class homes and homemaking, though it must be acknowledged that even a focused collection like this will inevitably fall short of capturing the breadth of these conflicting, contradictory, and varied experiences.

Somewhat paradoxically, our choice of a Canadian collection is led by a sense that the Canadian context of home is as unique as the Canadian experiences of home are diverse. The Canadian urban experience is uniquely mid-Atlantic, neatly reflecting neither the American pattern of sprawl and racialized urban cores nor the European pattern of dense urbanization and increasingly racialized working-class suburbs. Our rural landscapes and hinterland communities, suffering both population decline and resource-led booms, offer particular homemaking practices and experiences that are often at odds with or defined against those of the urban core(s)—but again in ways that are not neatly captured by either European or American models. Moreover, the postwar political economy of Canada, especially regarding gendered labour-market participation and neoliberal restructuring, positions Canada awkwardly. Though we will leave this for our closing remarks, we believe that the unique experiences of contemporary Canadian homemaking and home feeling offer important insights into what inclusive, socially and ecologically sustainable homemaking might look like.

Finally, this is a work of public and humanist sociology. The following chapters take on Duyvendak's (2011) challenge to create "an empathetic sociology that understands why people need to belong while showing the conditions under which they can peacefully do so" (p. 123). These chapters describe and analyze the difficulties faced by those engaged in homemaking practices; they, sometimes brutally, trace multiple crises of home, but they also celebrate relatively successful homemaking practice. While prescriptive action, implied or explicit, varies significantly, these chapters collectively and individually suggest that, despite the reactionary nature of many "home" politics in Canada and beyond, it is not a political option to dismiss these struggles.

In our conclusion we offer some preliminary speculation on what these chapters might collectively suggest to those engaged in progressive struggles for home. What can be said here is that each of the chapters can be read as part of a larger conversation about how home might provide for both individual agency and collective well-being. Each of these chapters has something to say about what inclusive homemaking practice might look and feel like. Though as editors our hand has been gentle, the writing reflects this intent. We have excluded abstract theoretical works and asked that each contribution be readable by a general audience familiar with the quirks of academic discourse. The subject of home, we believe, is too central to contemporary politics to leave solely to academics or, conversely, to be decided upon without consideration of academic voices.

THE LANDSCAPE OF THE SOCIOLOGY OF HOME

Defining the terrain of the sociology of home is an exercise in poetics and taxonomy, and it has become standard practice to introduce such collections with an extensive review of the literature that both frames and surveys the field. Readers interested in a comprehensive literature review of this type can look to other sources for useful surveys (see, for example, Kusenbach & Paulsen, 2013). Our goal in this introduction is more modest, in that we simply wish to signal some key debates, themes, and questions in the literature of home that inspire this collection.

There is a sociological tradition of equating home with a domestic "haven" separated from, and often a defence against, a "heartless" public sphere (Lasch, 1977), a distinction that has been mined with very different political implications (see, for example, Parsons & Bales, 1955; Hochschild, 1997). While historians and historical sociologists have demonstrated that such a distinction is relatively recent, intimately tied to changes in class and (re)productive structures, and less complete than often suggested, this distinction continues to have cultural resonance and consequence (Hall, 1992; Scott, 2009).

At the heart of this stream of home research is the contention that a relatively stable home is necessary for an individual's sense of self. From this vantage, homes are "article(s) of identity equipment," key elements of the situation within which identities are performed (Scott, 2009, p. 57) through homemaking projects of decoration and display (Hurdley, 2013). This does not imply that homemaking is simply a private performance, that there exists a firewall between home and political, cultural, and economic environments. Homemaking practices, even the most intimate or private, are said to reflect class position and aspiration, announcing not only which groups one might be a part of but those one rejects (Scott, 2009). Bourdieu (1984) and Douglas (1991) have been influential here, with Bourdieu's concept of *habitus* being widely employed. What makes homes special places for such performance, however, is the relative privacy they provide. Homes are said to have an element of the "backstage" (Goffman, 1956), which affords individuals greater control of their performances and a relative freedom from the constraints and expectations of more public spheres (Kusenbach & Paulsen, 2013; Saunders, 1989).

This raises the question, however, of what this all might mean when such privacy or backstage space is not available—or is a dangerous place. There now exists a rich line of inquiry into homemaking in difficult situations, whether it be for telecommuters faced with the intersection of work and "home" space (Johnson et al. 2006), those in institutions where privacy is intentionally or not limited (Wasterfors, 2013), or marginalized individuals whose homemaking practices occur in often very public spaces (Borchard, 2013; Robertson, 2012). The study of such circumstances foregrounds not only the hardships faced by those without enough home but also the agency employed in getting by when faced with such constraint.

Further problematizing the home as haven are those studies that squarely confront the home as a place of abuse or neglect, places where perpetrators are sheltered from the public sphere. Beyond the institutional settings mentioned above, private homes also are the principal setting for spousal abuse and the neglect and abuse of children. Feminist scholarship, meanwhile, has drawn attention to the isolating and alienating effects of a gendered division of labour in and outside the home, which has left women trapped in private spaces, engaged in routinized homemaking activity. The criticism of the postwar North American "orgy of homemaking" is an important moment in this critique, as is the study of the "escape" into paid labour that many women experienced during World War II (Klausen, 1998; Friedan, 1963; Pierson, 1986). As women's rate of participation in paid labour rose in the postwar period, the strain of the "Second Shift" of labour in the home became a critical focus. Most recently, the study of home in North America has acknowledged a "crisis" of home brought on by extended hours of paid work, stagnating wages, and the dismantling of welfare state supports—a crisis unequally borne by women (Anderson & Moore, 2014). This line of inquiry brings to the fore the extent to which homemaking projects are shaped by the political and economic forces and social struggles directly addressed in the third part of this book.

Identifying home as a haven (or hell) has allowed for a diverse range of empirical and theoretical inquiry, a body of work that takes seriously mundane homemaking activities and with empathy explores the deeply humane struggle to bring a small part of our environment under our control (Vachhni & Pullen, 2011). It also brings into relief the way that homemaking activities are shaped and constrained by social and cultural circumstance and the way such constraints weigh heavier on particular individuals and social groups. The study of the small things of homemaking makes clear that these "small things matter to large processes" (Fine, 2010, p. 361).

There are, however, limits, even risks, to centring this notion of home. Not the least of these is the naturalizing of a definition of home that is, as we have noted, historically and culturally specific. This line of inquiry does much to uncover microlevel agency in relatively private spaces and the macrolevel structures that shape this homemaking. Ideas and practices of home, however, are never fully captured by such relatively private and backstage places. When we leave our doorways and enter the street, have we left home behind? When we speak of hometowns and neighbourhoods, do we not also speak of home places?

Freeing the definition of home from its connection to intimate and private spaces suggests that we also experience home feelings and go about homemaking projects at the community level. Here we mean a specific sense of community, delineated to some extent by the grounds upon which we walk, bike, or drive. Our streets, our neighbourhoods, our towns, and even our cities are potential sites for home building and home feelings, *and* these sites are recreated through such home building. This is exciting and uncertain territory, bringing the sociology of home into debates about globalization, mobility, and place, questions of inclusion and exclusion, and into the more applied terrain of urban planning and social cohesion studies.

While it is common for many of us to speak meaningfully of hometowns and *our* neighbourhoods, it is equally clear that these towns, these neighbourhoods have undergone sometimes dramatic structural and cultural change in the postwar period. Prairie towns have disappeared, suburban sprawl has remade cities, creating vast tracts of new neighbourhoods that are structurally rather different than either the urban centre or traditional "streetcar suburbs" (Hayden, 2003), and urban and rural gentrification have reshaped long-established communities. Canada ranks only slightly behind the United States in residential mobility, with 41% of individuals having changed residences in a recent five-year period (Lockheed, 2008). Postwar immigration has shaped urban neighbourhoods and increasingly those of smaller communities. Popular and political discourses in Canada have echoed the more general North American anxiety over the loss of community.

The notion that feelings of home and homemaking projects require some attachment to a particular place, and that neighbourhoods are particularly appropriate places for these activities, is not a settled question in the literature. Indeed, sociologists and, more generally, social scientists have been skeptical of such claims. Duyvendak (2011) identifies skeptics as "universalists" who argue either that increased mobility is a liberator of possibility or that with increased mobility we either cannot or need not forge attachments to particular places (p. 12). Within this fold, Wellman, Carrington, and Hall (1988) have used Canadian data to suggest that community attachment now takes place largely through placeless social networking, rendering earlier forms of neighbourliness and community building obsolete. Springs and Allen (2005) go further in a critique of social-housing reform in Britain, arguing that "policy strategies to create stability are out of place in a world of movement" (p. 407). In a biting questioning of the political and disciplinary implications of this stance, Jasper (2000) has argued that it is grounded in the biography of academics who exist in and benefit from a rootless state, and who then have "suppressed any voices arguing for an allegiance to place" (p. 248).

This collection is not about to settle such matters. Instead, we question how and when it might be appropriate to make home by forging connections with others nearby one's place of residence—and how and why such attempts might be thwarted. Disadvantaged groups, including racialized immigrants and sexual minorities, have engaged in community/neighbourhood homemaking to establish places where they can lead public and semipublic lives—"heavenly" places, to use Duyvendak's terminology. And what happens when heaven becomes too heavenly? We must also question the limits of homemaking in communities and neighbourhoods by tracing the exclusionary practices upon which both gay villages and yuppy heavens can be built. If we are to take seriously the need for many to establish home in a neighbourhood community, we should explore how this might be accomplished in an inclusionary fashion. Exploring the possibility of concepts such as "elective belonging" (Savage et al., 2005), "trust amongst strangers" (Jacobs, 1992), and "the right to the city" (Lefebvre, 1968), the collection retains Sennett's (1992) wariness of the "repressive gemeinschaft" that can accompany the extension of home into public space, while also questioning those who would abandon any sense of home in community.

Three decades in, the neoliberal rebooting of Canadian economy and politics has impacted political and social policies and, in turn, homemaking in Canada. As Harvey (2005) argues, neoliberalism announces not only a restructuring of existing political and economic forms but also of "ways of life and thought, reproductive activities, attachments to the land and habits of the heart" (p. 3). While housing policy and markets have been remade in neoliberal form, so have homemaking practices and home feelings. To understand the neoliberal home, one must trace the effects of deregulation, mortgage-lending policies, the withering of welfare state provisions *and* altered familial relations, intensified consumer identities, and compressed experiences of time and space.

Feminist political economy (FPE) is useful for the unpacking of neoliberal politics of home. FPE has identified neoliberalism with twin processes of familialization, whereby social reproduction costs and responsibilities are shifted from the state onto families and into homes, and defamilialization, whereby family lives and homemaking practices are increasingly commodified. This is a world where "work becomes home and home becomes work" in a myriad of ways (Hochschild, 1997). By incorporating insights from urban theory and environmental sociology, a sociology of home can extend FPE's interest in how the home becomes a contested site for social reproduction and how homemaking practices are shaped by the power balance of state, market, and household (Bezanson & Luxton, 2006; Vosko, 2006).

In Canada, as elsewhere, the neoliberal period has seen dramatic shifts in where and how we experience home. There has been dramatic growth in major cities such as Toronto, Montreal, Calgary, and Vancouver. Each of these centres has become "unbound," according to Lorinc's (2006) terminology, marked by both sprawl and the transformation of bedroom suburbs into ethnically and racially diverse edge cities. It is also a period of escalating real-estate speculation and economic displacement in urban cores. While homes have become central sites for the intensified consumption that sustains neoliberal economies, at the same time economic inequality has increased through a polarization of those "over homed" and those "under homed," the latter including significant numbers of homeless. That the most significant crisis of the neoliberal period, the so-called Great Recession, was expressed in a large part in the United States as a housing crisis should not be surprising.

It is not by coincidence that social movement responses to neoliberal crisis have also been expressed, at least in part, as a politics of home. The Occupy movement saw thousands of protesters take up home in urban public spaces—a reaction to neoliberal crisis, for certain, but also a material expression of an alternative home politics (Jaleel, n.d.). More recently, in response to the threat of bitumen and natural-gas pipelines being built through traditional territories, some First Nations have commenced home building on pipeline routes (DePape & Darwish, 2014). Urban farming, alternative transportation, squatting, and degrowth movements each can be understood as intersecting responses to crises of home (Cattaneo & Gavaldàb, 2010). These responses trace political possibilities in a world where, as Harvey (2008) describes, "the planet as building site collides with the 'planet of slums,'" a place where ecological and social home politics intersect (p. 37).

THE STRUCTURE OF THIS BOOK

This collection is not intended as a comprehensive survey of the experience of home in Canada. Instead, it reflects what we feel are representative sociological arguments with a bias towards Canadian works of the materialist and humanist bent that we have described. We have divided the book into three parts and have provided introductions to each. Part 1 examines the interior experience of home and explores how the structures, design, and aesthetics of housing affect the meaning of home. Part 2 focuses on the struggles of homemaking and includes the voices of those who may be on the margins of home. Part 3 addresses the relationships between home and community, and takes up questions about how home is constructed by place and how home feelings extend beyond houses into neighbourhoods.

It would not be wrong to read into the three-part structure of this book a scalar structure: from the microlevel of personal homemaking to the meso-level of neighbourhood community, building to the macrolevel of political ecology. While intentional, this structure is more a matter of convenience than anything else. While each has its own bias, none of the readings settles too long on any single plane; each acknowledges, though often implicitly, that the most intimate of homemaking practices is shaped by the most macro of socio-economic forces, and that the political ecology of home is rebuilt through mundane microlevel experience. It is worth reiterating that the experience of home is not captured by any one of the scalar moments. It is telling that with a small change of emphasis most of these chapters would read nicely in any one of the others. Readers should, and undoubtedly do, feel free to bounce between parts. In so doing, one might even better capture the interplay between the experience of home as intimate accomplishment and socially conditioned experience.

We also hope, indeed fully expect, that in their encounters with these chapters readers are brought to reflect and act upon their own experiences of home. This may not be entirely comfortable. It certainly is not for the editors, and we can surmise this is also true of the contributors. This discomfort comes not only from personal sorrows attached to home but also from what Mills announced as the "terrible" lesson of sociology, that our homemaking and home feelings are as bound up in history as those we encounter in these pages (1959, p. 5). We anticipate, however, that, like us, readers will also take away the magnificent lesson of our discipline: that in engaging with our own homemaking practices and with those of others, we can strengthen and spread the possibility of home.

REFERENCES

Anderson, G. & Moore, J. G. (2014). "Doing it all ... and making it look easy!": Yummy mummies, mompreneurs and the North American neoliberal crises of the home. In M. Vandenbeld-Giles (Ed.), *Mothering in the Age of Neoliberalism* (pp. 95–115). Toronto: Demeter Press.

Bezanson, K. & Luxton, M. (2006). Introduction: Social reproduction and feminist political economy. In K. Bezanson & M. Luxton (Eds.), *Social Reproduction: Feminist Political Economy Challenges Neo-Liberalism* (pp. 3–10). Montreal: McGill-Queen's University Press.

Borchard, K. (2013). Homelessness and conceptions of home. In M. Kusenbach & K. E. Paulsen (Eds.), *Home: International Perspectives on Culture, Identity and Belonging* (pp. 113–134). New York: Peter Lang.

Bourdieu, P. (1984). *Distinction: A Social Critique of the Judgment of Taste*. Cambridge, MA: Harvard University Press.

Cattaneo, C. & Gavaldàb, M. (2010). The experience of urban squats in Collserola, Barcelona: What kind of degrowth? *Journal of Cleaner Production*, 18 (6), 581–589.

DePape, B. & Darwish. L. (2014, March 4). Momentum building against extreme energy and mining projects on West Coast. Retrieved from www.rabble.ca/blogs/bloggers/council-canadians/2014/03/momentum-building-against-extremeenergy-and-mining-project

Douglas, M. (1991). The idea of a home: A kind of space. *Social Research*, 58 (1), 287–308.

Duyvendak, J. W. (2011). *The Politics of Home: Belonging and Nostalgia in Western Europe and the United States.* New York: Palgrave Macmillan.

Fine, G. A. (2010). The sociology of the local: Action and its publics. *Sociological Theory*, 28 (4), 355–376.

Friedan, B. [1963] (2013). *The Feminine Mystique.* New York: W. W. Norton.

Gieryn, T. F. (2000). A space for place in sociology. *Annual Review of Sociology*, 26 (1), 463–496.

Goffman, E. (1956). *The Presentation of Self in Everyday Life.* New York: Doubleday.

Hall, C. (1992). *White, Male and Middle Class: Explorations in Feminism and History.* Malden, MA: Polity Press.

Harvey, D. (2005). *A Brief History of Neoliberalism.* New York: Oxford.

Harvey D. (2008). The right to the city. *New Left Review*, 53, (September/October), 23–40.

Hayden, D. (2003). *Building Suburbia: Green Fields and Urban Growth, 1820–2000.* New York: Pantheon Books.

Hochschild, A. R. (1997). *The Time Bind: When Work Becomes Home and Home Becomes Work.* New York: Metropolitan Books.

Hurdley, R. (2013). *Home, Materiality, Memory and Belonging: Keeping Culture.* New York: Palgrave Macmillan.

Ingold, T. (2012). Building, dwelling, living: How animals and people make themselves at home in the world. In C. Briganti & K. Mezei (Eds.), *The Domestic Space Reader* (pp. 31–34). Toronto: University of Toronto Press.

Jacobs, J. (1992). *The Death and Life of Great American Cities.* New York: Vintage Books.

Jaleel, R. (n.d.). *A Queer Home in the Midst of a Movement? Occupy Homes, Occupy Homemaking.* Retrieved from www.what-democracy-looks-like.com/a-queer-home-in-the-midst-of-a-movement-occupy-homes-occupy-homemaking/#sthash.PDBBzmBq.dpuf

Jasper, J. (2000). *Restless Nation: Starting Over in America.* Chicago: University of Chicago Press.

Johnson, L. C., Audrey, J. & Shaw, S. M. (2006). Mr. Dithers comes to dinner: Telework and the merging of women's work and home domains in Canada. In V. Shalla (Ed.), *Working in a Global Era: Canadian Perspectives* (pp. 301–325). Toronto: Canadian Scholars' Press Inc.

Klausen, S. (1998). The plywood girls: Women and gender ideology at the Port Alberni plywood plant, 1942–1991. *Labour / Le Travail*, 41 (1), 199–235.

Kusenbach, M. & Paulsen, K. E. (Eds.) (2013). *Home: International Perspectives on Culture, Identity and Belonging.* New York: Peter Lang.

Lasch, C. (1977). *Haven in a Heartless World: The Family Besieged.* New York: Basic Books.

Lefebvre, H. [1968] (2007). The right to the city. In G. Bridge & S. Watson (Eds.), *The Blackwell City Reader, Second Edition* (pp. 367–74). Malden, MA: Blackwell Publishing.

Lockheed, C. (2008). A moving story: How geographic mobility affects families. *Transition*, 38 (2), 36.

Lorinc, J. (2006). *The New City: How the Crisis of Canada's Cities Is Reshaping Our Nation.* Toronto: Penguin.

Mills, C. W. (1959). *The Sociological Imagination.* Oxford: Oxford University Press.

Murphy, R. (1995). Sociology as if nature did not matter: An ecological critique. *The British Journal of Sociology*, 46 (4), 688–707.

Parsons, T. & Bales, R. F. (1955). *Family, Socialization and Interaction Process.* Glencoe, IL: Free Press.

Pierson, R. R. (1986). *They're Still Women After All: The Second World War and Canadian Womanhood.* Toronto: McClelland & Stewart.

Robertson, L. (2012). Taming space: Drug use, HIV, and homemaking in downtown eastside Vancouver. In C. Briganti & K. Mezei (Eds.), *The Domestic Space Reader* (pp. 314–320). Toronto: University of Toronto Press.

Saunders, P. (1989). The meaning of "home" in contemporary English culture. *Housing Studies* 4 (3), 177–192.

Savage, M., Bagnall, G., & Longhurst, B. (2005). *Globalization and Belonging.* London: Sage Publications.

Scott, S. (2009). *Making Sense of Everyday Life.* Malden, MA: Polity Press.

Sennett, R. (1992). *The Fall of Public Man.* New York: Norton.

Sprigings, N. & Allen, C. (2005). The communities we are regaining but need to lose. *Community, Work & Family*, 8 (4), 389–411.

Vachhni, S. J. & Pullen, A. (2011). Home is where the heart is? Organizing women's work and domesticity at Christmas. *Organization*, 18 (6), 807–821.

Vosko, L. F. (2006). Crisis tendencies in social reproduction: The case of Ontario's early years plan. In K. Bezanson & M. Luxton (Eds.), *Social Reproduction: Feminist Political Economy Challenges Neo-Liberalism* (pp. 145–172). Montreal: McGill-Queen's University Press.

Wasterfors, D. (2013). Fragments of home in youth care institutions. In M. Kusenbach & K. E. Paulsen (Eds.), *Home: International Perspectives on Culture, Identity and Belonging* (pp. 113–134). New York: Peter Lang.

Wellman, B., Carrington, P. J., & Hall, A. (1988). Networks as personal communities. In B. Wellman & S. D. Berkowitz (Eds.), *Social Structures: A Network Approach* (pp. 130–184) Cambridge, UK: Cambridge University Press.

PART ONE
Home as Domestic Space

One need not look past the magazines at the grocery-store checkout to note that homes have become a key vehicle for lifestyle consumption. The makeover boom ushered in by reality television solidified the notion that better homes lead to better, happier lives. The material consumption of home makes the claim that consumption is the magic that transforms a house into a home. In media such as online blogs we get to peek inside people's homes, and we are encouraged to seek out our own interior transformations. We might envision our home interiors as sanctuaries of individual taste, or we might seek to have our homes speak a common language of builder's beige. In either case, the interior of our homes is a kind of enchanted space, whereby a material world can be cast with home feelings. What should we make of the demands for interior transformation of home? What does a home say about the people who occupy it? What if an interior experience of home is limiting rather than transformative? How does a space become a domestic space?

All of the chapters in this section explore the domestic and interior experiences of home and ask important questions about the possible relationships between houses and homes. These chapters enrich the material analysis of home by speaking to home objects. The authors suggest that we must look at aspects of houses such as walls, building codes, and collected objects to explore how people live in homes. As discussed in the next section of the collection, not all Canadians achieve a connection between house and home, and many do not have basic shelter. While the chapters in this section discuss people who are housed, they also speak to the ways in which home feelings can be manipulated, disciplined, or absent. Alan O'Connor, for example, discusses how condominium living in Toronto may be far from the lifestyle promises of the accompanying marketing and advertising campaigns. Some condo dwellers may experience their home as a kind of broken promise, and in this sense, their interior experience of home becomes a site of stress and disappointment.

The larger theme of the public nature of home is also relevant to the discussion of the private experience of home. Each of the chapters reflects on the question of how home interiors connect to neighbourhoods and communities and problematize the inside/outside distinction between private homes and public lives. While they address home dwellers as subject to power structures like colonialism and neoliberalism, they ask readers to think about home dwellers as creative and agent homemakers. The chapters also push the question of whether the claim that home is a private refuge is a problematic one, and ask readers to think about how our interior experiences of home speak to public citizenships.

The first chapter in this section offers a portrait of diverse experiences of domestic interiors in Vancouver. Kathy Mezei and her coauthors discuss how home interiors provide pathways to citizenship, social relations, and psychological interiority. On these terms, domestic interiority is an engaged process of living and never very far from the collective experience of social life. The seven contributors met in each other's homes once a month and offered observations both on how their own homes spoke to them and on their experiences of their fellow contributors' homes. The reflections on home are diverse and particular to each person. One contributor sees a kind of horror in the detached house that contains rooms that seem "hidden" and provides a kind of self-exile to the dweller. Another speaks to how a house can be honoured by what is collected within it. By discussing the travels between homes, the objects in homes, and the design of homes, the contributors let homes speak and reveal that sometimes homes speak on their own terms, and sometimes homes are subject to imposed narratives of power. The chapter demonstrates the deeply subjective nature of the experience of home.

In the next chapter, Lisa-Jo K. van den Scott offers an interesting exploration of the introduction of permanent walled housing in the non-Western context of the Inuit of Arviat, Nunavut. She argues that we must see walls as a form of "mundane technology" and as material objects that demand further sociological investigation, particularly in terms of power relations and normative implications. Van den Scott demonstrates how *Arviammiut* exhibit reflexivity in their relationship with walls and that they have both passive and active engagements with this mundane technology. She argues that walls are not simply a cultural imposition but are used by the Inuit in creative and useful ways, such as a tool for storage of such diverse items as certificates to pin cushions. Her research demonstrates that if we are to understand the full scope of the materiality of our homes, we need to think carefully and deeply about seemingly banal technologies so that we can uncover the dynamics of homogeneity and cultural diversity "woven into the fabric of our lives."

In the third chapter, Alan O'Connor follows Bourdieu's earlier forays into the analysis of housing in his classic work *Distinction*. O'Connor offers some preliminary reflections from a larger research interest in the recent condominium boom in Toronto. In this chapter, he explores the promise of highly glamourized, potentially sexualized, social exchanges offered by promoters of condominium living. He discusses the fact that many condos are not designed for social exchanges, as they lack shared living spaces, like laundry rooms. Moreover, poor building codes and construction standards often lead to inadequate noise protections. He notes that a condo dweller's first encounter with a neighbour may likely be a noise complaint. While the glossy advertising promises a certain "condo lifestyle," O'Connor concludes that individual condo buyers have little power or control to enact this dream.

Part 1 concludes with Ondine Park's exploration of the works of some Canadian visual artists who have confronted and reflected upon our increasing suburban landscapes. She grounds her analysis in the claim that homes, including suburbs, are ongoing social productions defined and conditioned by materiality. In this chapter, she also emphasizes the ways in which "immaterialities" also contribute to the making of home. Our expectations and hopes for suburban living, she notes, are deeply marked by the "suburban imaginary." The suburb also requires attention to the relationship between exteriors and interiors. Park notes that contemporary visual art often sees the suburban exterior as ugly and repetitive, even as a "non-place," and in turn, it is the suburban interior that gets marked as a "home." Park engages selected artists' works alongside classic philosophical and political debates about the dialectical relationship between home as an expression of and as a producer of individual identity. Her work encourages us to think carefully about how conceptions of home interiors, and suburban interiors in particular, can produce a "spatialization of individuals," whereby the interior is a *retreat* into a kind of privacy that is depoliticized and asocial.

CHAPTER 1

LIVING THE DOMESTIC INTERIOR: SEVEN CHARACTERS IN SEARCH OF HOME IN VANCOUVER, 2008–2010

Kathy Mezei, with Margaret Archibald, Patrick Chan, Emily Fedoruk, Kay Higgins, Fran Moore, and Jillian Povarchook

This project concerns a journey undertaken by seven characters, from 2008 to 2010, through the domestic spaces of Vancouver, a postmodern pastiche city in the process of globalization, a city and a globalization marked by edginess.[1] For Vancouver is a city on the edge of Canada, edgy in literature, architecture, art, and photography, and edging to accommodate its hugely diverse and increasing population in a limited physical space and an overheated housing market. As Charles Demers (2009) wryly noted in his pre-Olympics publication, *Vancouver Special*: "Vancouver is at a crossroads in its history—host of the 2010 Winter Olympics and home to the poorest neighbourhood in Canada; a young, multicultural city with a vibrant surface and a violent undercoat; a savvy urban centre with an inferiority complex" (backcover blurb). We seven embarked on a journey to map, textualize, collect, and live domestic spaces across the city, generations, and experiences, hoping—out of our own experiences and readings—to generate a domestic discourse that encompasses the practical, the theoretical, the civic, and the private. The object of our study was to model our own living spaces as a kind of imagined street in Vancouver and to consider the ways in which young people, artists, and retirees are responding to and changing the interiority of Vancouver through their living arrangements, movements, and networking. Although the architecture and built spaces of Vancouver—in particular the renowned buildings of Arthur Erickson (Simon Fraser University, the Law Courts, the Museum of Anthropology, and many private residences)—have received serious critical attention,[2] there has been, in contrast to the United Kingdom and Australia, until now relatively minimal discourse about Vancouver's domestic interiors and their affects.[3] In response to this deficiency, our project attempted to demonstrate the relevance and significance of engaging in discourses about local domestic spaces. As Alison Lurie (2014) pointed out in *The Language of Houses*, "A building is an inanimate object, but it is not an inarticulate one. Even the simplest house always makes a statement … architecture is a kind of language … that all of us hear" (p. 3). We have tried to listen to our interior spaces as they spoke to us.

FIGURE 1.1: MAP OF VANCOUVER AND SUBURBS

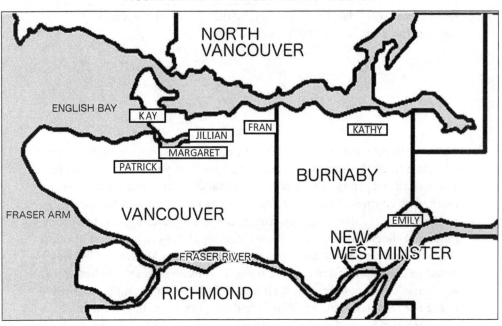

Source: Designed by Ria Kawaguchi, adapted from www.greatervancouverparks.com/
LowerMainlandMap.gif

Ranging in age from 23 to 62, in occupations of student, designer, literary scholar, public servant, arts consultant, social worker, and living in spaces varying from a postmodern apartment in a seedy downtown area in the process of gentrification to a leafy suburban street of heritage houses, our multidisciplinary study group formed a collectivity and a collection in the Benjaminian sense of keeping objects (Benjamin, 1969). To us, the process of collecting was as significant as the collection itself (Benjamin, 1969, p. 60). Although the collection of domesticities we represented was a narrow one, there was still diversity. We are settled, and we are transient. We have arrived, and we are becoming. Some have downsized. We live with parents, with partners, and alone. There are lovers and children who join us as occasional residents. We use our homes as "sleeping platforms and as offices" (Margaret).[4] "What we are producing (as a collectivity) is a collection in a literary sense, but also a material practice" (Emily).

GOALS AND METHODS

Our goal was to "show how an engagement with the domestic may lead to the formation of a map and a discourse that can help us better elaborate citizenship" (Pat). We understood citizenship in the sense of shared space, a kind of being together as a basis of common projects and the exercise of collective power (Gandesha, n.d.). Part of a larger research enterprise on "imagining citizenship," explored through study groups in religion, social justice, the environment, modernity, and media arts at the Institute for the Humanities at Simon Fraser University in Vancouver and initiated in 2008, our research group on domestic space felt that citizenship begins at home, at the level of the local, and in intimate relationships and spaces. We explored the "link between inner mind and inner dwelling," recognizing that the concept of interiority encompasses the material, psychological, and figurative, and also represents a "mental structure constructed over time, with inner chambers and inner walls" (Fuss, 2004, pp. 1, 7). In the arrangement and ambience of gardens, decks, rooms, neighbourhoods, and objects reside the detritus of our everyday lives (Fuss, 2004, pp. 1–21); these are the paths to our social relations, our citizenship, our interiority, our sense of belonging and well-being. As Daniel Miller observes in *The Comfort of Things*, "What was once the creation of societies is now in part accomplished at a domestic level under the auspices of effective, but distant state levels" (2008, p. 207). Yet we were aware that the design and impact of the private sphere upon social behaviour in our city has not been a subject of much inquiry, except in literature, such as in the novels of Ethel Wilson, Audrey Thomas, Wayson Choy, Timothy Taylor, and Daphne Marlatt.[5]

Our method responded to Henri Lefebvre's (1991) concepts of spatial practice (perceived), representations of space (conceived), and representational spaces (lived) (pp. 33, 38–39) in that each time we met we were *living* directly—travelling, visiting, eating, conversing in someone's home, rather than merely discussing or seminaring in an academic sense and in an institutional environment and thus only "passively" experiencing our lived spaces (p. 39). Our practice was to gather once a month at one of our homes. The host prepared a meal and outlined the history of his/her domestic space and neighbourhood; we then explored and discussed the space, as well as one or two assigned theoretical readings on some aspect of domestic space (see, for example, references). Some time after, we all sent posts to our private domestic-space blog, relaying and textualizing our experiences of the domestic space and reflecting on what we learned during this lived and living experience. We were conscious of the distinction between experiencing and then representing lived space through words and visual media, and in our writing tried to textualize the experience so that it resonated with immediacy—then and now. We investigated how writing (including the visual, performance, and textual arts) impacted the triangulation of subjectival interiority, the architectural interior, and the city (Pat). At the same time, we honed our skills of observation—by observing spaces, ourselves, and each other through a process of mapping and touring, of seeing and acting.[6]

We asked ourselves: how do we look at a building, and what is the relationship between looking and writing? That is, we did not see ourselves as domestic ethnographers but rather as domestic voyeurs or "home invaders," who enter in to tour, observe, and then recreate the immediacy of those lived spaces through our words (textualizing). With our backgrounds across many disciplines, we contributed specialized knowledge and standpoints: social work, history, heritage sites, architectural and design theory, literary texts and theory, the contemporary art scene, contemporary poetics, interior design practice. And, unlike design magazines, we were interested in human subjects and relations. In particular, we wanted to map the interiority of the subject in relation to interior space. As part of the project of exploring how this city sometimes acknowledges—or more often occludes—domestic interiors (there are only two university departments dedicated to the study of interior design in Canada), we also visited and participated in representations of Vancouver domestic spaces, such as exhibits, heritage houses, and conferences. As domestic missionaries, we organized conferences and exhibits.[7]

EMERGING MOTIFS

Certain recurring motifs emerged out of our visits, discussions, and subsequent posts; out of these recurring, somewhat obsessive motifs, a pattern emerged that could begin to constitute a domestic discourse shaped by Vancouver on the edge. For example, Kay's post on Fran's house (an early twentieth-century house on a quiet suburban street in East Vancouver) posed important questions: How do we attach meanings to buildings, how do we interpret interpretations and theories, and can we attain knowledge through a Bachelardian dream state?

1. Kay on Fran's House, May 2008

FIGURE 1.2: FRAN'S HOUSE

Source: Photo by Kathy Mezei

It's tempting to look at a building, or any physical object, but a building in particular in this case, and attempt to extract meanings from its shape, its colour, and other ways in which it engages the senses, as if those meanings were somehow intrinsic. Or, in the place of presumed absolute meanings, you could use Ideas from Important Thinkers, and wrap those ideas around some aspect of the building. Or, attach meanings based upon the aesthetic judgements (and attendant keywords) of Arbiters of Good Taste. There is a more mysterious approach, even: to enter the object as if it were a dream, and to try to capture what appears as knowledge in the dream state and bring it into the realm of language.

The "intrinsic" isn't really, and I think that is generally accepted. The observer is speaking from a particular set of expectations and experiences, in ways that are not always obvious. Uncovering the origin of a turn of interpretation can sometimes be illuminating, and sometimes tedious. Adopting that interpretation when your own position does not support it can be paralysing, or it can lead to unexpected leaps of understanding. This is also true of basing an interpretation on an authoritative (or even just trendy) work of theory. Without some examination of the relationship between the theorist's position and your own position, a pre-emption of real understanding can occur; but careful examination of the theorist's relationship to your own time and place (since Important Thought almost always appears as something foreign [but not too foreign]) can destroy the spell cast by the theorist's influence if it is not done with the proper reverence. We could turn to the writers of "house porn," who are often immensely clever, and like fashion writers are capable of constructing provisional systems of meaning in the blink of an eye, or maybe more appropriately, the twitch of a curtain. From them we can learn that an arrangement of cushions shows enormous wit and charm, or that a set of vertical surfaces intend to oppress us—items in a household not only convey meaning, but have intentions of their own.

These are other people's dreams, though, and dreams whose interpretation is highly determined by cultural assumptions, or the politics of academia, or the necessity to attract the proper readers to a magazine. (Kay)

Kay, an apartment dweller in Vancouver's crowded West End, then reflected more specifically on her experience of Fran's house, and through her turns of phrase, her textualizing of her reactions, created the immediacy of a "lived experience":

A house is not a painting or a photograph. It is more than a set of surfaces, so to some extent you would have to disregard what you see, and use other senses and other evidence to uncover what is beyond the surface. Beams creak and settle in response to movement, heat and cold, and other kinds of stress. Other sounds come from the physical and organic processes of the house. What I notice here is quiet. Without the sounds of traffic, and neighbours, and strangers in the street, I am disoriented. Rather than living inside a machine criss-crossed by humming pipes and wires, here I am inside of a box that clicks softly as beams and joists slide against each other.

There is a real division from the street here, and from neighbours: windows do not face other windows, crowds of passers-by do not stare at the front window trying to discern what is there. The entrance, and these windows, are separated by height from the ground the house rests on.

The geometry seems odd, different inside than out. One horror of the detached house is the mysterious hidden room, likewise spaces in the walls or attic or under the floorboards, or storage closets in the basement, where a previously unknown space can be revealed, containing what the surface denies is there. As a devotee of a particular type of horror film, I am highly disposed to see more, rather than less, potential for evil lurking in idyllic circumstances than in the more common reality of half-damaged existence. When a serial killer is arrested, don't the neighbours describe him as "normal," or even "nice" and "quiet" (although in retrospect, perhaps he "kept to himself" a bit too much)?

The early twentieth-century house, however, is not a perfect machine for incarceration, or even for the unquestioned exercise of authority. It is permeable to some extent by sound, by light and air, and by various forms of communication technologies. It is available as a vessel for oppression, but is not oppression itself. More than incarceration, it is either a place of sanctuary, or of self-exile. Sanctuary is largely symbolic, governed by a set of rules that vary from time to time and place to place. It is a matter of drawing a line around the space in which you find yourself, and having that line accepted by others. It is also a matter of determining who else will be granted sanctuary in that place, and under what terms. Shoeless, possibly. Bearing small gifts, possibly. Understanding that there are limits to the indulgence of their curiosity and exploration, quite likely. The place has to be prepared. Items commonly used, stored away. Stores of special provisions laid in. Spaces within the space prepared. The entrance prepared, and paths cleared for intended series of movements. If possible, all of this without the appearance of self-consciousness. (Kay)

In response to Kay's and the rest of the group's posts on her house and their comments on how the house reflects Fran herself, Fran pursued the relationship between space and subjectivity.

2. Fran's Response, June 2008

I've been pondering on the subjectivity of home—when does a house become home, what makes a house a home?

This place feels like home to me. I recognized it as home the moment my co-worker told me she was selling, and it has become even more so with each passing year. It is small, reminiscent of the home I was born into, and it is in a multi-cultural neighbourhood. Having grown up in small town Quebec, I am more at home in neighbourhoods where the dominant culture is "other."

But I'm not sure that those things are sufficient to make this "home." De Botton [Alain de Botton, The Architecture of Happiness] ponders on how sadness might be a requisite for relating to architecture. That may well be true. I think that at sixty years old, I am at a stage in my life where I am ready to claim "my home," where I am ready to "be home." More than at any other stage in my life, it is important for my home to reflect me, my personality, my idealized self. And this home fits with my sense of myself.

Whereas at other stages of my life, I made a home for my family to feel comfortable in, this house feels comfortable to me. Each piece of furniture, each picture tells a story. Either it was given to us by someone who made it, or we bought it at a particular place in our lives. I am surrounded, therefore, by my life.

We have made improvements in the house in keeping, we think, with what the house deserves. We have tried to honour the house. And this is because we feel the house is honouring us. It mirrors back our sense of ourselves and our place in society. We are of a certain age, we have worked in the health sector and have been active in unions, we both come from the working class, but have been educated into the middle class. This neighbourhood reflects all of that and so does this house. (Fran)

Fran also addressed the issue of how one relates the concept and experience of domestic space to the concept of citizenship, suggesting that by investigating domestic space, we expand and elaborate the meaning of citizenship:

This brings me to the second question I've been thinking about—does one's "home" enhance a sense of citizenship in the resident? And does this mean that one is less of a citizen if one does not have a home? While I emphatically do not think that citizenship should only be conferred on those with homes, I do wonder about the effect of place on one's sense of obligations and responsibilities to others. If I am happy in my home, will this make me more compassionate to my fellow human beings? Or does it do the opposite? Does "home" affect this at all? Also, if one is at home in one's neighbourhood, is it more likely that he or she will invest in the neighbourhood, the city, the country than one who feels "not at home"? (Fran)

In these posts, Fran and Kay explore the "link between inner mind and inner dwelling"; they draw attention to how the house (and home) reflect and enable one's subjectivity, noting changes in time and circumstance, the "mental structure constructed over time" (Fuss, 2004, pp. 1, 7). Fran zeroes in on her home as an example of the creation of society on a domestic level (Miller, 2008, p. 207); Kay compellingly argues that we should look to our own subjectivities and our experience of Bachelardian dream states rather than to authority and theory in assigning meaning to spaces.

In her post on Margaret's home, a two-bedroom apartment in Central Vancouver, Jillian explores the increasingly porous relationship between private and public spheres.

3. Jillian on Margaret's Home, March 2009

FIGURE 1.3: MARGARET'S HOUSE

Source: Photo by Margaret Archibald

More than anything, our visit to Margaret's home made me think about walking and the time we spend between domestic spaces. I had to hustle to Margaret's, willingly crossing the east/west boundary, something I rarely do unless on my way to work. I was not hustling too hard, however, to think about two things:

1. How accommodating Vancouver is that in the middle of February I can walk 5.8 km, in fairly stiff oxfords, and not be overcome with frostbite or other such maladies that are symptoms of the shared Canadian winter experience.
2. How the act of walking, whether with a purpose or not, is an extension of our domestic spaces, particularly for those of us housed in small, urban spaces.

Despite my unfamiliarity with the streets and houses west of Ontario St., I felt at home walking, laying a certain kind of ownership on the cracked sidewalks as I moved along, looking in the lit windows of old bungalows and the grandfather houses that tower above them. Lamp posts and rusty mail boxes are just as comforting as the wood and fabric with which we furnish our houses, the sidewalks and bike paths just as important as the foundations into which we pour our memories and collections.

I can't remember the exact phrase Margaret used, but she affirmed my thoughts when she mentioned how, because of their location, everything is accessible on foot. Mail, doctor, grocery, coffee … It seems as though when you give up a certain amount of square footage in your dwelling, the areas immediately surrounding you become a part of your domestic space. And, the act of traversing these otherwise unknown city plains becomes part of domesticity, or the domestic ritual.

As much as we become part of the city through walking, we in turn pull the city, neighbourhood, or even just our block into our home. Much as a glass of wine at the end of the day makes eight hours in front of a computer bearable, walking makes a life partially spent in 600 square feet bearable, or at least convenient. (Jillian)

The idea of home and citizenship and self is enhanced by walking or by what Virginia Woolf (1993) called "street haunting" in her essay "Street Haunting: A London Adventure." When Woolf concludes her excursion through her immediate London neighbourhood and returns to her "usual door" and the security of "old possessions" and "old prejudices" (p. 80), her "self," which has been blown about during her street haunting, will be safely and warmly sheltered and enclosed. In her street haunting through the streets of Vancouver, Jillian as *flâneur* similarly reflects on the elasticity of domestic space, the porous boundaries and fluid exchanges between the public space of the street and the private domain of the dwelling place; for her, walking becomes an extension of domestic space.

FIGURE 1.4: JILLIAN'S HOUSE

Source: Photo by Kathy Mezei

INTERIORITY, THINGS, AND THE PRIVATE/PUBLIC DIVIDE

From these and other responses and our ongoing discussions, the emerging domestic discourse seemed to emphasize the following motifs:

1. *Interiority*: In the context of globalization of economies and cultures, it is all the more vital to experience the urban environment from the inside, not merely to observe from the outside (Smith, 2006). Thus, as domestic voyeurs and home invaders, we peered into drawers, closets, cupboards, and bathrooms, and asked probing and personal questions of our hosts. The interior spaces of our homes then revealed our own interiority, subjectivity, performance of self, even as we may seek to hide or mask those selves. As Gaston Bachelard (1994) famously said, "The house image would appear to become the topography of our intimate being" (p. xxxii). For it is here in these lived spaces where the roots of our citizenship lie, whether projected inward to our families or outward to our communities. We learned that Fran's house, carefully and lovingly decorated, represents her ideal self (Fran), and that Pat is a global, mobile citizen, ready to up and move at the whim of a position, whose domestic interior here in Vancouver central transnationally mirrored his office as a graduate student in Melbourne. Pat recognized this about himself during the conversation and exploration of his apartment. But we have also reminded ourselves how our homes, our behaviour, and our interactions with our domestic interiors are subject to strategies of control and discipline (Deleuze, 1991), about which—especially in this age of mass globalized communication, marketing, and consumerism—many are surely oblivious.

2. *Things*: We learned about thingness and objects, how they mirror and shape relationships, are infused with meaning and history, inhabit domestic interiors sometimes in unexpected ways, and how they reveal our interior selves. We began to understand the vital and underlying connections between belonging and belongings. As Daniel Miller (2008) concluded in his study of households on a street in south London, "Material objects are viewed as an integral and inseparable aspect of all relationships. People exist for us in and through their material presence" (p. 286). Objects spoke to us in the sense that Alain de Botton quoting Ruskin meant when he noted that we want our buildings to shelter us, but also to speak to us—"to speak to us of whatever we find important and need to be reminded of" (as cited in 2006, p. 62). And so in our domestic visitations, we paused to observe Jillian's arrangement of books by colour, the rotation and placement of Kay's partner's paintings on the white walls, the light cast by Kathy's lamp in the kitchen. We tried to understand how people relate—or don't—to their objects as a first step to understanding larger networks and contexts of human interactions and communications. We tried to unpack the individual and diverse systems of objects (Baudrillard, 1996) we encountered and the significance and trajectory of their traces. We puzzled over and related to each other through the objects in our domestic interiors and to the host's relationship with those objects. We also thought about bodies and movement in these spaces, how family members in Emily's house meet or avoid each other on the narrow twisting staircase from the kitchen to the bedrooms, how Kay manoeuvres in her tiny galley kitchen.

3. *Public and Private*: Not surprisingly, our most persistently debated subject revolved around the public/private axis: "Not one of us is burrowed into our interior space. All of us are active in the public realm. I struggle with the distinction between public and private realm. I have a better understanding of public space. My sense of being shaped by open spaces is stronger than my appreciation of interiors" (Margaret).

Some of our lived spaces were small, even cramped, initiating discussion about privacy—what it constitutes, how important it is, how differently it is experienced. Both Kay and Pat, who lived in one-bedroom apartments, opened their front doors to communal hallways, and in Kay's case to a sudden flood of light and sky and a large plant-laden, furnished outside deck with a view over the Pacific Ocean. This blurring of private and public was perceived by some as a way of opening the self to the community and inviting the community inside. Others perceived such exposure as an invasion of privacy, of exposing the self to public view. We recognized that as citizens and domestic missionaries we must step out into the public, but we are also protective of our privacy, even during our group visits.

FIGURE 1.5: EMILY'S STAIRCASE

Source: Photo by Kathy Mezei

Not only doors but also windows function to blur the inside and outside. Windows in apartments and houses frame views of gardens, streets, mountains, and water, yet also stage and illuminate the interior for the passerby, the apartment dweller across the way, the inquisitive neighbour (Colomina, 1998, pp. 282–311). Sounds and smells trespass into the privacy of our homes, carrying with them reminders of other lives.

How do our bodies as private spaces resemble or contort themselves to the different levels of domestic privacy—in the detached home, in a high-rise, in a three-storey walk-up apartment? We seven are all city walkers, extending our domestic spaces into the public sphere, into our offices, coffee shops, the street, and appropriating this city's magnificent view corridors for ourselves. Yet the public also enters the home and our own interiorities through texts and words, in that we bring public and academic discourse into our private spaces, thus surrounding, unpacking, and investing our objects and domestic interiors with interpretations and critiques. As Kay reflected in her post, we need to be aware of the origins and effects/affects of these interpretations and critiques.

CONCLUSION

As a group of home invaders and domestic voyeurs, we have, through the process of observing, touring, and mapping our lived and living experiences, begun to "unpack" why and how the image of the "house is the topography of our intimate being" (Bachelard, 1994, p. xxxvi). Through multi-faceted representations of our spaces in writing, conversation, and papers, like this one you are now reading, we sought (as a group) to generate a domestic discourse that foregrounds the intersection of home and citizenship.

Our Group of Seven, like a house, is always under continuous construction and renovation; we have moved in and out of various rooms, apartments, houses, with some leaving the city. Since we embarked on our project, the idea of home and citizenship in this city has been thrown into even sharper relief and is being dramatically contested. Facing an ongoing dilemma in the numbers of homeless and destitute people, many of them moving here from other parts of Canada, Vancouver must also confront the contradiction and challenge of the exorbitant and still rising cost of real estate. Our housing prices now rank among the highest in the world. Given disruptive climate change and expanding war zones, thousands of refugees and migrants will seek to make Vancouver their home. In light of these dilemmas and the complicated presence of "guests," "foreigners," and "others" both within and from outside this city, how will Vancouver negotiate the laws and ethics of hospitality? As Jacques Derrida (2000) mused: "What does that mean ... if, for the invited guest as much as for the visitor, the crossing of the threshold always remains a transgressive step?" (p. 75). How then will hosts and "guests" position themselves, interact and live with each other, and navigate the codes of our civil society? Under such evolving and complex conditions, how will these diverse groups embark on their journeys to the domestic interior?

NOTES

1. I wish to thank and acknowledge warmly the participants in this project: Margaret Archibald, Patrick Chan, Emily Fedoruk, Kay Higgins, Fran Moore, and Jillian Povarchook. Dr. Chiara Briganti has been my partner in researching the domestic for over 20 years and has inspired some of the ideas here. I also wish to thank Mark Taylor and Gini Lee for permission to publish a revised version of this paper, originally appearing as Mezei (2010). Proceedings of the IDEA Symposium, *Interior Spaces in Other Places*, Brisbane, Queensland University of Technology, 2010; www.idea-edu.com/symposiums/2010-interior-space-in-other-places/.

2. For example, Douglas Coupland (1995); Lance Berelowitz (2005); Paul Delany (1994).

3. Domestic interiors, however, have been the subject of numerous works and installations by visual artists in Vancouver, for example, the exhibit *Ought Apartments* (2009) by Reece Terris, which reconstructed North American domestic interiors from the 1950s to the future at the Vancouver Art Gallery; Song Dong's *Waste Not* (2010–2011), exhibiting the contents of his mother's house; and the *Poetics of Space* exhibit (2015), also at the Vancouver Art Gallery, with photographs and paintings by internationally renowned photo-conceptual artists such as Jeff Wall, Stan Douglas, and Ian Wallace. Two exhibits, *Windows* (2009) and *Mongrel Histories* (2014), were mounted at the Republic Gallery by Gwenessa Lam. Peter Dickinson's play *The Objecthood of Chairs* presented the romance of two men through Western culture's romance with chairs (September, 2010, Woodward's, Studio T).

4. Comments by participants in the project are drawn from their posts to our private domestic space blog; attribution is indicated by names in parentheses following the comment.

5. See also the special issue of *BC Studies* 140 (2003) on domestic spaces in Vancouver.

6. Making a distinction between stories that are tours and maps, between acting and seeing, Michel de Certeau explains that "in narrations concerning apartments or streets, manipulation of space or 'tours' are dominant. This form of description usually determines the whole style of the narration" (1984, p. 119).

7. Pat Chan organized the "Showroom Symposium: A Discussion on Making Vancouver," at which Kathy and Emily presented papers (June, 2008); Kay has given presentations on the "Vancouver Special," a uniquely Vancouver home mass produced in the 1970s and 1980s, created a website, www.vancouverspecial.com, and published a monograph, *Higgins* (2010).

REFERENCES

Bachelard, G. (1994). *The Poetics of Space*. Boston: Beacon Press.

Baudrillard, J. (1996). *The System of Objects*. (J. Benedict, Trans.). London & New York: Verso.

Benjamin, W. (1969). Unpacking my library. *Illuminations*. (H. Zohn, Trans.). New York: Schocken.

Berelowitz, L. 2005. *Dream City: Vancouver and the Global Imagination*. Vancouver: Douglas & McIntyre.

Colomina, B. (1998). *Privacy and Publicity: Modern Architecture as Mass Media*. Cambridge, MA: MIT Press.

Coupland, D. (1995). *City of Glass*. Vancouver: Douglas & McIntyre.

De Botton, A. (2006). *The Architecture of Happiness*. London: Hamish Hamilton.

De Certeau, M. (1984). *The Practice of Everyday Life*. (S. Rendall, Trans.). Berkeley: University of California Press.

Delany, P. (Ed.). (1994). *Vancouver: Representing the Postmodern City*. Vancouver: Arsenal Pulp Press.

Deleuze, G. (1991). Postscripts on the society of control. Retrieved from www.n5m.org/n5m2/media/texts/deleuze.htm. *October 59* (3), 3–7.

Demers, C. (2009). *Vancouver Special*. Vancouver: Arsenal Pulp Press.

Derrida, J. (2000). *Of Hospitality: Anne Dufourmantelle Invites Jacques Derrida to Respond*. (R. Bowlby, Trans.). Stanford: Stanford University Press.

Fuss, D. (2004). *The Sense of an Interior: Four Writers and the Rooms That Shaped Them*. New York & London: Routledge.

Gandesha, S. (n.d.). "Imagining Citizenship": Introduction. SFU Institute for the Humanities. Retrieved from www.sfu.ca/humanities-institute/citizenship.htm.

Higgins, K. (2010). *How to Look at a Vancouver Special*. Vancouver: Publication Studio.

Lefebvre, H. (1991). *The Production of Space*. (D. Nicholson-Smith, Trans.). Oxford: Blackwell.

Lurie, A. (2014). *The Language of Houses: How Buildings Speak to Us*. Harrison, NY: Delphinium Books.

Mezei, K. (2010). Living the domestic interior: Seven characters in search of home in Vancouver, 2008–2010. In M. Taylor, G. Lee, & M. Lindquist (Eds.), Proceedings of the IDEA Symposium: *Interior Spaces in Other Places*. Brisbane: Queensland University of Technology. Retrieved from www.idea-edu.com/symposiums/2010-interior-space-in-other-places/.

Miller, D. (2008). *The Comfort of Things*. Cambridge, UK: Polity Press.

Smith, J. (2006, March). The Vienna Memorandum and shifting paradigms for conservation. In Christina Cameron (Ed.), Procès-verbaux/Proceedings: "Le patrimoine et la conservation des paysages urbains historiques"/"Heritage and the Conservation of Historic Urban Landscapes" (pp. 67–71). Table ronde organisée par la Chaire de recherche en patrimoine bâti, Faculté de l'aménagement, Université de Montréal/Round Table organized by the Canada Research Chair on Built Heritage, Faculty of Environmental Design, University of Montreal, Montreal.

Woolf, V. (1993). Street haunting: A London adventure. In R. Bowlby (Ed.), *The Crowded Dance of Modern Life, Selected Essays: Volume Two* (pp. 70–81). Harmondsworth: Penguin.

CHAPTER 2

MUNDANE TECHNOLOGY IN NON-WESTERN CONTEXTS: WALL-AS-TOOL

Lisa-Jo K. van den Scott

When defining new technologies, we often think of cell phones or machines of great import, of whiz-bang technologies. Latour (1992), among others (Arnold & DeWald, 2011; Bijker, 1997; Michael, 2000; Taylor, 2012), asserts the need to take a closer look at technologies often overlooked for their banality but that have deep consequences and complex meanings attached to them. While a small, yet significant, literature has grown up following Latour's (1992) lead, those studies that do exist focus almost exclusively on the Western context. Arnold and DeWald (2011) highlight this limitation and issue a call for studies of mundane technologies, particularly in non-Western contexts.

This case study of permanent walls among the Inuit of Northern Canada takes up this call. Walls lack the obvious innovative flare of the wheel, the light bulb, or the automobile, what Michael (2000) calls "epochal" technologies, yet they are forms of mundane technology so deeply rooted in our daily lives that we must look upon them as obvious objects of study. By focusing on the interaction of users and mundane technology, two modes of use emerge as particularly important in non-Western contexts, namely *passive engagements* and *active engagements*. Passive engagements refer to instances where technology itself brings consequences to bear on society, often resulting in human adjustments. Active engagements refer to interactions that are human guided and that result in technological adjustments, either in form, function, or meaning. While studies have long acknowledged that technologies are both constraining and enabling (e.g., Bijker et al., 1987; Mukerji, 1994), recent work (Collyer, 2011) stresses the importance of turning attention to reflexivity. The concepts of passive engagements and active engagements offer a way to examine reflexivity more closely.

Permanent walls have only recently been introduced to the Inuit of Arviat, Nunavut, Canada, a small, isolated hamlet on the Arctic Tundra. This housing shift affects how *Arviammiut* (people of Arviat) negotiate their understanding of and relationship to house walls in non-Western contexts. I shall first discuss mundane technology, then its implications in non-Western contexts. From there I introduce the concepts of passive engagements and active engagements. After a brief discussion of the setting, this chapter focuses exclusively on active engagements, presenting the wall-as-tool for storage as an exemplar of an active engagement.

MUNDANE TECHNOLOGY

In 1948, Siegfried Giedion issued a call to historians to take up the study of "anonymous history." He saw objects around us as artifacts, which, due to their banality, are usually overlooked. He writes: "We shall deal here with humble things, things not usually granted earnest consideration, or at least not valued for their historical import.… In their aggregate, the humble objects of which we shall speak have shaken our mode of living to its very roots. Modest things of daily life, they accumulate into forces acting upon whoever moves within the orbit of our civilization" (Giedion, 1948, p. 3). We do not normally conceive of mundane technology as "invented" technical objects, and yet they have achieved a "technological frame" (Bijker et al., 1987). Among other commonplace items, Giedion delves into the history of the spoon, the chair, and the drawer. Few stop to consider them as inventions in the first place. They are, however, forms of technology so deeply rooted in our daily lives that we cannot look upon them as mundane artifacts of little notice. Giedion's call, however, went unanswered for many years.

In the early 1980s, technology studies took off, growing out of science studies and suggesting theoretical models that include Actor Network Theory (ANT) (Callon, 1986; Latour, 1983) and the Social Construction of Technology approach (SCOT) (Bijker et al., 1987), among others. Initially these approaches were interested in unraveling the mysteries of whiz-bang, "epochal" technologies. By the early 1990s, scholars began to emphasize the importance of studying more banal, mundane technologies (Bijker, 1993; Latour, 1992; Mukerji, 1994). As Mukerji (1994) avers, "material culture" shapes our everyday lives in profound ways. Michael (2000), for example, illuminates how walking boots changed our relationship with nature in unexpected ways. "Invisible technologies," as he terms them, can have more ramifications in our daily lives than more epochal technologies.

Mundane technology carries with it moral implications (Latour, 1992). As items in our world with moral prescriptions, it is important to study these "missing masses." Latour (1992) uses the example of door hinges to delineate moral prescriptions. Hinges are a form of leverage that allows a small item to do what would take a great deal of work by humans. This substitution comes with prescriptive messages. The door now discriminates against the aged or the very young, for example. Thus there is a moral ideology attached to the hinges. Winner (1980) describes another way in which technologies can carry moral implications. His work delineates the purposeful construction of low bridges in Long Island so as to impede the passage of buses, thereby blocking access to Jones Beach from the poor (Garvey, 2007; Winner, 1980).

The material culture of mundane technology is both a residue of the achievement of patterns of social life and a manifestation of power and social categories in the built environment around us (Mukerji, 1994). Winner's (1980) bridges are one example of this, but Mukerji pushes us to think further. Power relations are reflected and carried out in the spread and use of (mundane) technology as a facet of material culture.

MUNDANE TECHNOLOGY IN NON-WESTERN CONTEXTS

Arnold and DeWald (2011) argue that we should move away from diffusionist models that privilege Euro-American influence and attend to the "social life of things" (Appadurai, 1986) *within* a colony or non-Western context (Arnold & DeWald, 2011, p. 971), attending to local agency (Arnold & DeWald, 2012). Arnold and DeWald (2011) maintain that colonizing regimes have less control over mundane technology than over epochal technology, and although this technology is still inflected with moral prescription, a study of "everyday" technologies exposes the researcher to a user-based, person-oriented level of analysis (Arnold & DeWald, 2012). They call for researchers to look beyond "dominant paradigms of colonialism, nationalism, and development, to explore the multivalent nature of 'everyday life' and enquire into 'the social life of things' as locally constituted, to examine modernity's diverse material forms, technological manifestations, and ideological configurations" (Arnold & DeWald, 2012, p. 1).

Mundane technologies in non-Western contexts must be studied in that local context, "on the ground." By observing use, first championed by Cowan (1987), we jolt our preconceived notions of how a people might receive an imported technology and discover how they cope with the technological artifact's imported moral prescriptions, embodied by the creators or inventors. In this way we can examine the reception of an object that is technical and also cultural (Griswold, 1994). In non-Western contexts, imported mundane technologies act in some sense as "boundary objects" (Star & Griesemer, 1989), and the negotiation of a technological artifact becomes a negotiation of differing cultural norms, values, or beliefs. Thus the everlasting ebb and flow continues. The sands of the shore shape the waves, and the waves shape the shore.

This chapter takes up the call with a case study of a mundane technology, permanent walls, in a non-Western context, among the Inuit of Arviat, Nunavut, and seeks to discover how an imported mundane technology "came to be constituted as local goods, subject to local usages and vernacular under-standings" (Arnold & DeWald, 2012, p. 3). *Arviammiut* build their "way of life" (Williams, 1958) around permanent walls, which slip in under the radar both theoretically and empirically, tricking us into hardly seeing them at all. How do *Arviammiut* form relationships with those walls at the local level?

PASSIVE/ACTIVE ENGAGEMENTS

Mundane technology does shape everyday lives and does carry moral pre-scriptions, but people also exercise agency. It is not mere recursiveness that arises but reflexivity, in the sense that, while there is a recursive relationship, participants are also consciously active in shaping their own norms and pat-terns of use of the mundane technology according to their cultural prefer-ences. Attention to reflexivity, however, is eclipsed in literature dealing with non-Western, and particularly colonized, locales. Groups like the Inuit are too often regarded as helpless victims constrained by imported technologies. While colonized groups are victims and have experienced constraint, the power dynamics at play are not sufficient to suppress completely the mecha-nism of reflexivity and agency.

New technologies, mundane or not, are engaged with previously existing cultural resources. Taylor stresses that, while there are some homogeniz-ing aspects, cultural adaptions to modernity (in this case technologies of modernity) are not identical across civilizations and "a given society will, indeed must, adopt the mode for which it has the cultural resources" (1999, p. 164). This study finds that reflexivity emerges as particularly salient in the relationship between *Arviammiut* and exogenous walls.

"Interpretive flexibility" (Bijker, 1993; Pinch & Bijker, 1984) constitutes a key tool in considering walls because it chronicles the flux of the polysemic nature of symbols (Schudson, 2002). Different relevant social groups (RSGs) negotiate shared meaning or meanings for the technological artifact through use (Bijker, 1997). When a technology develops its "technological frame"—the set of congealed meanings, uses, practices, and norms surrounding a technological object—it achieves "closure" (Bijker, 1997), but not before previously existing schema, or ways of thinking (DiMaggio, 1997), influence the technological frame.

I introduce here conceptual tools that allow us to emphasize the reflexive nature of the relationship between the social and the technical: passive engage-ments and active engagements. Added to the concepts of RSGs and "interpretive flexibility," these concepts help achieve a more sophisticated understanding of mundane technology. These terms are consciously anthropocentric. Although both passive and active engagements are operating at all times, one process might be more salient in any particular given moment. These engagements do not impose a dominant cultural model. By conceptualizing passive and active engagements, not only can we investigate the "technological frame" in the full glory of its relative firmness and fluidity, but we can dig right into the reflexive process, sorting the sand from the waves while still viewing them as part of one social process. While I introduce both concepts here, this chapter will focus on active engagements within the data analysis.

Passive Engagements

1. *Passive engagements are those in which individuals, at the microlevel, and societies, at the macrolevel, are affected by the technology.* They are not actively engaged in shaping the technology but rather bear the consequences of the technology. Within passive engagements, technology itself, while agentic and part of a social equation, has no motivation—while human beings are laden with motivation.

2. *Included in passive engagements are unintended consequences.* Telephones changed not only how we communicate but also our social expectations, and the airplane had global ramifications that we perhaps have still not entirely understood.

3. *The effects of passive engagements are homogenizing.* When a new technology is introduced, there are some ways in which it will reach across cultures to have similar impacts on different societies. The printing press will always make more material more easily accessible and have impacts on the importance of literacy, although in varying degrees across class. Some impacts of the technical on the social are quite predictable across societies.

People are not unaware of passive engagements or of how technology has intruded into and changed their lives. As Schroeder (2007) correctly points out, when a new technology infiltrates any given town around the world, it is "initially concerned mainly about the impact on 'morality' and on the disruption of 'tradition'" (2007, pp. 106–107). These concerns are raised in reaction to the homogenizing effects of passive engagements. Rather than implying a technological determinism, this interaction illustrates the negotiation between passive and active engagements.

Active Engagements

1. *Active engagements involve some agentic movement or work on the part of the human component to engage with the technology,* either as an individual or an RSG.

2. *This can occur either consciously or unconsciously.* These engagements are the means by which people give the artifact meaning, transform it, establish conscious uses of it, and react to passive engagements, socially constructing the artifact at hand and its technological frame, both in meaning and use. This can occur through identity work, boundary work, or emotion work, to name a few, as they construct or reaffirm meaning in the moment.

3. *Active engagements entail diversifying effects.* When a new technological artifact is introduced, the pre-existing cultural institutions combine with

novel agency and innovative engagements with the object, producing a locally specific, socially constructed use of the technology. At the outset, there are a number of ways in which the object might be used—there is no innate meaning. Which of those uses will surface depends on the schema of the pre-existing culture and how it combines its schema with this new technology.

By taking up the specific case of the introduction of permanent walls to *Arviammiut*, we can empirically analyze passive and active engagements of this mundane technological form. In so doing, we can observe how passive engagements have an indiscriminate effect on culture, while active engagements have the potential to vary greatly across societies according to cultural context.

SETTING AND METHODOLOGY: PERMANENT WALLS IN ARVIAT, NUNAVUT

Arviat, Nunavut is a small, isolated Inuit hamlet in the Far North of Canada. The hamlet has and is experiencing a rapid influx of technology. It provides an excellent group for an examination of use, since the physical content of walls has previously been achieved in the "South." The government or (a few) individuals ship up all of the housing today, choosing from a relatively small selection of prefabricated houses. Circumstances have relegated Arviat citizens, at this point, to creating, stabilizing, and achieving closure of their technological frame, the wall, with little input as to its physical development.

The hamlet itself has a population of roughly 2,500, accessible only by airplane, although at certain times of year one can make the arduous journey to other communities by snowmobile or dog team, the closest hamlet being roughly 210 kilometres away as the crow flies. There are approximately 480 inhabited houses within the clutch of buildings that make up Arviat. Aside from a handful of transient *qablunaaq*[1] (southerners, from south of Churchill, Manitoba, usually white but not always), the population is almost entirely Inuit.

Until the early 1960s, a nomadic lifestyle with ingenious and creative survival-based technology provided the basis of Inuit culture. They lived in *igluit* (snow houses) and *tupik* (caribou-skin tents) according to the season. Once the authorities rounded up the nomadic Inuit and forced them "off the land" into the newly created town that persists today, they introduced the Inuit to permanent structures. The Inuit of the area, now *Arviammiut*, have been living in these foreign structures for approximately 50 years.

Although there are no nomadic Inuit remaining in this area, *Arviammiut* still value traditional iglu-building and hunting skills, and incorporate them into the everyday fabric of the community through conversation, the consumption of traditional foods, and participation in these activities. These elements are deeply woven into the *Arviammiut* Inuit identity, an identity that *Arviammiut* strive to reinforce through the active engagements they have with the walls. Much of this performance of identity involves the struggle for authenticity.

Much that gave Inuit their distinct set of cultural resources was based on "the land," the tundra surrounding the hamlet. This is still the case. Eating traditional foods, for example, means knowing the land, hunting, and the preparation of the meat. These activities are all indelibly linked to the land, a place the Inuit now visit rather than live in. Walled-in to Western spaces means physical separation from the locus of their cultural way of being. These walls, then, require reflexive negotiation to accomplish Inuit identity performance and boundary maintenance.

Permanent walls have been in use for long enough that they have become mundane. It sometimes took a great deal of work to explain to participants that they had not misunderstood that I was indeed studying their relationship with walls and why I was interested in such a mundane object in their lives. At the same time, not only are there elders still living from "before" walls, but there is ample evidence that this technological frame has not yet fully congealed or achieved closure in how *Arviammiut* interact with their walls. Walls are used in extremely varied ways from home to home. Some families have largely ignored the walls, allowing paint to chip or children to draw on them or to paste stickers willy-nilly on the nearly bare walls. Other families have pictures thumbtacked all over the walls, have displayed newspaper articles, and have stapled on photocopies of religious passages. Still other families have framed and mounted photographs, and the walls more closely resemble the walls of the colonizers. These are but a few examples of how the use of the walls has not fully congealed into a set of norms. This community, then, where walls are both mundane and in flux, provides a rare opportunity for study. As mentioned above, reflexivity emerges as the mechanism from which patterns in use of the walls are emerging. These patterns emerged inductively from my data.

Attending to active engagements in this chapter, I present below the importance of performing the Inuit traits of creativity and ingenuity as they interact with their walls. The act of being separated from the locus of their identity, walled-in to Western homes, invokes seemingly mundane acts, such as using the wall as a tool for storage, with profound meaning for my participants.

Having previously lived in Arviat for five years, I returned in the summer of 2010 to conduct more field research. My data consist of field notes, ethnographic experience, as well as 28 in-depth interviews. During the interviews, I asked participants to take me on a tour of their walls. As we slowly meandered through the main rooms, participants told me the stories (or lack thereof) behind each of the items on their walls and answered questions about choice, placement, or meaning. Following the tour, we sat down, and I asked questions about the use of the different spaces in the home, the number of people living in the home, their feelings about their home, their beliefs and perceptions about the purpose of walls and windows, and their beliefs and perceptions about the change from living in *igluit* and tents to living in houses. With elders, who had lived on the land as children or in their young-adult lives, I asked about their experiences with the transition and their observations about "before" and "afterwards" (a dichotomy expressed by the participants themselves).

In all cases I encouraged storytelling, as this has particular value in Arviat. Having lived in Arviat as a resident, and having developed friendships with the Inuit population before it ever occurred to me to do research, allowed both my participants and me to feel at ease with each other. I transcribed the interviews and read and reread them for themes. Through an inductive approach and a close reading of the sociology of technology literature, I found that the reflexivity was especially relevant in this context and that the data allowed me to extend and develop a more nuanced formulation of reflexivity.

WALLS IN ARVIAT

Permanent walls are an "invisible" technology (Michael, 2000), slipping in under the radar both theoretically and empirically, tricking us into hardly seeing them at all. While the term "walls" can refer to many things—screens, fences, or physical walls between borders—in this paper I use the term "wall" and "permanent wall" to refer to those inside of houses, both dividing the space within the home as well as the walls that divide "inside" from "outside." Mine is not the first to regard walls as a technological artifact (Adams et al., 2008; Gieryn, 2002; Latour, 1992) or to assert that knowledge is needed to negotiate these walls as a technological system (Marshall, 2006). Marshall, in a study for the Canadian government on policy and housing design, states that "the Inuit are resources-conscious but do not understand their present housing systems and receive no training" (2006, p. 2).

Permanent structures are displays of power (Levinson, 1998). Churches were the first structures in town along with the health centre. These buildings were key in establishing religion and the Canadian government as dominant institutions. The Hudson's Bay Company was also among the first to set up permanent structures, especially in areas outside of the communities where it had trading posts. These walls meant safety from the elements for the traders, separation from the Inuit (as interactions with the Inuit were mediated by the traders' ability to go indoors and away from them), and a way to store and protect goods—especially from theft, something which must have seemed very odd to the Inuit at that time, who did not work within an economy where goods could be hoarded by one person or group with no expectation of sharing.

Both governmental and religious institutions have now been taken over either by local *Arviammiut* or by the territorial Inuit government, although many advisors are southern. In 1993, the Inuit were granted self-governance, and in 1999 Nunavut became its own territory. Larger buildings (relative to homes) represent the local government level. The government has an interest in defining those buildings as centres of power and maintaining them. These include the school, hamlet office, health centre, post office, and "Blue Building," which houses the Department of Education and the Nunavut Housing Corporation. Within these walls, some individuals find legitimacy as "experts," while those outside the walls often do not have their local knowledge bureaucratically legitimated.

I now turn to a specific active engagement but would like to stress that the passive engagements are equally important in a full analysis of walls. In this case study, passive engagements include radically changed relationships with the weather and the idea of "inside" and "outside"; novel notions of public and private, as internally divided spaces, bedrooms, and doors are introduced; and the transmission of family-knowledge changes in gender-based ways that make more difficult the passing on of skills, such as sewing, from mother to daughter.

ACTIVE ENGAGEMENTS: WALL-AS-TOOL

Active engagements involve a relationship with the technical artifact, in this case the wall, mediated by time, needs, perceived needs, and resources. This is where "work" on the part of the user happens and the social affects the technical and the technological frame surrounding it. This work occurs within the social and cultural context of the users. For the *Arviammiut*, this context involves a focus on creativity and ingenuity.

Inuit Identity: Creativity and Ingenuity

Although the introduction of a new technology might inspire any group to reach new creative heights, the Inuit are actively striving towards this in performance of their Inuit-ness. Creativity and adaptability are part of the Inuit self-image (Berkes & Armitage, 2010). They greatly value *aturunnarniqasiajungaaq* (improvisation) and *asiajuuqsaraittunnarniq* (resourcefulness). As the Inuit engage in boundary work to maintain their hold on a distinctive and solid identity, they espouse these values in particular as Inuit values.

This is the schema, historically and socially informed, with which *Arviammiut* approach a new artifact. The resources available to the Inuit of this area changed dramatically and unpredictably, and the schemas extant from previous living conditions and material resources are now being transposed to make sense of permanent walls.

By exercising resourcefulness, an individual can perform positive Inuitness and boundary work. These values, therefore, play a significant role in how the Inuit of Arviat relate to objects in their lives. Walls are not exempt. Individuals actively and purposefully invoke these values as "strategies of action" (Swidler, 1986), attempting to maximize them in their relationship with walls. Traditionally, when living nomadic lives centred on basic survival, the Inuit needed to make use of everything possible. The wall cannot simply stand there. It must serve an active purpose, it must be used in all possible ways. By engaging with the wall and determining ways to make it more useful, the wall itself is subsumed into everyday life, normalized within the community, and, in its usefulness, becomes a tool. In short, walls are made over as tools for practising traditional cultural activities and values, such as creativity and ingenuity.

Active engagements that emphasize these, among other, Inuit values include the enaction of the Inuit value of *aktuaturaunniqarniq* (interconnectedness) through the elaborate gifting of items to be displayed on others' walls; the performance of personal and family identity through the display of family photographs; wall-as-tool for remembering, with the new ability to collect and maintain souvenirs such as graduation hats;[2] and the reclamation of history through the appropriation of photographs of relatives taken by early explorers and mounting these photographs along with contemporary photographs of family inset in the frame.

This chapter now focuses on the specific active engagement "wall-as-tool" for storage. This use of the walls in this way provides an opportunity to actively perform Inuit-ness. There are different levels of storage for which the wall can be used. These range, temporally, from rarely touched articles stored over long periods of time to often-used articles stored on the wall for easy access. I shall proceed through the continuum from long-term to short-term storage of artifacts on walls and connect each to the performance of Inuit values.

Wall-as-Tool: Long-Term Storage for Important Documents or Mementos

The homes in Arviat have little storage space, in particular for items such as paper or other miscellaneous small items that one might collect over the years. When the owners are at a loss as to how to store articles that they do not want ruined, they invoke the wall as a useful space. Several participants explained that they had put certain artifacts on the wall to keep them from getting destroyed either from lying around the house or by the presence of several children. Nadia,[3] for example, explains why a small rose painting is not framed: "I wanted to put the frame in it, but before somebody wrecks it, I just put it up there."

The desire to keep things safe on the walls comes up across the board. Oliver, a widowed elder who did not move into permanent structures until he was a young adult, also expressed to me that "whatever you leave anywhere in the house, it would get wrecked, so [I] decided to put them [certificates] up on the wall." Phoebe, who frequently has grandchildren present, echoes this sentiment. Thus the wall is a very useful place to put up anything that the participant would like to keep from getting damaged or destroyed.

The wall is considered the safest place for important documents, certificates, or mementos. Hallways are often a convenient location for the accumulation of such storage (see figure 2.1), which is not frequently accessed. Once "in storage," many of these certificates will be forgotten in the same way that more southern filers might forget about a certificate sitting in a filing cabinet.

FIGURE 2.1: CARMEL'S HALLWAY, FULL OF CERTIFICATES AND AWARDS

Source: Photo by Lisa-Jo K. van den Scott

Other articles may also be stored on the walls for the long term. Phoebe, for example, is storing a plastic floral arrangement that reads "Mom" on her wall until she passes away, when it will be placed at her gravesite. Marcus has tacked a lock of his son's hair to the wall. For *Arviammiut*, this is a creative solution to a problem. How does one keep important documents or mementos safe? Where? The solution of using the wall is an active engagement with that wall and, in this case, also demonstrates Inuit creativity in problem solving.

"So I Just Put It Up"

For some, wall storage is more of a last resort. When confronted with small gifts, the participants often turn to the wall as a tool to be used in the resolution of the storage dilemma.

Int.: What made you put it [a plaque with a photograph of a sunset] there?

Jaimie: When they gave it to me, *I just hang it up.* [author's emphasis]

Int.: And how 'bout the basket?

Ruby: Um, somebody gave it to me, and I didn't know where to put it, *so I just put it there.* [author's emphasis]

Participants faced with a storage dilemma conceptualized the wall as a storage area to "just put" things that needed to be kept and needed to find a home. In many of these cases, the wall could then serve the dual purpose of storage and display. The above quotations are but a selection of similar responses: "I just put them up" (Gabriella); "I just hanged it out there" (Ruby); "It's just up there" (Phoebe); and "Don't know where else to put it, so they put it on the door" (Gabriella).

Gifts make up the majority of this category, but there are a range of items that were "just put up" on the walls for storage. Margy knew that she wanted to keep her wedding bouquet, and so it rests cradled by caribou antlers on the wall: "That's from my wedding too. Like, I didn't know where I should put my bouquet, *so I just put it there*" [author's emphasis] (Margy; see figure 2.2).

FIGURE 2.2: MARGY'S WEDDING BOUQUET CRADLED IN CARIBOU ANTLERS

Source: Photo by Lisa-Jo K. van den Scott

While walled-in to a Western space, Margy and others can access an identity rooted elsewhere, bringing their culture *indoors* through the use of walls to store and display various items.

Display as Use: Maximizing Use for Otherwise Useless or Broken Artifacts

The desire to make use of things facilitates the transformation of the wall into a tool for storage. It is also a tool for display, and there is some overlap. An object that is broken or has served its purpose will not immediately be thrown out. If a use can be conceived of for this object, it will be put to that use. Display is a valid use for an object, and thus some of these items end up on the wall and out of the way in storage and also on display.

Oliver automatically tries to make use of everything, having grown up "on the land" and having had to make use of everything for basic survival. On his wall is a rifle: [Oliver through translator] "When it stopped working, um, he put it up on the wall *'cause it won't be any use if he just left it on the ground. So* when it stopped working, he put it up on the wall for decoration" [author's emphasis]. Through this use, Oliver is indirectly performing his Inuit-ness. While consciously adapting the utilization of the gun in order to ensure its continued value as a useful item, Oliver demonstrates his ability to be resourceful and creative in his approach to solving the "problem" of the nonworking rifle.

This wall artifact is not merely out of the way: it now serves an aesthetic purpose. There is a conscious "re-engagement" happening. Margy, for example, has a spatula that is no longer usable for its intended purpose. It now sits in her window sill serving an ornamental function (see figure 2.3). Part of what is aesthetically pleasing about this object is that it demonstrates obvious ingenuity in action. She has re-engaged with this artifact. Abigail underscores this point when I ask her about the stickers on her range hood. She tells me that her mother decorated the range hood and then continues: "Yeah, *my mum's pretty creative.* She even put a sticker, *illa* [I mean], she received the card and she cut it, birthday card, and she, uh, taped it on her helmet. Something different, she said" [author's emphasis] (Abigail). While some cultures may not see the meaning behind a decorated spatula or a cut-out from a birthday card taped onto a helmet, within the community these acts are quite meaningful. In this way, *Arviammiut* are actively engaging with the wall and using it as a tool to enable these acts; as a locus, it is the medium through which an aesthetic purpose for an artifact can be accomplished.

FIGURE 2.3: DECORATED SPATULA

Source: Photo by Lisa-Jo K. van den Scott

Lily's home is the most extreme example within the community. Explaining to me an old flour sack she has framed on the wall, Lily accentuates the importance of display as a valid aesthetic purpose and a way to keep old items, which are no longer useful in their intended purpose: "So my husband, Brennan, found that between the stuff, and 'Look what I found!' And then ... I said, 'I'm gonna keep it. I'm gonna put it in the wall.' I was so surprised 'cause it has the price in there, four dollars thirty-one cents, but the English part, they use it for repairing a canoe. When there's a hole, they have to repair, so it's only in French [laughter]" (Lily; see figure 2.4). This flour sack has undergone not two but three stages of usefulness—twice re-engaged.

FIGURE 2.4: FLOUR SACK, FRAMED

Source: Photo by Lisa-Jo K. van den Scott

The centrepiece of Lily's home is her artwork on the wall (see figure 2.5). In 1990, Lily and Brennan chartered a helicopter and went back to where her family had lived on the land before she was born. They saw white rocks there and began to collect them. Over the years, and several trips later, they amassed quite a collection. Today the rocks reside on the wall. Lily tells me about the wall: "First, at home, we kept them in the jar. But *it doesn't look like any use*, so I sketch on a paper and ask my husband, 'If I large my sketching, could you please cut the ones that I need you to cut?' And he said, 'Yes.' … So instead of displaying the rocks [in] the jar, we wanted to do something special with those rocks" [author's emphasis] (Lily). Not only do these scenes serve to connect her to her past, but she is actively and viscerally engaging with the wall to create an aesthetic use for rocks that were serving no purpose stored in a jar.

FIGURE 2.5: LILY'S WALL

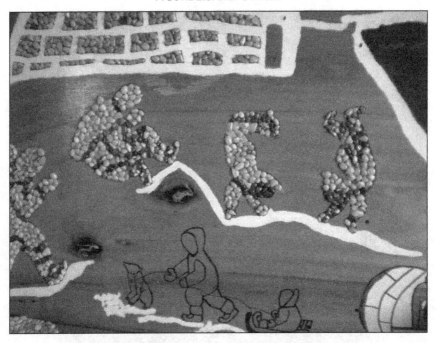

Source: Photo by Lisa-Jo K. van den Scott

Occasional Access

Along the continuum, there are also items that are stored for occasional access, such as Christmas decorations. In some homes, Christmas decorations stay in place year-round, "stored" in plain view on the walls; however, they are only "used" during Christmas time. How are they used? They are attended to only during the Christmas season. For the rest of the year, residents and visitors are "clutter blind" to these items on the wall. When I questioned participants on these decorations in the summer, Ellen, Marcus, and Oliver gave responses similar to Trevor's:

> Uh, Christmas decorations, like during the Christmas time of the season. Maybe most of us put some decorations inside the house, and so we feel that there's a meaning to a Christmas, is what it means to us too, so we can show it to other peoples, like, from outside of this house, so we can tell those people too that we feel the Christmas spirits, so some, we decorate our house too, like during the Christmas time of the season. (Trevor)

While not all participants have Christmas decorations up year-round, but in storage for part of the year and in use during the month of December, most have some articles whose "away" place is on the wall and that are used occasionally. A knife on Felix's wall is one example of this. Other examples include notepads, pin cushions (see figure 2.6), schedules, fly swatters, and back-scratchers. Ruby explains about the pin cushion, "We always use it for sewing, needles, pins. [It's on the wall] so that it will be easy to take, and it's far from the children."

FIGURE 2.6: PIN CUSHION TACKED TO THE WALL

Source: Photo by Lisa-Jo K. van den Scott

Easy-Access Storage: Keys, Sunglasses, and Knives

There are also easy-access storage solutions on the walls. These include hooks for keys, which are almost without exception handmade, and other more creative displays of resourcefulness. Sunglasses, for example, need to be easy to access and yet will get scratched if they are not stored safely. Sunglasses are quite important because they prevent snow-blindness in the spring. By implementing creative storage areas on the wall with string or wire, *Arviammiut* are enacting their Inuit-ness by practising what they are known for: ingenuity. Tori takes pride in her solution for sunglasses (see figure 2.7). New ideas, new ways of doing things are part of her membership in the community and her own expression of her personal identity as an Inuk.

FIGURE 2.7: SUNGLASSES AT TORI'S HOME

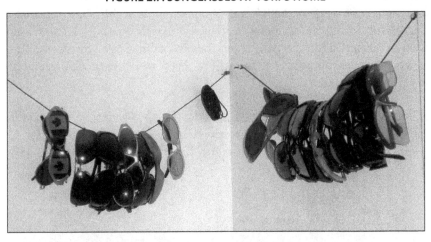

Source: Photo by Lisa-Jo K. van den Scott

Innovation is tied to practical purpose. Tori did not sit down and think about how she could be innovative that day, and thus more Inuit. When presented with a problem, she found a solution. The Inuit find solutions. This is a treasured part of their cultural tool kit (Swidler, 1986). Tori and others pride themselves on their solutions. The wall provides another avenue for solutions.

Ruby has found an easy-access storage solution for knives that might make southern housewives swoon: the trim above the counter provides an ideal location for knives (see figure 2.8).

FIGURE 2.8: EASY-ACCESS KNIVES

Source: Photo by Lisa-Jo K. van den Scott

Other items stored on walls for quick and easy access are CDs, bills, scissors, pens, and phone numbers. House or phone numbers may be taped up, on a Post-it Note, or even written directly on the wall such as at Deborah, Oliver, Ruby, Hyacinth, Gabriella, Elise, and Felix's homes.

These uses of the walls are active engagements in action. Walls came with no handbook of uses and meanings. The Inuit were able to approach them with fresh eyes and to determine a meaning, through use, which—while not entirely unique—consciously reflects their firm practice of and belief in resourcefulness and practicality. The wall becomes a convenient location in a way that would not have occurred to these participants had they been restricted to the layered and historical meanings that others from a more southern background, give to walls. Wall-as-tool for storage is one of the meanings that *Arviammiut* have ascribed to the technological artifact through their use of that artifact, a use that was mediated through the social: through the performance of their definition of Inuit-ness in their intentionally and consciously creative and innovative uses for the new technology.

CONCLUSION

A special kind of technology—mundane technology, banal and demure—can be found woven into the fabric of our lives. These technologies are not immediately understood as invented, and yet technological innovation and change can apply just as equally. It is important to pay attention to these banal technologies if we wish to understand the full spectrum of our relationship with technology and technological artifacts. Studying mundane technology grants us access to the day-to-day, taken-for-granted aspects of technology that affect, and are affected by, greater proportions of the population. This work, however, has mainly been carried out in Western contexts. In Arviat, walls interrupt life-as-it-was. Passive and active engagements, with a focus on use, tease out how the Inuit are affected by this technological artifact and how they in turn do have agency and shape the technological frame.

There are implications of passive and active engagements that warrant further study. Passive engagements, for example, seem to pull cultures towards cultural convergence. Active engagements, on the other hand, seem to encourage the kind of identity and boundary work that fosters unique cultural identities and cultural divergence. It is possible that these concepts may be transposed into studies of modernization to help us discover which processes boost cultural diversity and which lead to homogeneity. Further comparative empirical work may yield answers to these questions.

NOTES

1. This is commonly spelled *qallunaaq*; however, in Arviat dialect *qablunaaq* is the appropriate spelling.

2. This practice is particularly important in an oral culture where the "remembering" songs have been lost.

3. All participant names are pseudonyms.

REFERENCES

Adams, A., Schwartzman, K., & Theodore, D. (2008). Collapse and expand: Architecture and tuberculosis therapy in Montreal, 1909, 1933, 1954. *Technology and Culture*, 49(4): 908–942.

Appadurai, A. (1986). *The Social Life of Things*. Cambridge & New York: Cambridge University Press.

Arnold, D., & DeWald, E. (2011). Cycles of empowerment? The bicycle and everyday technology in colonial India and Vietnam. *Comparative Studies in Society and History*, 53(4), 971–996.

————. (2012). Everyday technology in South and Southeast Asia: An introduction. *Modern Asian Studies*, 46(1), 1–17.

Berkes, F., & Armitage, D. R. (2010). Co-management institutions, knowledge, and learning: Adapting to change in the Arctic. *Inuit Studies* 34(1), 109–131.

Bijker, W. E. (1993). Do not despair: There is life after constructivism. *Science, Technology, & Human Values*, 18(1), 113–138.

————. (1997). *Of Bicycles, Bakelites, and Bulbs: Towards a Theory of Sociotechnical Change*. Cambridge, MA: MIT Press.

Bijker, W. E., Hughes, T. P., & Pinch, T. J. (Eds.). (1987). *The Social Construction of Technological Systems: New Directions in the Sociology and History of Technology*. Cambridge, MA: MIT Press.

Callon, M. (1986). Some elements of a sociology of translation: Domestication of the scallops and the fishermen of St Brieuc Bay. In J. Law (Ed.), *Power, Action, and Belief* (pp. 196–233). London: Routledge & Kegan Paul.

Collyer, F. (2011). Reflexivity and the sociology of science and technology: The invention of "Eryc" the antibiotic. *Qualitative Report*, 16(2), 316–340.

Cowan, R. S. (1987). The consumption junction: A proposal for research strategies in the sociology of technology. In W. E. Bijker et. al. (Eds.), *The Social Construction of Technological Systems: New Directions in the Sociology and History of Technology* (pp. 261–280). Cambridge, MA: MIT Press.

DiMaggio, P. (1997). Culture and cognition. *Annual Review of Sociology*, 23, 263–287.

Garvey, J. (2007). The moral use of technology. *Royal Institute of Philosophy Supplement*, 82(61), 241–260.

Giedion, S. (1948). *Mechanization Takes Command: A Contribution to Anonymous History*. New York: W. W. Norton & Company Inc.

Gieryn, T. F. (2002). What buildings do. *Theory and Society*, 31(1), 35–74.

Griswold, W. (1994). *Cultures and Societies in a Changing World*. Thousand Oaks: Pine Forge Press.

Latour, B. (1983). Give me a laboratory and I will raise the world. In K. Knoor-Cetina & M. Mulkay (Eds.), *Science Observed: Perspectives on the Social Study of Science* (pp. 141-170). London: Sage.

———. (1992). Where are the missing masses?. In W. E. Bijker and J. Law (Eds.), *The Sociology of a Few Mundane Artifacts: Shaping Technology, Building Society: Studies in Sociotechnical Change*. Cambridge, MA: MIT Press.

Levinson, S. (1998). *Written in Stone: Public Monuments in Changing Societies*. Durham, NC & London: Duke University Press.

Marshall, S. 2006. Arviat community and housing design charrette. In *Technical Series* (pp. 1–10). Ottawa: Canada Mortgage and Housing Corporation (CMHC).

Michael, M. (2000). These boots are made for walking: Mundane technology, the body and human-environment relations. *Body & Society*, 6(3–4), 107–126.

Mukerji, C. (1994). Toward a sociology of material culture: Science studies, cultural studies and the meanings of things. In D. Crane (Ed.), *The Sociology of Culture: Emerging Theoretical Perspectives* (pp. 143–162). Oxford: Blackwell.

Pinch, T. J., & Bijker, W. E. (1984). The social construction of facts and artefacts: Or how the sociology of science and the sociology of technology might benefit each other. *Social Studies of Science*, 14(3), 399–441.

Schroeder, R. (2007). *Rethinking Science, Technology, and Social Change*. Stanford: Stanford University Press.

Schudson, M. (2002). How culture works: Perspectives from media studies on the efficacy of symbols. In L. Spillman (Ed.), *Cultural Sociology* (p. 141–148). Malden, MA & Oxford: Blackwell.

Star, S. L., & Griesemer, J. R. (1989). Institutional ecology, "translations" and boundary objects: Amateurs and professionals in Berkeley's Museum of Vertebrate Zoology. *Social Studies of Science*, 19, 387–420.

Swidler, A. (1986). Culture in action: Symbols and strategies. *American Sociological Review*, 51, 273–286.

Taylor, C. (1999). Two theories of modernity. *Public Culture*, 11(1), 153–174.

Taylor, J. G. (2012). The sewing-machine in colonial-era photographs: A record from Dutch Indonesia. *Modern Asian Studies*, 46(Special Issue 01), 71–95.

Williams, R. (1958). *Culture and Society, 1780–1950*. New York: Columbia University Press.

Winner, L. (1980). Do artifacts have politics? *Daedalus* 109(1), 121–136.

CHAPTER 3

Condo: The New Structure of Housing

Alan O'Connor

Pierre Bourdieu has a lot to say about the sociology of home. There is, of course, his famous diagram of the Kabyle house (Bourdieu, 1990), in which he demonstrates a homology between the structure of the house and the Kabyle world view. This schematic diagram should always be shown along with his photographs of these homes with their roofs removed by the French Army, the occupants having been forced into camps during the Algerian War. There is always this complex seeing in the work of Bourdieu, and I hope he would not mind my observation that the floor plan of the Kabyle house is oddly reminiscent of condo floor plans in the sales brochures that realtors produce to market new condo buildings. Both the Kabyle house and the condo are small dwellings.

There are many photos of homes in Bourdieu's *Distinction* (1984). We are invited to look into the elegant but rather old-fashioned bourgeois reception room, with its carpets and antique chairs. But this is the 1960s, and the theme of Bourdieu's book is the rapid social changes that are happening. So we see a young couple in a more informal apartment, with light modern furniture, the table laid for a simple evening meal. And then there is the working-class kitchen, with the mess of breakfast, one child reading a large book at the table, and another being washed by Dad in the kitchen sink. Bourdieu, with a bitter irony, will call this the choice of necessity. The photos all have a kind of intimacy, and I wonder if Bourdieu took them himself. Certainly he considered photos such as these a kind of evidence.

As usual, there are multiple forms of evidence in Bourdieu's major study of the housing market around Paris, published with the unhelpful title *The*

Social Structures of the Economy (2005). This is a study of the market for
single-family homes in the region around Paris. These are mostly houses
for people who cannot afford anything else. Bourdieu looks at the ways in
which the state (including the local state) structures the market for housing
through urban planning, building codes, and regulations concerning home
mortgages. He examines the field of housing construction, dominated by a
small number of large firms. He studies the advertising material in which
developers tout the modern engineering of a house made from prefabricated concrete slabs, or the traditional values of a mason-built home. He
interviews buyers and observes the tactics used by experienced sales staff.
They quickly assess if the person is serious or just out for a Sunday afternoon drive. Next they have to find out the buyer's income and eligibility for
mortgage financing. Many buyers find this intimidating. The salesperson
smiles and helps in a friendly way. In many cases the buyer cannot afford
what they want, and the salesperson's job is to get them to accept something
that is not their first choice: a smaller house or one very far away. Bourdieu
sees the buyer as a victim of symbolic violence or of their own desire to be
a homeowner at any cost.

Matthew Lasner's (2012) history of co-op apartments and condo living in
the United States up to the 1960s repeatedly touches on issues of social class
and distinction (including, until the 1940s, outright discrimination based on
race and religion). A desire for community often meant a desire for social
exclusion. Many buyers were swayed by advertising and marketing; they often signed up with little understanding of the condominium bylaws (p. 199).
Issues of condominium management come up frequently in the narrative.
Noise problems from children are mentioned (p. 217), noise from upstairs is a
problem in apartment-style buildings (p. 229), and adequate soundproofing is
expensive to install (p. 230). The emphasis is on studies of cultural landscape
and the built environment. The experiences of ordinary people enter Lasner's
book only from printed sources: he does not use the methods of oral history
or ethnography. He hopes other researchers will take up this challenge (p. 26).

All things considered, Lasner comes down in favour of condo living. In an
earlier book, he says there is much to applaud (Lasner, 2011). The dissertation
on which his book is based is dedicated to his grandma, who thought condo
living was paradise. It is not clear how relevant this judgment is to the contemporary condo boom in Toronto. Leslie Kern's (2010) research on women
and new-construction condos in downtown Toronto is much more critical.
She finds evidence of commodification, privatization, and limited social
contact with the surrounding neighbourhood. Buyers mostly seek financial
gain from increased resale values of their units. (International financial organizations have repeatedly warned about over-priced condos in Toronto; for
financial losses on upscale Toronto condos, see Pigg, 2015.) Many downtown
condo corporations achieve a quorum for annual general meetings only by

having building managers gather signed proxy forms. Rosen and Walks (2014) give a useful overview of the condominium boom in Toronto, where by 2011 condos accounted for 18% of all housing units. The article has some useful criticisms of public policy but is mainly descriptive of factors influencing this restructuring of the city. They briefly mention problems such as shoddy workmanship, but their article is not based on interviews with condo owners and residents. Further work is needed to evaluate the quality of life of those who have bought into the condo lifestyle.

An early research paper in the United States by Silverman and Barton (1984) lists conflicts between condo developers and owners; between owners and renters in the same building; and conflicts between owners, sometimes leading to litigation. They suggest that there is a high level of dissatisfaction among condo owners. From preliminary research at two housing developments, they conclude that the fundamental problem is a tension between the values of home ownership and the realities of condominium living. Whereas there are norms for noise, wandering children, overgrown weeds, and car parking for neighbourhoods of single-family homes, there are no norms for dealing with comparable issues in condominium buildings. Whereas it is possible to have little interaction with neighbours in single-family dwellings, in a condo building the owners share a party wall with the next unit. (For social studies of noise, see Hendry, 2013; Radovac, 2011.)

In a study of gated communities in China and England, Blandy and Wang (2013) repeatedly describe homeowners who feel powerless in the face of problems and property governance. Blandy, Dupuis, and Dixon (2010) report that residents of multiowned housing feel powerless in relation to the developer and managing agent: "Lack of knowledge at the outset often puts owners and residents in a weak position on a day-to-day basis" (p. 9). Noting that the experience of living in such buildings has received little attention, the same authors relate that "many of the individual owners in such developments report that they lack control over the management of the site and its facilities, despite their rights of legal ownership" (Blandy, Dixon & Dupuis, 2006, p. 2366).

My own research is based on the sociology of Pierre Bourdieu. Issues of housing and home recur throughout his work. *The Social Structures of the Economy* (2005) includes:

- A study of marketing materials and advertisements
- Observation of the strategies used by sales agents and realtors
- Interviews with homeowners about their experience of acquiring the property and the reality of living there

Bourdieu shows how the field of housing is structured by several levels of government, by regulations surrounding mortgage eligibility and interest rates on mortgages, and by the domination of the field by a fairly small number of property developers. Buyers are influenced by marketing and advertisements. Bourdieu points out that material goods such as clothing and housing, which last and are on public display, say a lot about the cultural capital of the owner and their location in the social field (Bourdieu, 2005, p. 19). The purchase is not simply an economic decision. Sales agents and realtors play a crucial role in managing the real-estate purchase, which many buyers find intimidating. "Before making up their minds, they mainly studied advertisements" (Bourdieu, 2005, p. 190). From interviews with property owners, we can document their experiences of this process and of living in their new home. Bourdieu found much disappointment, including problems of poor construction, lack of facilities, and noise from neighbours. He concludes that housing is not so much a market (the main focus of real-estate news is on the market) as a field in which purchasers with low volumes of economic and cultural capital have little power.

This method can be followed in the study of the condo market in Toronto. We may start with the constant marketing of condo lifestyles in free magazines such as the *New Condo Guide*, published biweekly by the Yellow Pages Organization. It is distributed free in boxes outside subway stops and at large supermarket chains in the Greater Toronto Area. The *New Condo Guide* has the feel of a magazine, with its front cover, table of contents, regular columns, and feature articles, usually on new condo projects. But the entire magazine is written by industry insiders and not by independent journalists: it is completely upbeat about your condo adventure. The *Toronto Star* has its "New in Homes and Condos" section in its Saturday edition. A doctoral dissertation at the University of Toronto found that it makes some attempt at journalism—the articles are specially written for the *Star* by freelance writers—but its coverage is almost entirely uncritical of the condo industry (Langlois, 2012). (I asked a reporter at the *Star* about this lack of balance, and she responded that "New in Homes and Condos" is not an editorial section of the paper. I wonder how many readers make this distinction. It is not identified as an advertising supplement.) My own content analysis of one month of the *Toronto Star* arrives at a very similar conclusion, though there has since been an occasional article on fraud by a condo developer or complaints about poor building construction. By far the most frequent type of story is a report on the market for condos, usually based on quarterly reports by realtor organizations or by the banks. The overall effect is sometimes confusing, with a headline one day about brisk sales compared with last year, and another day a warning about a price bubble in the condo market. The weekly free paper *NOW* also gets into the action. It used to have a regular "What I Bought" feature, and now publishes a glossy monthly supplement. In *NOW* the emphasis is on how smart young people turn their condo into a unique personal space, expressive of their personality and creativity. Critical investigative reporting by Philip Preville in *Toronto Life* (July, 2012) and Tamsin McMahon in *Maclean's* (April 28, 2014) is the exception to the rule. Even front covers such as "Trouble in Condoland" and "Why Condos Are a Living Nightmare" are unable to counter the field effects of advertising and marketing by the condo industry.

TABLE 3.1: TOPIC OF CONDO ARTICLES IN THE *TORONTO STAR*

Article topic	Number of articles
Market report	23
Traffic gridlock	2
Island Airport expansion	2
King Street proposal	2
Kensington Market proposal	2
Stores close due to development	2
Problems with glass construction	2
Trees removed by developer	1
Muslim condo complex	1

Source: Monday to Friday editions, *Toronto Star*, Dec. 2013–Feb 2014. N=37.

Future research must supplement content analysis with qualitative research to enhance the understanding of condo living and to get at individual experiences of condo living. As I approached this research project, I was surprised to realize that I could draw on my own experience. I have lived in three different condo buildings in downtown Toronto, for at least a year in each unit. My experience recalls the classic sociology of the early twentieth-century city, because I would say that the experience is one of intimate strangers. For example, condos are defined by not having a shared laundry room, as in rental apartment buildings. (The engineering difficulty of exhausting clothes dryers exists in both apartment and condo buildings. In the first it is solved by a single laundry room; in the second by exhaust pipes installed throughout the building.) But although there is no shared laundry room, the image of condo living always includes the promise of social exchange. The condo image is one of encounters, frequently sexualized, of the glamorous young person you might meet in the gym or in the lobby. In all three buildings I've lived in, you can hear your neighbour pissing. A strange intimacy. I've put this in ordinary language because the more polite "bathroom noises" does not hit the mark. And it is quite audible in the main living area. In fact, all three units had serious noise problems. The first two apartments had problems of acoustic noise through the walls: you could distinctly hear the television, computer games, and loud voices through the wall of the next unit. My third condo had problems of acoustic noise travelling through the entrance doors. A few days after I moved in, I heard terrible screams coming though my entrance door. When I opened the door, it was obvious that the screams were coming from behind the door of my neighbour. It was one of those difficult moments, and I seriously considered phoning the police to report possible domestic violence. Then I realized that it was Hockey Night in Canada, and the screams came from my neighbour watching the game on television. There was also serious acoustic noise from the shared balcony on the other side. Floor-to-ceiling glass windows have poor sound insulation (about 25% of the minimum required for party walls), and I could hear my neighbours when they took mobile phone calls on their balcony. When they entertained guests at a dinner party on the shared balcony, the loud voices disturbed quiet enjoyment even with all my windows tightly closed.

These are all examples of acoustic noise. Impact noise is caused by banging that is transmitted though the building frame: kitchen cabinet doors banging, toilet seat dropped, heavy footsteps overhead, furniture scraping on the floor. Whereas there are minimum standards for acoustic noise in the Building Code, there is no standard at all for impact noise in condo buildings.

Part of the study of the field must also include an investigation of how the Building Code is written. It is one of the complex ways in which the state structures the field, but most buyers of condos give it little thought. Any question about building construction to the architect or developer will likely bring the response: the condo meets the requirements of the Building Code. How is the code written? A recent example of changes allows for wooden-frame condo buildings of six stories; previously, wooden buildings could only be four stories high. This change was lobbied for by the condo industry and the lumber industry. It has recently been passed in Ontario, having previously been accepted in British Columbia. It is unlikely that buyers will be alerted that their condo building is not made from poured concrete. Or that there are no standards for impact noise carried by the wooden frame. Or that the standards for acoustic noise are judged by engineers (including those at government agencies) to be woefully inadequate for buildings where people live in such close proximity.

The experience of condo buyers is mediated by marketing. Some good studies have focused on the image, which started with the theme of value for money (condos are a good investment) and quickly shifted to lifestyle themes, often aimed at young female buyers. The most frequent picture of condo developments contains modernist images of buildings soaring into the sky, with a few matchstick figures and young trees at street level. The other motif comprises expensively dressed and attractive young people, often women. (These images are indistinguishable from cosmetics advertisements.) The experience of condo buyers is also mediated by realtors, and it is important to interview these professionals to understand how the field of condo sales is constructed. I have had mixed experiences with realtors, but I would say that Bourdieu is on the mark: realty is about managing the client's expectations. I turned down one unit because the balcony overlooked six or eight industrial-sized garbage containers. "Whoever thought that was a good idea?" I asked. "They have to go somewhere," replied my realtor, though later she admitted that particular unit was not selling very quickly. The experience of living in a condo is also mediated by building managers. I actually have a lot of sympathy for people doing this job. Building managers are currently seeking professional status and autonomy within the industry, and this change certainly should be encouraged. It is clear that building managers are in the unfortunate position of having to manage all the problems created by poor building standards. In many respects, they seem to hold an impossible position. For example, some noise problems could be ameliorated, but this improvement would require admitting on a website or in a residents' handbook how poorly the building is actually constructed. Out of fear of legal action, building managers feel pressure from the condo developer and from current owners not to name the problems. But if problems are not named, they cannot be solved.

The condo industry is surrounded by the neoliberal language of the market. Most stories in the *Toronto Star* are market reports of one kind of another. Yet my conclusion is that, considered as a field, individual condo buyers and residents have little power. Issues of the Building Code, construction standards, and building design are collective matters over which condo buyers have little say. The glamorous marketing image of condo living is very far from the reality of living in these buildings; this contradiction is similar to what Gillian Tett (2010), drawing on Bourdieu's work, calls "silences" in reporting and academic writing. Commentators accept the marketing image that condos are a quality product, silencing other voices.

At the conference where this paper was originally delivered, there was an interesting discussion of the meaning of home. The theme emerged that home does not end at the front door. In different ways, people described how home reaches out beyond the walls, for example, in the desire to invite people inside, if only their rented apartment were not so cramped and rundown. The marketing for condo lifestyles includes the theme that there will be other people like you using the gym or in the lobby. Even suggesting the most impossible sexual fantasy, condo living promises something that reaches beyond the walls of each private unit. It is possible that this utopian impulse may be the foundation for a movement of condo owners that will make real demands on the industry. The tragedy of these buildings is that one's first encounter with a neighbour will probably be a noise complaint.

REFERENCES

Blandy, S., A. Dupuis & J. Dixon (Eds.). (2010). *Multi-Owned Housing: Law, Power and Practice.* Burlington, VT: Ashgate.

Blandy, S., J. Dixon & A. Dupuis. (2006). Theorizing power relationships in multiowned residential development: Unpacking the bundle of rights. *Urban Studies*, 43(13), 2365–2383.

Blandy, S. & F. Wang. (2013). Curbing the power of developers? Law and power in Chinese and English gated communities. *Geoforum*, 47, 199–208.

Bourdieu, P. (1984). *Distinction.* Cambridge, MA: Harvard University Press.

Bourdieu, P. (1990). *The Logic of Practice.* Stanford: Stanford University Press.

Bourdieu, P. (2005). *The Social Structure of the Economy.* Cambridge, UK: Polity.

Bourdieu, P. (2012). *Picturing Algeria.* New York: Columbia University Press.

Canada News Wire. (2013, May 23). Building industry releases report: Industry calls for changes to Ontario Building Code that will result in safe, affordable homes for GTA residents.

Canadian Mortgage and Housing Corporation. (n.d.). *Quieter Condominiums: Cite Bellevue Phase III* (Innovative Buildings Case Study No. 12). Retrieved from www.cmhc-schl.gc.ca/en/inpr/bude/himu/inbu/upload/CitÄ-Bellevue.pdf [February 16, 2015].

City of Vancouver. (n.d.) *Noise Control Manual.* Retrieved from www.vancouver.ca/files/cov/noise-controlmanual.

Davidson, M. J. (1981). *An Analysis of Condominium Consumer Complaints in the State of Florida: 1975-1980* (Unpublished doctoral dissertation). Florida State University, Tallahassee, Florida.

Hendry, D. (2013). *Noise: A Human History of Sound and Listening.* New York: Harper Collins.

Keil, R. (2002). "Common-sense" neoliberalism: Progressive Conservative urbanism in Toronto, Canada. *Antipode*, 34, 578–601.

Kern, L. (2010). Selling the "scary city": Gender, freedom, fear and condominium development in the neoliberal city. *Social & Cultural Geography*, 11(3), 210–230.

Langlois, P. (2012). *Meaning, Media and Dwellings: The Public Image of the High-Rise Toronto Condo* (Unpublished doctoral dissertation). University of Toronto, Toronto.

Lasner, M. G. (2011). Behind this facade: The generic condo as a space of autonomy. In J. Williams (Ed.), *Tarp, Architecture Manual: Spring 2011, Insidious Urbanism* (pp. 45-49). Brooklyn: Pratt Institute, School of Architecture.

Lasner, M. G. (2012). *High Life: Condo Living in the Suburban Century.* New Haven & London: Yale University Press.

Lasner, M. G. (2015, February 17). Reform the condominium. *New York Times.* Retrieved from http://www.nytimes.com/2015/02/17/opinion/reform-the-condominium.html?_r=0.

McMahon, T. (2014, April 22). Condo hell. *Maclean's.* Retrieved from http://www.macleans.ca/society/life/condo-hell/.

O'Connor, A. (2008). *Punk Record Labels and the Struggle for Autonomy.* Lanham: Lexington Books.

Pigg, S. (2015, July). Trump hotel investors lose legal battle. *Toronto Star*, S12.

Preville, P. (2012, July). Faulty Towers. *Toronto Life*, 36–44.

Radovac, L. (2011). The "War on Noise": Sound and space in La Guardia's New York. *American Quarterly*, 63(3), 733–760.

Rosen, G. & A. Walks. (2014). Castles in Toronto's sky: Condo-ism as urban transformation. *Journal of Urban Affairs*, 37(3), 289–310.

Silverman, C. & S. Barton. (1984). *Condominiums: Individualism and Community in a Mixed Property Form*. Berkeley: Institute of Urban and Regional Development, UC Berkeley.

Tett, G. (2010, July). Silences and silos: Why so few people spotted the problems in complex credit. *Financial Stability Report*, 14. Retrieved from https://www.banque-france.fr/fileadmin/user_upload/banque_de_france/publications/Revue_de_la_stabilite_financiere/ etude14_rsf_1007.pdf.

CHAPTER 4

PRIVATE SUBURBAN HOME: THE PHANTASMAGORIC INTERIOR AND THE GHOSTLY INDIVIDUAL

Ondine Park

The ever-increasingly ubiquitous suburban house, tucked away within residential enclaves, is the site of home for a large and increasing portion of Canada's population.[1] The *idea* of home as being suburban is even more compelling.

The following chapter is embedded in the tradition of social spatial theorizing—a perspective that sees places and spaces as social *spatializations*. This means that all places and spaces, including the suburb, are ongoing social productions (Lefebvre, 1991; Shields, 2013): that is, rather than simply being an independently existing container, product, or thing, space is an always emerging becoming, contingently formed through routine, habit, and discourses. In this view, the suburb is in part defined and conditioned both by its materiality and by the way it is enlivened by those who make use of it, including making a home of it; but, in addition, it is also always more than this materiality and enactment. The suburb also consists in such immaterialities as the affective, the desired and desirable, the mythic, and, importantly, the imagined. It is this imaginary aspect of the suburb on which this chapter focuses; in particular, it considers the suburban imaginary.

The suburban imaginary is a concept I use to describe the culturally and historically specific set of meanings, expectations, images, and ideas about the suburb that is shared and formed in the popular imagination, particularly through cultural mediation (Park, 2014). The suburban imaginary is a social production: it is something that we co-produce both personally and socially;

and in turn it is also something that comes to us in various preconstituted ways and helps condition and produce our interactions with and understandings of the suburb. This imaginary informs how we come to expect or know the spatialization of the suburb prior to, in concert with, or even in tension with our direct experience of it. Despite the suburb's varied history and a great deal of nuanced suburban scholarship, the suburban imaginary changes very slowly and continues to be generic, simplistic, and easily recognizable. The dominant image of the suburb persists. Even personal experience does not deter belief in the dominant image. Ideas people have about "suburbia" often contradict their own experience of it (Teaford, 2008; Corcoran, 2010). It is important to regard this still operative dominant imaginary as lively and very powerful because it has material consequences: the way the suburb is imagined influences the policy and financing decisions made about cities (Teaford, 2008, p. xiv) and the decisions and conditions that shape people's lives. In the following chapter, I consider the ways the suburb is imagined and what we might be able to learn from this imaginary. In particular, I consider the idea of home as deeply informed by and constitutive of the suburban imaginary as it emerged historically and philosophically, and look at ways it is represented in the work of contemporary Canadian artists. These works of art articulate and interrogate the ways in which the suburb is imagined and can be understood as providing interpretation of and critical reflection upon the suburb as site of home.

THE SUBURB

The contemporary suburb as a spatial form emerged as an effect of the Industrial Revolution, starting to form around the 1800s, first in England and then in the United States of America (Hayden, 2003; Fishman, 1987). There are many different versions of suburban history, owing to the various ways in which "suburb" can be defined,[2] but the version that locates the beginning of the modern suburb in response to the Industrial Revolution is a view supported by observers from that time such as Friedrich Engels (1987/1845), who described the newly forming spatial arrangements of the industrial cities as reflecting newly emerging social class and gender organization. The middle classes began to build houses at a remove from the city in order to maximize the healthful benefits newly believed to be offered by the physically, morally, and spiritually hygienic private, domestic dwelling located away from the hustle and pollution of the city. Yet this commutable distance still allowed businessmen to stay engaged with city commerce while women (ideally as wives and mothers) stayed home to nurture children (Fishman, 1987).

In contemporary visual art, the suburb is represented as a serial spatialization (Park, 2014); that is, it is imagined as a series of mutually separate spaces that provide different functions and enable different kinds of activities and affective attachments. Accordingly, in representations of the suburb, two distinct categories of space can be found: the exterior and the interior. These two spaces stand not only distinct from each other but indeed in opposition to each other. The suburban exterior is represented as ugly and too large and repetitive in scale—making the human seem irrelevant in an all-too-human-made environment (Park, 2014). Moreover, the exterior is presented as a *non-place*: a space in which social meaning has been prevented from accreting or from which social meaning has been evacuated.[3] In contrast to the suburban exterior described thus as a space unfit and unavailable for human dwelling, the suburban interior shuns exteriority and offers protection against it. The suburban interior figures as a space of, and ineluctably marked by and for, the private individual and family and their things: the suburban interior is home.

HISTORICAL AND PHILOSOPHICAL CONDITIONS FOR THE DEVELOPMENT OF THE SUBURB

The social theorist Walter Benjamin, recounting changes to technologies of perception and life in nineteenth-century Paris, noted that the *interior*—a new type of spatialization—historically emerges in this period of modern industrial urbanization as living space separate from the place and sphere of work. This interior, this place of private dwelling, was a retreat for the private citizen from both social life and business life (Benjamin, 1999, pp. 8–9). The interior was opposed to the place of work, and both commercial and social considerations were kept out of this space of privacy. In the interior, the private individual was able to mark out and affirm his individual existence (Benjamin, 1999, p. 14). (This imagined individual capable of self-hood and self-fulfillment was historically a man.[4]) The interior, the private space of the private individual, offered coziness, comfort, and a space of individuality (to the middle-class man). It was the "universe of the private individual; it is also his étui.… It is as if he had made it a point of honor not to allow the traces of his everyday objects and accessories to get lost" (Benjamin, 1999, p. 20). An étui is a small case for holding small articles such as needles (derived from an Old French verb that means to enclose, to guard, to hold). The implication here is that the interior holds, contains, and collects together all the smallest traces of the individual's existence so they might not get lost: "The traces of its inhabitant are molded into the interior" (Benjamin, 1999, p. 20). The residence was, then, conceived as a container for the individual that perfectly fit and was fitted to the particularity and the peculiar contours of the inhabiting individual (Benjamin, 1999, p. 220). The inhabitant's imprint was so precise and so deeply moulded, Benjamin asserts, that the interior could be read accurately, in the inhabitant's absence, as clues to piece together his individual personality.

To be clear, the division between an inside and all that is excluded from the inside was not itself what was new in the nineteenth century. The division between inside and outside is not what Benjamin was describing as a historically new development. Indeed, the house has been understood as a means by which to separate inside from outside since antiquity, enabling the related conceptual separation of nature (outside) and human (inside), public (outside) and private (inside) (Kaika, 2004, p. 265; Arendt, 1958). Yet, despite this long-standing understanding of the house as enabling spatial division, the particular character of the public and private spheres, which the house was imagined to separate, shifted during and since the Enlightenment. Specifically, "the right to a private space became closely linked to the idea of individual freedom (of the white, Western male subject) that constituted the core of Enlightenment thinking, and access to an isolated private sphere became part of a broader social project of emancipation" (Kaika, 2004, p. 265). The private house was the spatial manifestation—that is, the private house both confirmed and acted as evidence—of this individual freedom. In this reimagination of the house's role emerged the ideologically imbued idea of the *home*: "a place liberated from fear and anxiety, a place supposedly untouched by social, political and natural processes, a place enjoying an autonomous and independent existence" (Kaika, 2004, p. 265–266).

According to architectural historian John Archer (2005), the contemporary residential suburb is the large-scale articulation of this ideal of the home as the culmination of the strong aspirational ideologies of private property and individual selfhood. For Archer, the philosophical grounding of suburban architecture is in a series of shifting attitudes towards the meaning and design of the house in its relation to the homeowning individual. Beginning in the 1700s, the design of houses was increasingly influenced by Enlightenment conceptions of selfhood, property, and privacy, and especially by philosopher John Locke's articulations of the ideal of the individual as a rational, agentic actor separate from society and able most fully to self-actualize through private property. As a result, the privately owned house became a site of selfhood; that is, it began to be understood as an integral element of the full expression of the self. Houses began to be designed and decorated as a reflection of the individual homeowner's identity and personal criteria, moving away from the design of houses as the execution of architectural typologies appropriate to the owner's position in social hierarchies—which architects had been doing prior to this, since the Renaissance (Archer, 2005, p. 2). The house now reflected the owner in design and through the accumulation of things in a way that nothing else could. And, significantly, the house was increasingly a fundamental component of self-fulfillment: without privately owned property—in particular, without access to a private interior—one could not truly fulfill the conditions of achieving selfhood. For Archer, this is the driving philosophical underpinning that we see realized in the increasing ubiquity of the suburbs.

Further transformations in the early twentieth century brought about an intensified understanding of the house as a privatized enclosure that expresses the self. Among these developments that contributed to this transformation were "a legal definition of personhood as private property; the popularization of psychological discourses about the self; ... and the growing strength of market mechanisms designed to elicit and sustain specific attachments to home" (Blaustein, 2009, p. 40). Importantly, this nexus of private house as site of the self's interiorized home became more explicitly and ubiquitously spatialized as suburban. Thus, "individuality, independence, and moral virtue [were equated] with an overwhelmingly suburban conception of private space" (Blaustein, 2009, p. 42).

Consistent with the notion of the interior as the deeply individual and individualized site of the private individual, many contemporary artists who represent the suburban interior vividly catalogue the material edifices of suburban interior life and demonstrate ways in which suburban interiors bear the peculiar imprint of their inhabitants. For example, Guelph-based artist Susan Dobson's photographic series *Open House* explores this theme of the conveyance of biographical information in these "traces" of the inhabitants. Although these interiors are not filled with the velvety and plush surfaces that literally moulded and took the physical impressions of those nineteenth-century inhabiting counterparts Benjamin describes, the particularity of the objects and decoration of the suburban-home interiors photographed by Dobson create an impression of their inhabitants that is just as distinctive. Many of the rooms are highly idiosyncratic: in many cases, the walls are literally marked by the inhabiting owners, painted in murals. For example, in one colour photo, part of a bathroom can be seen through an open door, which is centred in the image. Both the door and the visible wall of the bathroom are adorned with hand-painted murals of scenes from Michelangelo's Sistine Chapel ceiling. On the door, a muscular, nude young man looks over his back. On the wall, Michelangelo's God, from the vignette *The Creation of the Sun, Moon and Vegetation*, is outstretched, pointing towards (and in the process of creating) the golden orb of the sun, accompanied by two smaller figures curled in his billowing robes. This trio hovers above the bathroom sink, a small mirror centred over God's abdomen. While the viewer cannot directly read the motivation behind the peculiar decorative decision to paint a bathroom with renditions of Michelangelo's masterpiece, it seems clear that by painting so ostentatiously, the inhabitant conveys something personal, even if not entirely legible. Many rooms featured in *Open House*, decorated thematically, unabashedly declare the personal interests, experiences, and likes of the inhabitants.

Dobson's photos intimate an intimacy: they seem to offer a private (potentially intrusive) glimpse at deeply personal and personalized spaces. Indeed, many rooms seem overflowing with a profusion of personal things and intimate decorative touches. A colour photo depicts a kitchen (see figure 4.1). Fairly large, white, and otherwise nondescript with its mass-produced cabinetry, the bland environment is layered with a superabundance of children's art—drawings, paintings, paper crafts—tacked onto almost every visible surface. Many clues, including children's boots, pink bag, and umbrella at a door, and the stuffed animal on the counter next to the stove, suggest that at least one school-aged girl lives in this home with someone who celebrates (or feels compelled to post) her art. This image suggests, seemingly less intentionally than the Michelangelo mural but no less strikingly (and perhaps more apparently legibly), the expression of an intimate and significant devotion.

FIGURE 4.1: THE SELF ON DISPLAY IN THE PHANTASMAGORIC HOME INTERIOR

Source: Untitled by Susan Dobson, from the series *Open House* (2002/2003). Lightjet print, 101.6 cm x 127 cm. www.susandobson.com/OpenHouse.html. Photo courtesy of Susan Dobson.

Although the images appear almost as snapshots of daily life, Dobson staged these interiors with the help of the actual inhabitants (Dobson, n.d.). *Open House* is, then, an invited tour of home interiors on display. The scenes represented in the photos demonstrate the constitution of individual, private life intentionally put on display by their respective inhabitants. In the image of the kitchen, the utter excess and almost manic display of personal and personalized embellishments seem playfully but insistently to suggest not only that there is a child in this home but also that perhaps she is the focal point of the home and of family life. At the same time, despite the intentionality of the displayed home, Dobson's works also suggest the degree to which the interior reflects the inhabitants in perhaps less-intended ways. There is another layer of impression imprinted upon the interior. The scenes present glimpses into expectations of what is presentable as home, revealing more deeply embedded desires, necessities, and expressions of the inhabiting individuals. Thus, in the kitchen, the overwhelming indirect presence of the child becomes strangely excessive upon a prolonged viewing of the scene. The image suggests the degree to which a home, styled and individualized by the choices of the adult homeowners, is overwritten by their children, less intentionally but more directly and insistently individuating the domestic interior. Thus, the intention to create an impression or a preferred reading of both the home interior and the homeowners is subverted yet reinforced by this element of display.

If the interior can be read as providing material evidence of the dwelling individual, it also helps to define and *produce* the dwelling individual. The interior is the result of, hosts, and produces both the individual and the need for endless aesthetic, consumer, and pragmatic decisions. Such decisions imbue and extend the individual self into the material and psychic making of the interior. Individuality, then, is not an attribute or essence that pre-exists the making of the interior but is one co-produced by these decisions, as well as by the requirement to decide. As Gaston Bachelard (1964) argues, the house—the interior—*inscribes* dwelling into the inhabitant: "Over and beyond our memories, the house we were born in is physically inscribed in us. It is a group of organic habits" (p. 14). In Bachelard's framing, the relationship of activity and reception is turned around. It is not merely the house that acts as an empty receptacle of the individual's activity, produced by and bearing the marks of this activity: the one who dwells in turn becomes a "diagram" of inhabitation. The particularity of inhabiting a first home inscribes itself into the inhabitants' habits—into the very way in which they use their body—and thus shapes all their subsequent iterations of inhabiting: "The word habit is too worn a word to express this passionate liaison of our bodies, which do not forget, with an unforgettable house" (Bachelard, 1964, p. 14–15). More than simply reflecting, representing, or embodying the character of its residents, the house reciprocally and actively marks the dwelling individual, producing the dwelling individual and making the inhabitant become the representation or expression of the particularity of dwelling within that specific house. In these ways, then, the interior creates the individual as much as the individual creates the interior.

THE SUBURBAN HOME INTERIOR AS PHANTASMAGORIA

The interior, in being imagined as a self-made, self-making environment—that is, an environment that is made by the self and that makes the self—is expected to be controlled, safe, and private enough to be able to reflect one's preferences and to help produce a self. In contemporary artwork representing the suburban-home setting, an excessive fulfillment of the expected guarantees of safety, insularity, and privacy easily turns into a sense of inescapability, secrecy, suffocation, suppression, perversion, and angst—making the interior an intense place overstuffed with private meaning: the interior retreats from an encircling non-place (Park, 2014). Under conditions in which the non-place proliferates, the individual is left responsible for meaning making. As such, the interior incorporates those who are accounted in the meaning making but shuns those who are not. Images of suburban homes reinforce boundaries that are both physical and, ultimately, social: exteriors and interiors are disconnected from each other, separated by impenetrable boundaries that render both spaces inescapable. Exteriors appear with menacing or guarded entries. Interiors appear without exits: doors and windows tend to be absent. When windows do appear, views through the glass are often blocked by curtains or give glimpses into an otherwise contained world, such as crowded rooftops with no sky or fenced-in yards with nothing beyond. Exteriors and interiors are mutually segregated and refuse relationality (Park, 2014).

As Benjamin describes, the citizen within his private interior became a collector of consumable culture, appearing to partake in the world by surrounding himself with the decontextualized material-cultural artefacts of a world from which he was separate: "The private citizen who in the counting-house took reality into account, required of the interior that it should maintain him in his illusions. This necessity was all the more pressing since he had no intention of adding social preoccupations to his business ones. In the creation of his private environment he suppressed them both. From this sprang the phantasmagorias of the interior" (Benjamin, 1969, p. 169). The private, categorically separated interior is a *phantasmagoria*. The phantasmagoria was a late eighteenth-, early nineteenth-century image-projection performance in which a procession of images were projected from hidden lanterns, creating a spectacle in which the viewer gained an impression of movement. Likewise, the domestic interior is phantasmagoric in making the private individual appear *as if* participating in the world, but not actually doing so—creating the impression or illusion of participation. Because the lantern—the source of the images and the means of the production of the phantasmagoria—was invisible to the audience, the transition between images "created a dream-like and ghost-like visual effect" (Pile, 2005, p. 19). Thus, not only did the phantasmagoria create the illusion of movement, but additionally the mechanism of this illusion created a hallucinatory quality. As such, the effect of both aspects of the phantasmagoria—the appearance of the spectacle and the concealment of the processes that produce it—is one of alienation (Pile, 2005). Similarly, the private individual, nestled within the comforting confines of the newly emergent domestic interior of the nineteenth century, was alienated by the simulation of engagement with the larger world, which was, in fact, merely an effect—the production of a semblance of lively reality. This interior "represented the universe for the private citizen. In it he assembled the distant in space and in time. His drawing-room was a box in the world-theatre" (Benjamin, 1969, p. 169). The interior-dwelling individual was also alienated by the inability to see the social conditions that produced and maintained the phantasmagoria of the interior: the spatial-ization through which the domicile offered a retreat and protection from a (social) reality that seemed only to exist beyond the limits of the domestic home interior. As Benjamin observed, "To live in these interiors was to have woven a dense fabric about oneself, to have secluded oneself within a spider's web, in whose toils world events hang loosely suspended like so many insect bodies sucked dry. From this cavern, one does not like to stir" (Benjamin, 1999, p. 216).

In contrast to the interior, in which the private individual man may mark out and affirm his individual existence, in the places of work and particularly in the streets, "people appear only as types" (Benjamin, 1999, p. 14). The withdrawal and retreat of the citizen into the phantasmagoric world of the private interior was the spatialization of a concomitant political and social withdrawal of the citizen—the "demonstrable flagging of the social imagina-tion" (Benjamin, 1969, p. 167). Individuals no longer imagined their efficacy through their action as social citizens but rather through having children: that is, the citizen reimagined his capacity to impact the future through pri-vate familial means rather than social and political ones (Benjamin, 1969, p. 167). Such a conceptualization of the individual has larger-scale implications.

In creating this private home interior—this phantasmagoria—the indi-vidual ostensibly creates a space safely outside of the realm of public life. In it, the private individual suppresses concern for not only his business inter-ests but also his social function (Benjamin, 1999, p. 19). In other words, the reimagination of the citizen as a private individual contained such a political figure safely within a private, apolitical, asocial home. This is why, for Maurice Blanchot (1987), the interior cannot be the space of political possibility. For Blanchot, the conditions of the possibility of being and living otherwise—dif-ferently and freely—are grounded in *everyday life*, which is in the city streets, "if it is anywhere" (Blanchot, 1987, p. 17). Understood in these spatial terms, political and social possibility grounded in daily life is not to be found in the coziness of the interior of home. Whereas the "man on the streets" is always on the cusp of becoming political, the man ensconced within "the four walls of his familial existence" is depoliticized, consuming spectacle in a waking half sleep, unaffected by the images that parade before his eyes; meanwhile, the political citizen in him sleeps (Blanchot, 1987, p. 15). The vitality of the political man on the streets is dulled, as the man in his four walls renders the world desiccated (like Benjamin's insect bodies sucked dry). He falls into a hallucinatory state as he consumes the world, feeding off of small and trivial units of the world as simulation in the phantasmagoric interior. Thus, able to consume the spectacle of the world without being called to action or feeling involved by it, the individual safely contained in his homely interior is also safely unthreatening in the social and political world beyond. Viewing the world as spectacle for entertainment, he does not experience himself as part of that world and, in particular, as one who can affect that world or effect any collective world.

It is important to highlight the particularly suburban character of such an orientation to depoliticized privacy in the interior of the home. As a result of the above-noted historical changes to the notions of the self brought about by the Enlightenment, it became important to be able to differentiate one's individual identity from larger society. A key means by which to accomplish this "categorical differentiation of identity" was through the individual's relationship to privately held land. Specifically, differentiation

> "could be accomplished most obviously by establishing one's residence, that is, one's site for establishing one's personal and private identity, in a locale that was both literally and rhetorically contrapositional to that most social and urbane of places, the city. The answer was the suburb. In other words, the city came to be identified as the social or public domain against which personal identity necessarily was defined" (Archer, 2005, p. 27).

In other words, the Enlightenment's demand to categorically differentiate oneself "led to an incipient suburban imperative" (Archer, 2005, p. 27): a demand to live in the suburbs.

Furthermore, in the early twentieth century, with emerging configurations and effects of a spreading notion of privacy, in order to "be a good citizen of a stable nation, it was assumed (and arguably still is) across large sections of built, textual, and visual worlds, one must inhabit an autonomous, detached unit with identifiable boundaries that at once announce its contents to the social world and seal, stabilize, and defend them from it" (Blaustein, 2009, p. 42). The accomplishment of such an ideal of individual house ownership on such a universal scale, so as to fulfill (or attempt to fulfill) the ideal of the good citizen and of the stable nation, is the suburb.

GHOSTS IN THE HOME INTERIOR

Hannah Arendt (1958) describes the domestic interior of the modern individual as an escape—not from political life but from public, social life (p. 38)—into the petty, albeit pleasurable concerns with "small things" in which the modern individual tends to trifling domestic items "within the space of their own four walls" (Arendt, 1958, p. 52). For Arendt, such an orientation to trivial domestic things historically emerges as a symptom of the alienation the individual experiences from the larger historical, political, and social forces, as well as from the pace and relentlessness of change under conditions of modernity and particularly of rapid industrialization. Arendt acknowledges why immersion into such a comfortable domestic sphere is eminently humane and desirable: here, everyday life is comforting. Interiority is the sphere of intimacy, privacy, comfort, and withdrawal, and offers a disengagement. Unlike in public life, in the interior, the modern private individual presumably does not actively feel a sense of alienation and anonymity but one of fulfilled individuation and an actualized (if small sense of the) good life, even if the conditions are ultimately annihilating. One is not "an anyone" (that is, anonymous), as in Blanchot's man in the street, but a particular, distinct someone—one who is located and locatable in his particular place. However, for Arendt, such a reorientation of the conditions of happiness to such a small domain forfeits "the grand, fully human happiness of the public realm" (Kogl, 2009, p. 520). In contrast to the possible grandeur of the public realm, the private realm is *charming*—captivating in its capacity to "harbor the irrelevant" (Arendt, 1958, p. 52). The public realm, in being unable to harbour the irrelevant, can never be charming. For Arendt, to live a private life is not to live a "truly human life" (p. 58) or even within "reality," because it is an entirely subjective life, lacking the confirmation of or permanence achieved by and enabled within sociality. According to Arendt, private life is a life marked by a consciousness of *privation*—a lack, an insufficiency. This privation is the lack of other people, of the social. The private man is one who, from the perspective of others, "does not appear, and therefore it is as though he did not exist. Whatever he does remains without significance and consequence to others, and what matters to him is without interest to other people" (Arendt, 1958, p. 58).

The status of the private individual, understood in these terms of privacy, should be alarming. The individual who is private in this way—the one who remains within interiors, retreating from the social world, the one who is unrecognized or unrecognizable by others, the one who cannot or will not participate in public life—is, in anthropological terms, the one who is socially dead (Patterson, 1982)—that is, someone who no longer lives in the social world. The interiorized, private individual as socially dead can then be understood as a ghost inasmuch as the one who is socially dead is a presence that cannot be explained because their presence does not fit into recognizable shared-meaning systems. Unencumbered by the weight of political and social responsibility, the ghost floats through the social world but does not participate in it. In this way, it haunts the social. Significantly, ghosts are instructive figures:

> Ghosts appear when the trouble they represent and symptomize is no longer being contained or repressed or blocked from view.... The whole essence, if you can use that word, of a ghost is that it has a real presence and demands its due, your attention. Haunting and the appearance of specters or ghosts is one way ... we are notified that what's been con-

cealed is very much alive and present, interfering precisely with those always incomplete forms of containment and repression ceaselessly directed toward us. (Gordon, 2008, p. xvi)

Ghosts direct attention to the emergent process in which that which has been made to pass out of perceptibility, markedness, or questionability is erupting. While the private individual is socially dead, in the form of a ghost, they are resurrected as a troublesome figure that has something social to tell us.

FIGURE 4.2: PHANTASMAGORIC GHOST HAUNTING THE SPACE BETWEEN INTERIOR AND EXTERIOR

Source: Winter Kitchen by David Hoffos (2007) from the series *Scenes from the House Dream*. Single-channel video, audio and mixed-media installation. Trépanier Baer Gallery, Calgary. Courtesy of the artist and Trépanier Baer. Photo credit: David Miller.

Lethbridge-based artist David Hoffos's multimedia piece *Scenes from the House Dream: Winter Kitchen* (see figure 4.2) suggests a haunting narrative that is not quite legible. In this miniature diorama, the viewer sees the inside of a kitchen at night. A coffee pot sits on the stove to the left. Below it, on the ground, a coffee mug lays overturned. The only sources of light are from the inside of the refrigerator, which is slightly ajar, and the lights outside, visible through patio doors and the window over the sink. The window is open and seems to have been open for some time because snow appears to have blown in through it, forming piles on the countertop and floor, although it is not now snowing. Curtains billow hauntingly around the window, and the sound of howling wind can be heard. The curtains are not material, and they are not present in the diorama space: they are phantasmagoric. Hoffos created the illusion of blowing, spectral curtains through a series of projections and mirrors.

The source and mechanics of the illusion is on display in the exhibition space, but these are not immediately present in the dioramic space, rendering the effect of the glowing, blowing curtains ghostly and unsettling. The visibility of the technique that creates the ethereal, moving effect, however, adds a layer of illegibility: Why are the curtains the only moving element of the display? To what do these ghostly apparitions direct us to pay attention? This interior space seems to have been violated and abandoned or silenced: the mug, which seems at one time to have fallen or been dropped, stays overturned on the floor; the refrigerator and window have been left open, while the door remains shut. The home has been either intruded upon or exited from. It is unclear, however, what has happened or when. There is just a creepy affective charge, giving the sense that something sinister may have transpired.

The effect of such a violation of the interior is unsettling and unsettles the home as the site of security and privacy. The curtains—both in and yet not present in the scene—at the threshold between inside and outside, blown in and out by the howling winds of the exterior, remind us that whatever the ideals of privacy, of seclusion from social and political life, the private interior can never be perfectly sealed and separated from the larger social and political world: social and political life blows through and sets the very conditions of possibility for every household. Hoffos's kitchen is a miniature stage set—a false environment created precisely for the ghostly to be projected onto it. Just as for Benjamin, this interior is a phantasmagoria, an illusion created by a projection onto and covering over the actual material conditions. Enchanted by the phantasmagoric, the interior is rendered more violable precisely because of its failure in the social imagination.

INTERIORITY

If the interior is characterized as a spatialization of the private individual, then *interiority* can be understood as the qualities of, relationships to, or associations with the interior. Interiority, as the quintessential characteristic of the interior, can, then, be dislocated from the particular spatialization of the interior; that is, the quality of interiority, such as privacy, need not be attached to the interior. Worryingly, Arendt (1958) observes that under the conditions of mass society, the realm of privacy—of interiority—has expanded (p. 38) so that an entire population might be enchanted by the charm—the captivating irrelevance—of private life. The private is not by this enlarging made public but instead causes the public realm to recede (p. 52). Accordingly, contemporary life is lived not only within the privacy of the domestic interior: extended realms of privacy and interiority have also supplanted the public, common realm. The residential suburb extends the home interior to the backyard, with its carpet-like lawn and outdoor living-room patio set, to the cul-de-sac, with its assumed guarantee of safety for children's games, and to the neighbourhood as an extended safety zone. The interiority of the home is extended through the car into a personal bubble of interiority that renders commuter routes long strings of consecutively arranged interiority bubbles. For Arendt, this expansion and overtaking of the public by interiority has also destroyed the private sphere, "because it has become the only common concern left" (p. 69): the interior's capacity to shelter and comfort and act as a substitution for a fully human public life has been obliterated by the expansion of interiority.

FIGURE 4.3: EXTENDED INTERIORITY

Source: Backyard (Daytime) by Kristopher Karklin (2014). Inkjet print, edition of 7, 36" x 54". Barbara Edwards Contemporary, Calgary. Photo courtesy of Kristopher Karklin.

In Alberta-based artist Kristopher Karklin's *Backyard (Daytime)* (see figure 4.3), a nude man stands slightly off-centre, facing away from the viewer towards a backyard. This suburban backyard is a representation of Karklin's father's backyard located in Fort MacMurray, the site of the expansive Canadian tar sands. An eerie, suffocating feeling pervades the image. At a glance, the photo appears to be indefinably odd: there is a desolate intimacy to the image. The man's body is tensed, holding a baseball bat poised in a ready position to hit a ball that will never arrive: the man is alone in this space. He stands in this posture on a wooden deck that overlooks a grassy backyard. The yard is enclosed on two sides by a fence and on the third side by a driveway that ends in an empty garage. Boreal forest crowds around the other side of the fence. Above the trees is a sparsely clouded but otherwise clear blue sky. The image in the photograph is jarringly artificial and seems to have strange proportions and lighting. This is a photo of a dioramic collage. The fence marks not only the limits of the backyard but also the walls of the diorama model. The image of the man has been digitally placed in a photo of a miniature set comprised of miniature three-dimensional models (the garage, the deck, the fence, and a firepit) and images of outside elements (sky, trees, grass) rendered from collages of photographs affixed to the surfaces of the space. The trees and the sky are a wallpaper mosaic of tree and sky photos, respectively. The ground is a tessellation of patterned tiles that give the sense of "grass" and of "cement." This backyard scene is, then, a realist image comprised of a photograph of simulated and assembled images and objects. It is an extended interior space enclosed by surfaces that present the expansive outdoors as a multiply removed two-dimensional simulation. The man is situated in an outside-looking interior. Here, nature appears as a phantasmagoria projected onto and simultaneously forming the walls. Nature is simulated as a lively world stretching beyond the bounds of human inhabitation but in fact acting as a cover that disguises the expansion of the desiccated, antisocial interior. The man is a social ghost whose presence is marked in and by this interior, but whose existence cannot be confirmed by others—because there are no others. Not only is this an extended interior—a backyard and forest as room—but it is also an interiorized exterior: there is no outside beyond this charmed, expanded private interiority.

CONCLUSION

Suburban architecture and the house-ownership ideal had their roots in trans-formations of thought surrounding the self and its relation to the private home interior. The private realm characterized by an orientation to interior dwelling is an insistent orientation: one that shapes understandings of what it means to be a person, a good citizen, and how to live a good life. It is also a particularly suburban orientation specifically counterposed to everyday life, understood as unfolding in a public, politically potent, and social realm. In contemporary Canadian art, the suburb is imagined as the extension and fullest expression of this logic of separating the spheres of life. These artworks illustrate and open for analysis the ways in which the interior enfolds and represents the individual—in their absence or in their ghostly presence: the suburban interior is imagined as a spatialization of the individual. Moreover, these interiors also produce the producing individual. Indeed, the interior and the individual reciprocally cre-ate each other in their individual and mutual articulation. With the formation of the interior comes an attendant retreat into depoliticized, asocial privacy into which one may escape from the demands of the incommensurate worlds of work and especially society. The expansion of interiority and the extended in-teriorities of the suburban backyard, neighbourhood, or car on the commuter highway cannot constitute the public sites of the everyday, which is redolent with political and social potentiality.

Importantly, the work of art attunes us to the phantasmagoric interior of the suburban home haunted by the ghostly individual, thus illuminating the alienation of everyday life within the very core of comfort. These haunting figures enable an affective legibility of the problem of the difficulty of social and political life and simultaneously hint towards potent hidden desires and promises for a life lived with meaning.

NOTES

1. An estimated two-thirds of the population of Canada live in the suburbs (Gordon, n.d., n.p.).
2. As Sies (2001) notes, "Suburbs come in a diverse range of densities, planning forms, land use mixes, and relationships to nearby urbanized areas and ... they may boast a confusing array of dwelling types and costs" (p. 316).
3. See Augé (1995) for an extensive discussion of the non-place. What is of particular importance about the non-place is that it is based on an anthropological understanding of place, in which *place* describes spaces that are imbued with agreed-upon social meanings. Non-places, in contrast, are spaces, peculiar to super modernity (what Augé describes as the current version of modernity, in which we live marked, among other things, by hyperindividuality). In non-places, spaces do not have shared social meanings but rather a multiplicity of possible individual and contingent meanings.
4. As such, the spatial segregation of the spheres of public and private life describes only, at best, a small, middle-class, masculine population—and even then, only imaginarily or for heuristic purposes. In my discussion of the theoretical origins of the individual and the interior in particular, I use the masculine pronoun explicitly and intentionally.

REFERENCES

Archer, J. (2005). *Architecture and Suburbia: From English Villa to American Dream House, 1690–2000*. Minneapolis and London: University of Minnesota Press.

Arendt, H. (1958). *The Human Condition*. Chicago: University of Chicago Press.

Augé, M. (1995). *Non-Places: Introduction to an Anthropology of Supermodernity*. (J. Howe, Trans.). London and New York: Verso.

Bachelard, G. (1964). *The Poetics of Space*. (M. Jolas, Trans.). Boston: Beacon Press.

Benjamin, W. (1969). Paris: Capital of the nineteenth century. *Perspecta* 12, 165–172.

Benjamin, W. (1999). *The Arcades Project*. (H. Eiland & K. McLaughlin, Trans.). Cambridge, MA and London: Belknap Press.

Blanchot, M. (1987). Everyday speech. (S. Hanson, Trans). *Yale French Studies* 73 (Everyday life special issue), 12–20.

Blaustein, J. (2009). Counterprivates: An appeal to rethink suburban interiority. *Iowa Journal of Cultural Studies*, 3(1), 39–63.

Corcoran, M. P. (2010). "God's Golden Acre for Children": Pastoralism and sense of place in new suburban communities. *Urban Studies* 47(12), 2537–2554.

Dobson, S. (n.d). Susan Dobson homepage. www.susandobson.com/

Engels, F. (1987/1845). *The Condition of the Working Class in England*. London and New York: Penguin Classics.

Fishman, R. (1987). *Bourgeois Utopias: The Rise and Fall of Suburbia*. New York: Basic Books.

Gordon, A. (2008). *Ghostly Matters: Haunting and the Sociological Imagination*. Minneapolis and London: University of Minnesota Press.

Hayden, D. (2003). *Building Suburbia: Green Fields and Urban Growth, 1820–2000*. New York: Vintage Books.

Hoffos, D. (n.d). David Hoffos homepage. www.davidhoffos.com/

Kaika, M. (2004). Interrogating the geographies of the familiar: Domesticating nature and constructing the autonomy of the modern home. *International Journal of Urban and Regional Research, 28*, 265–286.

Karklin, K. (n.d.). Kristopher Karklin homepage. www.kristopherkarklin.com/

Kogl, A. (2009). A hundred ways of beginning: The politics of everyday life. *Polity, 41*(4), 514–535.

Lefebvre, H. (1991). *The Production of Space*. (D. Nicholson-Smith, Trans). Malden, MA: Blackwell.

Park, O. (2014). *The Suburban Imaginary: Ambivalence, Strangeness, and the Everyday in Contemporary Representations of the Suburb*. (Unpublished doctoral dissertation). Edmonton, University of Alberta.

Patterson, O. (1982). *Slavery and Social Death: A Comparative Study*. Cambridge, MA: Harvard University Press.

Pile, S. (2005). *Real Cities*. London and Thousand Oaks: Sage Publications.

Shields, R. (2013). *Spatial Questions: Cultural Topologies and Social Spatialisation*. London and Thousand Oaks: Sage Publications.

Sies, M. C. (2001). North American suburbs, 1880–1950: Cultural and social reconsiderations. *Journal of Urban History, 27*(3), 313–346.

Teaford, J. C. (2008). *The American Suburb: The Basics*. New York and London: Routledge.

PART TWO

Not at Home: Homemaking on the Margins

As stated at the outset of this collection and by many of our contributors, commonsensical ideas of home tend to either embrace home as a feeling or equate home with a physical space, most often those private spaces in which we live. Home is conceived of as a concrete dwelling where we feel safe, loved, and well cared for, where our basic social needs of food, clothing, and shelter are met. But what sociological insights may be gleaned from analyses of home located in the narratives of individuals whose home lives and homemaking experiences fall outside the confines of these narrow, everyday constructions? What does home mean for racialized working-class women, poor single mothers, for youth-in-care or young persons living on the street? What does it mean to be home and/or to engage in the making of home in provisional, liminal, and/or institutional settings? And for those who lack a material space to call home, what does it mean and, relatedly, what are the implications of being homeless?

These are some of the larger questions raised in the second part of *Sociology of Home: Belonging, Community, and Place in the Canadian Context*. Each of our contributors offers timely analyses of home and/or homelessness that enhance our understanding of the sociological meanings attributed to homemaking activities and practices in important ways. First, all of our authors speak to issues related to the historical and/or contemporary realities of social exclusion, inequality, and marginalization in relation to the social reproduction of home and home-based lives. They capture the lived experience of homemaking in difficult spaces and the precariousness of said homemaking, as narrated by those who make or construct meanings of home while not at home but in semipublic spaces (see, for example, Borchard, 2013), including rescue homes, foster or group homes, care facilities, shelters, the homes of family and friends, or the street. Second, these chapters point to and/or challenge the relationship between the private and the public, and draw attention to the in-between or overlapping spaces that often characterize the intersection of the private or domestic and the more public or institutional aspects of home. And finally, these works collectively emphasize the ongoing tensions that exist between home (or lack thereof), homemaking and citizenship, agency, citizenship rights, and responsibilities—and how these relations are increasingly complicated in a neoliberal society.

A number of these themes are reflected in Shelly Ikebuchi's chapter, "At the Threshold: Domesticity and Victoria's Chinese Rescue Home, 1886–1923." Here the historical relationships between the private/public, foreign/domestic binaries are interpreted vis-à-vis the homemaking experiences of Chinese women housed in Victoria, BC's Rescue Home, ca. 1886–1923. Though one of the Home's stated goals was to save Chinese women and girls from the perils of slavery and prostitution, Ikebuchi's research shows how, in the absence of private space, women as wives, mothers, and workers engaged in homemaking in an institutionalized setting reminiscent of a "total institution" (Goffman, 1961). She employs the concept of "threshold space" to theorize and analyze the rescue home both as a domestic space and simultaneously as a public place, one that mediates women's private and public lives and in doing so reveals what she terms the "slippages" between the two. She further questions what it means "to be home" and examines how legal, religious, and state-based constructions of home not only informed gender, familial, and race relations in the past, but serve to (re)create and regulate foreign and domestic subjects or citizens in the present.

The intersections of home, family, and citizenship are also taken up by Kate Butler in her chapter, "Negotiating Family Relationships in the 'Home': Examining Constructions of Home for Youth-in-Care in Greater Victoria." Drawing on semistructured interview data, Butler's research explores how youth-in-care (i.e., biological, foster, or group-home care) come to understand and experience home as wards of the state in an increasingly individualistic society. She stresses the difficulties youth-in-care encounter in their attempts to negotiate and practise citizenship when their family lives are subject to change and their homes are transient, temporary, or transitional spaces mediated by governmental child and welfare systems. While her findings indicate "safe," "stable" homes are more conducive to engaged citizenship, she suggests the entrenchment of the neoliberal state and the privatization of family life may only serve to further marginalize youth-in-care.

Constructions of home have been and continue to be central to the study of both family and gender relations, especially within feminist political, economic, and sociological traditions. Situated within this framework, Amber Gazso's chapter, "Low-Income Lone Mothers and 'Home': The Importance of Social Relations," offers feminist analyses of social reproduction and homemaking on the margins that reveal women's multiple and interrelated conceptualizations of home. Her narrative approach, grounded in the stories of poor women, affirms the importance that social-support networks play in maintaining mothers and families' day-to-day lives. The absence of a place "to call home" highlights the meanings mothers ascribe to their shared networks, familial and community connections, or what Gazso terms "social interactions" with respect to their "creation" or "practice" of home. Contrary to popular understandings of home as a "place," her research suggests "home" often resides in mothers' accounts of their social relationships that foster and sustain home feelings.

Part 2 is rounded out by Jennifer Robinson's chapter, "Lacking the Safeguards of Home: Experiences of Youth Homelessness," which centres the narratives of homeless youth and illustrates how the lack of home negatively impacts young people's relations (i.e., with the general public and police) and limits opportunities to exercise "political and legal rights" in comparison to those who are housed. Inhabiting public spaces, homeless youth are subjected to social control, stereotyping, and stigmatization. She argues that homeless youth are perceived as "deviant" or a "nuisance," and are viewed as "non-persons" and are dehumanized. To counter individualized, reactive responses to homelessness, Robinson concludes that further structural analyses are warranted. She recommends the pursuit of collective action to address persistent poverty contributing to social exclusion and more proactive solutions to eradicate homelessness.

REFERENCES

Borchard, K. (2013). Homelessness and conceptions of home. In M. Kusenbach & K. E. Paulsen (Eds.), *Home: International Perspectives on Culture, Identity and Belonging* (pp. 113–134). New York: Peter Lang.

Goffman, E. (1961). *Asylums: Essays on the Social Situation of Mental Patients and Other Inmates.* Garden City, NY: Anchor Books.

CHAPTER 5

AT THE THRESHOLD: DOMESTICITY AND VICTORIA'S CHINESE RESCUE HOME, 1886–1923

Shelly Ikebuchi

L ocated in Victoria, British Columbia, the Chinese Rescue Home (the Home) was administered by the Woman's Missionary Society (WMS) from 1886 until 1942. Although its mission would change over the years, it originated as a benevolent mission whose goal was to rescue and reform Chinese (and later Japanese) prostitutes and slave girls or those who were thought to be at risk of falling into one of these categories. Both an institution and a home, this space helped to define the limits and possibilities of the home and, in some ways, the nation. The Chinese Rescue Home inhabited a space on the threshold between the private and public realms, and, as an institution, the Home blurred the lines between the foreign and the domestic. This chapter, thus, exposes the slippages between the private and the public, as well as between the foreign and the domestic.

Susan Gal has pointed out that "since the emergence of the doctrine of 'separate spheres' in the nineteenth century, social analysts in Europe and the United States have repeatedly assumed that the social world is organized around contrasting and incompatible moral principles that are convention-ally linked to either public or private: community vs. individual, rationality vs. sentiment, money vs. love, solidarity vs. self-interest" (Gal, 2002, p. 77). Yet, as feminists have pointed out, these dichotomous notions are far from incompatible: "The principles associated with public and private coexist in complex combinations in the ordinary routines of everyday life" (Gal,

2002, p. 78). The line between the public and the private realms, if it can be said to exist at all, is fraught with ambivalence and contradiction. Ideas and practices that have traditionally been associated with the public realm continually insinuate themselves into the private realm. Likewise, the emotive and affective elements that have long been associated with the private realm have always existed within the public realm. Just as bodies continually cross between private and public spaces, so too do practices, emotions, and ideas. Some scholars have begun to question the integrity of the spaces themselves by asking whether private spaces such as the home are truly separate or distinct from the public spaces outside of them (Legg, 2003; Gowans, 2003; Blunt, 1999).

In this chapter, I interrogate theoretical spaces and physical spaces associated with the Chinese Rescue Home, as they transcended or merged the public and private. I argue that these *in-between* spaces help to deepen our understanding of how the public and private inform each other. Thus, this chapter uses the metaphor of the threshold to explore what it means to be *home,* both in a national sense and a familial one. The threshold of the home might be considered both an emotional and physical transitioning between the public and the private. The physical threshold of a home is a place where the public realm is shed, sometimes quite literally. Shoes may be left behind in favour of comfortable slippers. Outerwear is discarded, as the warmth and protection of the home deems it unnecessary. The threshold is a place of transition and transformation. But it is not a clean place. The residue of the public remains within this private space. The dirt from one's shoes mingles with rain from discarded umbrellas. At the threshold, the remnants of the public world literally enter and settle into the private spaces. By examining the messiness, the instability, and the contradictions of the threshold, we can come to see a more nuanced representation of that which lies outside of and within home spaces. The threshold is not simply an empty space between two spaces: it is a space where practices and ideologies from both sides are negotiated, played out, embraced, and sometimes discarded.

In what follows, I use the metaphor of the threshold in two ways. First, the threshold is considered as an organizing environment that defines what must be maintained and/or set aside in an effort to ensure the purity and clear delineation of each realm. As such, the negotiations that take place within the threshold help to (re)define both the public and the private realm. While this study does not provide an analysis of strictly private or public spaces, if indeed these can be said to exist, my argument is that what occurs within threshold spaces informs all of those spaces that exist in proximity as bodies move across, through, and between. Second, the threshold is a space that has the potential to disrupt the existing order. It is a messy and contradictory space where the demands and expectations of both realms must be suspended to allow for the coexistence and mingling of multiple and diverse bodies, discourses, and practices. As a temporary and transient space, the threshold thus has the potential both to order and to break down order. It is not a space of strictly private relations or of public interactions, but instead is a preparatory space for each. As such, what happens at the threshold, what is ordered or resisted there, determines how both public and private spaces are inhabited, resisted, and redefined.

I begin by exploring how the productive spaces of the Chinese Rescue Home built on and challenged discourses of the foreign versus *domestic* through the proposed *domestication* of foreign subjects. By productive spaces, I refer to the physical and theoretical spaces where discourse and ideologies were produced. Discourses of domesticity were produced both within and outside of the private realm and sometimes in between. The merging of the private with the public, both discursively and materially, created a space for the creation of the Chinese Rescue Home. It was precisely this interplay of the private and public that allowed for the Chinese Rescue Home to function as a threshold space that provides insights into the production of both public and private discourses and spaces. Through an examination of the two Royal Commissions, the Home's records, photographs, and official Woman's Missionary Society reports, this chapter thus considers the material and productive spaces that defined and challenged what it meant to be home.

Following my discussion of the Home itself, I trace the discourses that informed it by asking how and why the Chinese Rescue Home came to exist in the first place. Discourses of home and family, I argue, were produced in the courts, just as they were produced through intimate relations. As productive spaces that informed the Chinese Rescue Home, both the courts and Royal Commissions played important roles. Judges ruled on custody of Chinese women, thus cementing legal and social ideas of proper familial relations. Likewise, Royal Commissions defined (white) citizenship by defining the limits and possibilities of what it meant to be *home*. Although the Royal Commissions took place within the public realm, here I theorize them as constituting a type of discursive threshold, as they catalogue, organize, produce, reproduce, and challenge both public and private narratives. Through an examination of the Royal Commission on Chinese Immigration (1885) and the Royal Commission to Investigate Chinese and Japanese Immigration into British Columbia (1900), I offer a semiotics of the domestic which reconsiders the interplay of the private and the public. It is important to note that while I rely on binaries of the private and public and of the foreign and domestic, the goal here is to challenge the notion that these binaries represent categories that are either static or distinct. Although the domestic realm has often been associated with women, men and women have routinely crossed the threshold between the domestic realm and the more public, male-dominated realm. The in-between or threshold spaces thus provide insights into how gendered ideas and bodies filter into and through both realms.

THE CHINESE RESCUE HOME AS A THRESHOLD SPACE

Although the Chinese Rescue Home was often considered to be a domestic space, it was also framed in other, much more public ways. Within court documents, Home records, and the Royal Commission of 1902, the Chinese Rescue Home was described as a refuge, an educational and training facility, and a religious mission. It was a space where the private and the public intersected and overlapped. As evident in its name, being a home for Chinese and Japanese women was one of the primary functions of the Home. Duncan and Lambert (2004) describe the home as "perhaps the most emotive of geographical concepts, inextricable from that of self, family, nation, sense of place, and sense of responsibility toward those who share one's place in the world" (p. 395). That the home was all of these things was evident in the following wedding announcement that was placed in the *Victoria Daily Times* in 1895 by the missionary women who ran the Home.

> Mr. and Mrs. Sam are the eighteenth couple married from the Home, all of whom are comfortably settled and in the enjoyment of the blessings of Christian citizenship. This speaks well for the work of the Home and affords a strong claim for the continued support and sympathy on the part of the Christian people of this city and province at large. Every one of the 18 women thus settled in peaceful and reputable homes of their own, have been won from a state of slavery to which death itself would have been infinitely preferable.[1]

This announcement was meant to draw attention to the successes of the Chinese Rescue Home. For the women who resided in the Home, becoming a success usually meant one of four things: Christian marriage, domestic service, missionary work, or, in rarer cases, obtaining an education. As the announcement implied, Christian marriage would garner the resident the blessings of Christian citizenship, as well as peaceful and reputable homes. Thus, private concerns such as marriage spilled over into the public realms of citizenship. In order to achieve these successes, training and discipline were necessary. Proper domesticity was not something that was seen as natural for Chinese and Japanese women but was instead something to be achieved through domestication. Thus, domesticity was something to be institutionalized and produced within the walls of the Chinese Rescue Home.

The domestic realm has been a site of intervention for many who have been interested in the material ways that the home informs gender and gender relations. While many scholars initially viewed the domestic as part of the private realm and juxtaposed this realm against the male-dominated public realm, others have charted women's movements both within and outside of the domestic realm, thus troubling the boundary between the private and the public in significant ways. Stephen Legg (2003), Georgina Gowans (2003), and Alison Blunt (1999), for instance, examined how women in India used home spaces as political spaces of anticolonial resistance, which helped to define not only the domestic but the national and imperial as well. These studies indicate the usefulness of destabilizing notions of truly private or public spaces. They ask us to consider the boundaries, or thresholds, between the private and the public as being fluid or porous, as women and men routinely crossed these boundaries. It is such boundaries that this chapter interrogates in order to consider how domesticity was used to alleviate public concerns and mandates.

Within threshold spaces, we cannot separate the dirt of the public world from that which enters into the spaces of the private world. It collects in the crevices of threshold spaces, yet it cannot be completely shed in these spaces, as it is tracked deeper into the home. Theorizing the Chinese Rescue Home as a threshold space allows us to consider not only how the public and the private mingled and settled in one space, but also how this mixing was influenced by and also shaped the relations and practices on either side. The threshold was not just a place *between* the danger of the outside and the purity and sanctity of the home, but it was a place that allowed for both to exist in one space, as it facilitated the movement of the public into the private and the private into the public.

The Home was literally home to the Chinese and Japanese women who were rescued or otherwise recruited. Yet it was also institutional, governed and administered by a religious organization; it was simultaneously private and public. There, women were prepared and trained for their work in private spaces. But in these spaces, women also negotiated public interventions and discourses in order to resist these private imperatives. How these negotiations were resolved was based on both race and gender. Given that the Home was an institution run by women and for women, the logical form that it would take would be as a domestic space. The buildings that were chosen or constructed were houses, despite the fact that they would function as schools or institutional spaces. The house that the Chinese Rescue Home occupied from 1888 to 1909 was well maintained and had a simple charm, with its wide decorative veranda and the ivy-covered posts flanking the front entranceway. Although a domestic space, the colonial style was a reminder of the historical legacy of empire, the wide veranda and decorative finishing reminiscent of Victorian values of home and hearth. The building itself, the *home,* was to represent both domestic citizenship and proper (white) domesticity. There was a small picket fence in front of the house, which marked off the space as a home. The existing gendered norms were carefully maintained, at least outwardly. Yet this space also challenged binaries of foreign and domestic, due to the racial mixing that took place within its walls.

In 1909, when the Women's Missionary Society decided that a new and larger facility was necessary, the construction of the new space once more mimicked traditional home spaces. Architecturally, the Home was fashioned in the manner of a Georgian manor home. It had parlours, sewing rooms, bedrooms, and a kitchen. These spaces informed the types of relationships that were subsequently forged within them, with discourses of family and motherhood being prevalent throughout the Home's records. One of the imperatives of the Home was the domestication of Chinese and Japanese women. In order for Japanese and Chinese women to be acceptable citizens, they had to be taught the rudiments of what it meant to be a *proper* woman. Training Chinese and Japanese women to be good Christian wives was part of this imperative. The women who ran the Home were deeply invested in the marriage of these women, and to this end they screened and selected husbands from the Chinese and Japanese male residents who applied to them for wives. Despite the fact that these women were expected to become wives to Chinese or Japanese men, the training they received linked proper domesticity with whiteness. Kitchens were meant to allow women to be trained in Western cooking, sewing rooms for the making of Western garments, and parlours for teaching the so-called proper way to build a fire. All of these domestic chores were part of what Foucault called the making of docile bodies (Foucault, 1995, pp. 149–156); at the same time, they were about both making a home and disciplining and domesticating a people. The work that was carried out in the Home was concerned with the private realm, but it also had more public and productive concerns given that one of its mandates was the production of citizens (although the Christian citizenship that was offered was not to be mistaken for Canadian citizenship). Thus, the domestication that was taking place was also concerned with maintaining a hierarchy of citizenship.

The Home served other purposes that, while not strictly private, were usually domestic. These spaces also served as training spaces for those young women who would go into domestic service. Domestic spaces lent themselves to gendered expectations but were also tied to multiple institutional imperatives. Although producing Chinese and Japanese women as wives and mothers produced one type of success story, in reality the Home was also training women in skills that were necessary for sending them out into service, thus supplying white women with much-needed service staff. The records often measured the success of their changes through references to the satisfaction of white women with their *girls*. In 1899 Matron Snyder reported that "most of the Japanese women who were with us have taken positions as servants when leaving the Home."[2] One young woman entered the mission after being rescued from a brothel at the age of 19. She stayed for two years, and was then "hired out" as a servant; it was reported that she was "giving satisfaction" in the home where she worked. Other women who went out into service were also described as "proving most efficient helps"[3] or "giving good satisfaction,"[4] although some were deemed "a great disappointment."[5]

Clearly, despite the necessity that the Home take on a domestic veneer, the public continually inserted itself into the private through the productive activities that took place within its walls. In addition to the benefits to white women who hired the Home's residents, the training of Chinese and Japanese women in domestic skills also served a different goal: that of supporting the Home financially, as the residents took on sewing and other needlework. Thus, the production that took place within the walls of the Home provided economic support for the women who resided there and for the institution itself. Within this space, white women worked to prepare Japanese and Chinese women to enter into both the domestic realm as wives and into the public one as workers. The organizational work that occurred within the Home allowed for domestic servants, wives, and mothers to be produced according to white standards of domesticity.

The Home also acted as a threshold between the legal domain and the familial one. The public realm, through the courts, police, and immigration officials, supplied the Home with a ready stream of what the missionaries referred to as inmates; however, it would be a mistake to imply that this confinement was uncontested. The placement of Chinese women into the Home was challenged by Chinese community members. Although the Home records were quick to frame court disputes as issues over familial custody, Chinese community members who challenged them did so by filing writs of habeas corpus. This strategy implicated the Home in the forceful confinement of these women. The writs contended that the women were held against their will and against the rights of their family or so-called owners. The judges who decided these cases did so through legal definitions of family, custody, *and* confinement, thus defining the Home as both familial and as institutional.

Within the spaces of the Home, the public and private mingled and coalesced. Through this mixing, the private and the public were challenged, negotiated, and often redefined. This intermingling had repercussions in terms of the types of Chinese and Japanese homes that emerged outside of the Home, as well as the types of productive and economic relationships that were produced by it. In order to understand the processes of domestication and their effects, the domestic must be considered as both constitutive of and constituted by institutional and state practices. Further, the Chinese Rescue Home, as an institution and as a domestic space, was informed by national and global discourses that helped to define what it meant to be home.

THE FOREIGN AND THE DOMESTIC

Understanding the home as a domestic space is only one way in which to define home. Not only the familial abode signals home. Conceptions of the nation as *domestic* soil also signal home. In her discussion of antebellum America, Amy Kaplan (1998) makes the argument that "the *domestic* has a double meaning that not only links the familial household to the nation but also imagines both in opposition to everything outside the geographic and conceptual border of the home" (pp. 581–582). She contends that the domestic, in both senses of the word, was defined against foreignness, in particular against racial demarcations of otherness. Even before the inception of the Chinese Rescue Home, the Chinese were central to discussions of what it meant to be home and who could reside there. The two Royal Commissions discussed here lend insight into how Chinese women in particular would be implicated in defining the domestic. The Royal Commissions were concerned with negotiating whether, how, and under what circumstances the so-called foreigner could become domestic. These commissions were the discursive thresholds where knowledge was catalogued and produced, and where suspect bodies were examined and evaluated in order to determine who could enter into the domestic realm and who must remain an outsider. Yet the delineation of the foreign and the domestic was not always straightforward. Even while these commissions sought to alleviate concerns around immigration and settlement of foreign populations, so-called foreigners were finding homes in Canada.

Defining a nation (*domestic* soil) necessitated both definition and delineation of the Other. Both the Royal Commission on Chinese Immigration (1885) and the Royal Commission to Investigate Chinese and Japanese Immigration into British Columbia (1900) investigated concerns raised by white community members about Japanese and Chinese populations, the threat they were seen to pose to the (white) nation, and the growing hostility towards them. The report of the 1885 commission was 731 pages and drew on discussions from inquiries in San Francisco, California, Portland, Oregon, and British Columbia. The report of the second commission was 430 pages and, like its predecessor, included transcripts of evidence taken during a two-and-a-half month inquiry. These commissions drew on, challenged, and (re)produced binaries of foreign and domestic.

Marilyn Lake and Henry Reynolds (2008) contend that the "nineteenth century was the great age of global mobility" and that "more than 50 million Chinese embarked for new lands in these decades, an equal number of Europeans and about 30 million Indians" (p. 23). In their groundbreaking book, they explore how "white men's countries" were created through the "transnational circulation of emotions and ideas, people and publications, racial knowledge, and technologies" (p. 4). While their book traces the transnational circulation of racial discourses, this chapter focuses on the intersections of the foreign and the domestic as they were negotiated in localized public forums, in order to ask not only how it was that discourses of the foreign helped to define the limits of citizenship but also how the foreign and the foreigner settled into the fabric of the nation. So-called foreigners did not just exist at the threshold of the nation but instead were a crucial part of the *work* of producing and organizing what it meant to be domestic. While the types of racial discourses that appeared in the Royal Commissions dealt with so-called foreign bodies—both within Canada and beyond it—as Lake and Reynolds (2008) remind us, the creation of a white nation relied not only on barring foreign bodies but on *defining* them as foreign (p. 23). In addition to producing the foreigner as the antithesis of white domesticity, part of the work of producing domestic citizens was concerned with domesticating and transforming the foreign *into* the domestic. Whiteness was certainly viewed as superior, yet part of that superiority relied on the idea that whites had a duty—a burden—to assimilate and raise up the so-called foreigner in their midst. Thus, part of the organizing work that was to take place during these commissions was around how the foreigner might find a place within the nation.

It is at the threshold that we are most apt to find matter out of place. Mary Douglas (1966), in her classic book *Purity and Danger,* posited that "dirt is essentially disorder. There is no such thing as absolute dirt: it exists in the eye of the beholder" (p. 2). Dirt in the garden is seen as order. In the home, it is disorder. Thus, dirt "offends against order. Eliminating it is not a negative movement, but a positive effort to organise the environment" (Douglas, 1966, p. 2). The two Royal Commissions discussed here were, by their very nature, attempts to organize the environment by ridding it of what were seen as contaminants. As Renisa Mawani (2009) explains, "Commissions of inquiry were often responses to the limits and failures of law. Emerging within circumstances of crisis that warranted official investigation and state response, commissions provide a rich site in which to examine the types of proximities, relations, and practices that were believed to endanger the settler regime" (p. 26). Although both the Royal Commission on Chinese Immigration of 1885 and the Royal Commission on Chinese and Japanese Immigration of 1902 were part of a larger state (public) response to concerns around Chinese and Japanese immigration, the discussion, in many ways, revolved around more private concerns.

Throughout the commissions, the foreign was defined as distinct from the domestic. Yet each was essential to the definition of the other. Definitions of foreign were necessary in order to cement what it meant to be domestic or *at home.* The defining of the domestic subject (citizen) was closely related to ideas of familial domesticity. In fact, it was precisely this relationship that allowed for the possibility that Chinese and Japanese women might be transformed from foreign subjects into subjects who might be conceived of as domestically compatible with the nation. Domestication and domesticity were to become vital to their assimilation. In fact, assimilability was a question of whether the foreign could be made domestic (Lake and Reynolds, 2008).

In the two Royal Commissions, there was considerable disagreement on how to deal with foreign bodies. Many argued that Chinese and Japanese populations were simply inassimilable. Inassimilability was measured, in part, through reference to the home and domesticity, as proper familial relations and

proper domesticity were to be assessed by the standards of the white population. In the first of the two Royal Commissions, the discussion around Chinese
in Victoria quickly turned to the domestic realm. When asked to comment on
the habits of the Chinese population in regards to public morality, public order,
and public health, Victoria's mayor, Joseph Carey, immediately made reference
to white standards of living, focusing on religion, home, and family: "As regards public morality, they are not the same as we are. They do not respect the
Sabbath or wives. Their wives here, as I understand, are their second wives, and
chiefly prostitutes; these living and bringing up their families whose children
are known to be illegitimate."[6] The mayor then went on to implicate the home
in particular: "As to public health, we have a great deal of trouble with them
in that respect. They do not feel the same as ourselves that it is necessary for
them to keep their houses clean."[7] This supposed lack of cleanliness was often
attributed to the lack of *proper* women. That Chinese communities were often
framed as bachelor communities meant that Chinese were viewed as both transient and unclean. Concerns around *public* health, order, and morality were
defined through reference to white standards of home and family.

Nayan Shah (2001) makes similar observations in his work on San Francisco's Chinatown. As in Victoria, references to cleanliness were one way to
distinguish the foreign from the domestic. Thus, the *private* domestic realm
was crucial to the defining of *public* health, morality, and order. The foreign
was defined as that which was outside of the standards of white domesticity.
In Victoria, opinions about the lack of Chinese cleanliness were not unani-
mous. When questioned by the commission, Chief Justice Sir Matthew Begbie
responded to allegations that Chinese were unclean by stating, "That they are
as a race dirty, or believed to be dirty, seems quite incompatible with the fact
that they are as a race unanimously invested with a virtual monopoly of the
two occupations requiring the highest degree of personal cleanliness, vis.,
cooking and washing."[8] Begbie's response points to the fractures that existed
within the white community with regard to the assimilability of Chinese
populations. Regardless, both Mayor Carey and Chief Justice Begbie drew on
the domestic to define the limits and the possibilities of citizenship.

Given that the domestic realm was so crucial to definitions of belonging,
it is not surprising that the domestic realm held promise and possibility
for those who wanted to enter Canada. During the second commission,
the Royal Commission on Chinese and Japanese Immigration of 1900, the
commissioners questioned Reverend Canon Beanlands of Victoria. Unlike
many of his colleagues and contemporaries, Beanlands did not oppose immigration to Canada; in fact, he advocated a very distinct type of immigration. His concerns were with the domestic realm. When asked if it was "in
the interests of a country to have an immigration of her people here who
will not assimilate," Rev. Beanlands replied that it was, as he "should always
like to see them as a servile class."

Q. From which you could draw help?

A. Yes.

Q. No intention of elevating?

A. I do not see it is our business in the least.

Unlike Reverends Perrin and Rowe, who were also interviewed and who saw it as a Christian duty to elevate the Chinese, at least in terms of their religious training, Beanlands was less concerned with this aspiration. But when asked if he thought this servile class could go to heaven, Beanlands magnanimously replied, "Oh, yes; we have no class distinction there."⁹ Here, Reverend Beanlands was clear: class and racial distinctions were necessary, but it was within the domestic realm that Chinese could find a place.

The domestication of Chinese men helped to maintain existing racial taxonomies. Although the domestic realm was to offer Chinese entry into the white community, their entry relied on their service to white populations. The slippages between the foreign and the domestic were evident in Beanlands's reply. Although welcoming Chinese immigrants as a servile class was meant to keep them always as foreigners, they were to be allowed to enter not into the public realm but into the domestic realm. They were to find their places within the *homes* of white Victoria residents. Although they would not be seen as at home in the nation, they were crucial to the making of homes. Further, given that many of the Chinese immigrants were men, the slippages that took place were also along the lines of gender. The feminization of Chinese men was seen as one way to *domesticate* them while they were on Canadian soil. Thus, discourses of national inclusion and exclusion both drew on and challenged ideals of proper (white) domesticity. Although both of the Royal Ccommissions were public hearings, they were concerned with policing the private realm, the home, as well as the public one. Both of these commissions served as thresholds where the foreign and domestic were sorted and organized. However, this threshold space was itself disordered. Within this discursive space, ideas around the foreign and domestic were entangled with narratives of public concerns and their links to the private realm. These entanglements provided opportunities for Chinese men and women to challenge prevalent discourses of inassimilability.

Although Chinese prostitutes were framed as domestic insurgents and as domestically delinquent, it was the domestic realm that held the promise of their transformation. During the first inquiry, Sergeant John Flewin testified as to his contact with Chinese populations in his role as a police officer. Like Mayor Carey, Flewin began his discussion with reference to the unsanitary conditions in Chinatown. His discussion then turned to Chinese women: "There are upwards of one hundred women here. Their characters are very low, almost all prostitutes. White people get into trouble with them."¹⁰

Chinese women were clearly a concern to the commission, not only because of their supposed immorality, domestic delinquency, and lack of conformity to white standards, but also because of the threats that they posed to the sexual propriety of white families and homes. The Royal Commission framed Chinese prostitutes as threats to white populations in terms of both disease and their corruption of "little boys,"[11] and the commissioners warned the Canadian government that the "Chinese are the only people coming to the continent the great bulk of whose women are prostitutes [*sic*]."[12] According to the Royal Commission, the "evidence is that Chinese prostitutes are more shameless than white women who follow the same pursuit, as though the former had been educated for it from the cradle."[13] The innate immorality of Chinese women, then, was seen to have originated in the domestic realm, as the commission implicated mothers, who ensured and produced their children's immorality. So the very foreignness of Chinese women, and arguably the entire Chinese population, derived from the deviance that originated in the domestic realm. Thus, as I have shown in the discussion of the Chinese Rescue Home, domestic training was one way to deal with this deviance.

What it meant to be domestic was defined in the public realm. The Royal Commissions helped produce domestic (public) citizens by both defining and blurring the lines between the foreign and the domestic. Further, producing the domestic (national) subject relied on notions of proper familial domesticity. It was not only Chinese men who were meant to be domesticated through their placement in the domestic realm. Although Chinese, and later Japanese, women were described as the antithesis of familial domesticity, it was precisely this reliance on the domestic realm in defining the national one that allowed for and necessitated missions such as the one that underwrote the Chinese Rescue Home. If the domestic was so important to how public citizens were measured, then the key to transforming or domesticating foreign bodies was also to be found in the domestic realm.

CONCLUSION

The space of the Home challenged the binary of private and public through its public function and its architectural design as a home. It functioned as both a domestic space and a space of productivity, in both an economic sense and an ideological one. This chapter has attempted to expose the slippages between the foreign and the domestic and between the public and the private. It has illustrated one method for exposing these slippages, by considering those spaces where mixing of the private and public was not only allowed but encouraged. This analysis has examined the influence of the private and public as it was encountered within threshold spaces and outside of them. Threshold spaces are both transitory and transformational. They are spaces where discourses, ideologies, and bodies come together in ways that transform them and the spaces around them. Here I have used the material analogy of the threshold to draw attention to how the private and the public organize, influence, and transform each other in complex ways.

Understanding how these binaries coalesced in the past helps us to understand the realities that are produced even in the present. The domestic was defined and produced in both the public and the private realms, in Royal Commissions and in the domestic space of the Home. Evidence of these same types of slippages can be found in present-day threshold spaces. The slippages between the private and public and between the foreign and the domestic are still evident in the recent debates on the Live-in Caregiver Program (see, for example, Pratt, 1999). These debates inform us that the public continues to be invested in and informs the concerns of the private realm. As in my discussion of the Chinese Rescue Home, what is often at stake is not only how racialized groups become subject to white domestication, but also how this is/ was, at the same time, framed as an opportunity for the so-called foreigner to *become* domestic. That this transformation from foreigner to *domestic* citizen takes place within the private realm is a reminder that the public and the private continue to inform and shape each other, forming a solid foundation for what it means, even now, to be home.

NOTES

1. *Victoria Daily Times*, Thursday, December 26, 1895, 5.
2. *Annual Report of the Woman's Missionary Society of the Methodist Church of Canada, 1899–1900*. Toronto: The Ryerson Press, xciv.
3. "Minutes of the Oriental Home and School Advisory Committee," April, 1913, *Oriental Home and School Fonds*: 1896–1914, Record Number MS-2439, British Columbia Archives.
4. "Minutes of the Oriental Home and School Advisory Committee," June, 1897, *Oriental Home and School Fonds*: 1896–1914, Record Number MS-2439, British Columbia Archives.
5. *Annual Report of the Woman's Missionary Society of the Methodist Church of Canada, 1899–1900*. Toronto: The Ryerson Press, xciv.
6. *Report of the Royal Commission on Chinese Immigration: Report and Evidence*. Printed by order of the Commission, 1885. 45.
7. Ibid.
8. *Report of the Royal Commission on Chinese Immigration: Report and Evidence*. Printed by order of the Commission, 1885. 75.
9. *Report of the Royal Commission on Chinese and Japanese Immigration: Session 1902*. Ottawa: Printed by S. E. Dawson, 1902. 29.
10. *Report of the Royal Commission on Chinese Immigration: Report and Evidence*. Printed by order of the Commission, 1885. 50.
11. *Report of the Royal Commission on Chinese Immigration: Report and Evidence*. Printed by order of the Commission, 1885. liii.
12. Ibid.
13. Ibid.

REFERENCES

Blunt, A. (1999). Imperial geographies of home: British domesticity in India, 1886–1925. *Transactions of the Institute of British Geographers, 24(4),* 421–440.

Douglas, M. (1966). *Purity and Danger.* New York: Routledge.

Duncan, J. S., & Lambert, D. (2004). Landscapes of home. In J. S. Duncan, N. C. Johnson, & R. H. Schein (Eds.), *A Companion to Cultural Geography* (pp. 382–403). Malden: Blackwell Publishing Ltd.

Foucault, M. (1995). *Discipline and Punish: The Birth of the Prison.* New York: Random House.

Gal, S. (2002). A semiotics of the public/private distinction. *differences: A Journal of Feminist Cultural Studies, 13(1),* 77–95.

Gowans, G. (2003). Imperial geographies of home: Memsahibs and Miss-Sahibs in India and Britain, 1915–1947. *Cultural Geographies, 10(4),* 424–441.

Kaplan, A. (1998). Manifest domesticity. *American Literature, 70(3),* 581–606.

Lake, M., & Reynolds, H. (2008). *Drawing the Global Colour Line: White Men's Countries and the International Challenge of Racial Inequality.* Cambridge: Cambridge University Press.

Legg, S. (2003). Gendered politics and nationalised homes: Women and the anticolonial struggle in Delhi, 1930–47. *Gender, Place and Culture, 10(1),* 7–28.

Mawani, R. (2009). *Colonial Proximities: Cross Racial Encounters and Juridical Truths in British Columbia, 1871–1921.* Vancouver: UBC Press.

Pratt, G. (1999). From registered nurse to registered nanny: Discursive geographies of Filipina domestic workers in Vancouver, B.C. *Economic Geography, 75(3),* 215–236.

Shah, N. (2001). *Contagious Divides: Epidemics and Race in San Francisco's Chinatown.* Berkeley: University of California Press.

CHAPTER 6

NEGOTIATING FAMILY RELATIONSHIPS IN THE "HOME": EXAMINING CONSTRUCTIONS OF HOME FOR YOUTH-IN-CARE IN GREATER VICTORIA

Kate Butler

In late modernity, youth are increasingly conceived of as rights bearers with particular responsibilities to themselves and others; at the same time, however, they are presumed to belong to a family unit that will take care of their major interests within the setting of a family home. For youth-in-care, this position of precarity is especially challenging, as their relationship to home is governed by the provincial-government care system. For youth-in-care, home is complicated: it can mean foster homes, group homes, youth detention facilities, or homes that they live in with family members, friends, or by themselves. Negotiating these very different understandings of home is an additional expectation placed on young people in the care system. Youth-in-care are expected to belong to whichever foster family or group home they are placed in, even though this can mean that the home experience is temporary, fragmented, and unsettling. For these youth, home is where their lives as wards of the state collide with that of the private family.

In this chapter, I explore how youth-in-care have understandings of home that are shaped by intersections of the state and the family. In other words, the experience of youth-in-care is one in which the public and the private realms overlap. In addition, not only is there a blurring of the public and private spheres, but also, in contemporary societies, there is a downloading of responsibility from the state to the home. Families—biological, foster, or otherwise—are increasingly called upon to carry out tasks for the well-being of children and youth, which used to be performed by the state. How youth enact citizenship claims illustrates the reality of these responsibilities in the home environment. The analysis of citizenship, therefore, is an important and useful way to assess young people's relationship to the home environment. While a stable home is not a prerequisite for the practice of citizenship, findings indicate that stability in the home environment shapes how youth-in-care come to see themselves as citizens. To better understand participant experiences with citizenship at home, I discuss the findings from my research on citizenship practices of 20 former youth-in-care in Greater Victoria and highlight what this tells us about youth citizenship.

I begin with a brief review of the literature on citizenship practices of young people, with an emphasis on citizenship of youth-in-care and what this means for understandings of home. I then outline the research on which this chapter draws by first discussing the methods used to conduct my research on youth-in-care. Next, I discuss the findings of my research as they relate to expressions of foster and group homes among the participants. Finally, I conclude by returning to the relationship between youth citizenship and the home environment, and the challenges for youth-in-care.

LITERATURE REVIEW

As other contributors to this book have illustrated, the home has long been a place where the personal collides with the public. The home is not a safe haven from the realities of the outside world; instead, our very constructions of that so-called outside world are an integral part of the home experience. Scholars writing about the concept of home draw attention to the ways that a sense of home can imbue our relationships to physical land, neighbourhoods, community, and national identity (Duyvendak, 2011; Kasinitz, 2013; Lasch, 1977). It is not new, therefore, to understand home in such a way that it illustrates the problems and fractures that exist among individuals, as well as the ties that bind people together. Like so much else in life, home is experienced differently depending on social location, context, and personal background. Understandings of home are necessarily complicated by intersections of the state and the family.

The state and the family intersect when young people practise citizenship in the home environment. T. H. Marshall (1964) famously delineated the historical trajectory of civil, political, and social rights in Western, liberal democracies. Marshall illustrated that rights are granted by the state to individuals. However, in late modernity nation-states have lost much of their control over significant matters in the lives of their citizens (Giddens, 1992). This means that collective identifications, such as allegiances to a particular country, are often replaced by processes of individualization (Beck, 1992).

The concept of individualization means that individuals are increasingly responsible for their own decisions, without the support of the state. In today's world, being a citizen goes beyond national ties or boundaries and extends into the global realm (Hall, Coffey & Williamson, 1999). In this sense, citizenship is best understood as contested and contextualized: it varies in meaning according to social, political, and cultural contexts, as well as different historical conditions (Lister, 2007). Citizenship is thus continually being negotiated and renegotiated, not only during childhood and youthhood but also across the entire life course (Hall et al., 1999, p. 440).

Youth citizenship, then, is fluid and dynamic, and not dependent solely on the state. Citizenship is not something that one attains when reaching adulthood: it is a way of behaving and acting in everyday life (Smith, Lister, Middleton & Cox, 2005). Understanding citizenship as comprised of processes and actions requires moving beyond the idea of youth as "future citizens" (see, for example, Marshall, 1964). Citizenship is much more than a goal that is achieved when one reaches the age of majority or becomes financially independent (Shaw & McCulloch, 2009, p. 10). With this in mind, youth citizenship refers to the legitimating quality through which young people are entitled to participate in communities and are recognized as members by other people both within their communities and within social institutions (Mortier, 2002, p. 83). This definition recognizes the fluidity and multiplicity of citizenship as it occurs in both public and private spheres; moreover, it recognizes the way that citizenship itself is continually being renegotiated (Smith et al., 2005, p. 440).

If there is an agreement, then, that youth citizenship must mean more than simply legal membership in a political community (Howe, 2005), what else must be included for young people to practise citizenship? There needs to be a recognition of the actions and behaviours that comprise citizenship, along with young people's actual lived experiences. In looking at the literature, a few key characteristics of youth citizenship emerge, including the ability to access rights and exercise responsibilities, opportunities for meaningful participation, and experiences of belonging (see Beauvais, McKay & Seddon, 2001; Howe, 2005; Lister, 2007). These criteria suggest that youth citizenship is about more than formal inclusion: youth must have opportunities to realize rights and to have a voice in decisions that affect them. When we apply the concept of citizenship to the home, therefore, we need to be aware of how young people are included and excluded as they practise and realize citizenship.

For young people who have been in government care, practising citizenship occurs at the intersection of the private family (foster, biological, and other) and the public sphere (provincial policies governing youth-in-care). The home is a crucial site for citizenship practices for youth, as it is the place and space where they spend considerable time, have relationships with adults, and grapple with questions of identity. Youth-in-care have both opportunities and challenges in accessing citizenship claims (Smith, Stewart, Poon, Saewyc & the McCreary Centre Society, 2011). The term *youth-in-care* itself encompasses a wide variety of individuals, who have had very different experiences with the care system.[1] However, despite the varied experiences, there are some similarities that are worth mentioning in terms of challenges for this population in enacting citizenship in the home.

Before I discuss the structural and systemic barriers that youth-in-care face, it is important to note that there are many former youth-in-care who are thriving. As the resiliency literature suggests, there are numerous internal and external protective features that young people develop, which allow them to do well even under difficult circumstances (Ungar, 2004). Furthermore, in British Columbia and across Canada, youth-in-care experience government care differently, and there are many young people who have gone through the system who are leaders in their communities (Andrews, 2008; RCY, 2009; Smith et al., 2011).

Notwithstanding these success stories, however, many youth-in-care face numerous challenges both while in care and when they leave care (Callahan & Swift, 2007; Parton, 2006; Parton, Thorpe & Wattam, 1997).[2] For instance, while children in care and those in the general population experienced the same common health conditions, those in care were diagnosed for these conditions 1.2 to 1.4 times more often than children in the general population (Child and Youth Officer for British Columbia, 2005, p. ii). Furthermore, young women in continuing care became pregnant four times more often than young women who had never been in care (Child and Youth Officer for British Columbia, 2005, p. 2). As for what these health statistics mean for young people, one telling indicator is that youth between the ages of 19 and 25 who used to be in care experience poorer health indicators than those who were not (p. iii). Youth in the care system also report high percentages of abuse (Beauvais et al., 2001, p. 62), as well as neglect. Furthermore, youth who have been in care are at a higher risk of being involved with the youth justice system: 36% of youth-in-care appeared before youth court, in contrast to less than 5% of the general youth population (RCY, 2009, p. 14). These youth are also more likely to be identified as having educational special needs as compared to the rest of the youth population (RCY, 2009). All of these health risks complicate the path to citizenship, as these youth remain on the margins (RCY, 2009).

Moreover, leaving care has been shown to be a traumatic and difficult experience for many youth, as their social support systems can be limited when they leave the home environment, be it foster care, group homes, or other situations (Munson, Lee, Miller, Cole & Nedelcu, 2013). Youth who have been in care tend to have fewer resources, both financial and otherwise, while in care, as well as when they leave (Fisher, Marsh, Phillips & Sainsbury, 1986; Masten, 2006). Some provincial government programs are aimed at helping former youth-in-care: in 2008, the Ministry of Child and Family Development (MCFD) established the Agreements with Young Adults (AYA) program that helps former youth-in-care, ages 19 to 24, transition into adulthood by providing financial assistance for living expenses, child care, tuition costs, and health care (MCFD, n.d.). However, this kind of program does not reach all youth who need it (according to Woolley [2013], only 7.5% receive AYA assistance most years), and many young people remain unaware of the help that is out there. Youth leaving care with mental-health challenges also face hardships when experiencing adulthood for the first time (Munson et al., 2013). Furthermore, many youth leaving care need practical help locating housing, educational programs, and jobs, as well as sustained and meaningful emotional support.

Finally, the demographics of the population of young people in care illustrate that some groups are overrepresented. First, Aboriginal youth are considerably overrepresented in the care system: in 2010, 4,628 Aboriginal youth were in care, comprising approximately 50% of the care population (MCFD, 2010, p. 1), while Aboriginal youth only make up approximately 7% of the general population of children in the province (Child and Youth Officer for British Columbia, 2005, p. ii). Second, in terms of sexual orientation, youth who identified as lesbian, gay, bisexual, and/or transgender (LGBT) are also more likely to have experiences in government care: in the 2011 Fostering Potential study, 12% of youth-in-care identified as lesbian, gay, or bisexual, while the numbers of LGBT youth in the province are likely lower (Smith et al., 2011, p. 12). LGBT youth face unique challenges within the care system and often feel like their voices are not being heard (Ragg, Patrick & Ziefert, 2006). Sources of support for youth can become sources of stress when youth reveal sexual identity (Ragg et al., p. 245). Finally, it appears that recent immigrants and refugees, or youth who are newcomers to Canada, also face particular challenges being in and leaving care, and may be overrepresented in care systems (Hare, 2007). Government care can be a time of great uncertainty for newcomer youth: not only are these youth dealing with the foster care system, but they also have to handle all of the challenges associated with immigration and/or refugee status. These youth are particularly vulnerable prior to coming into care and are vulnerable again during the transition to independence (Hare, 2007).

METHODS

In researching the lived experiences of youth-in-care and their citizenship practices in the home, I used a qualitative research strategy and conducted 20 semistructured interviews in Victoria, Canada with youth ages 14 to 24 who had previously been in government care in Canada.[3] Victoria, the capital of British Columbia, has a population of about 80,000 people, while Greater Victoria includes almost 350,000, making it the 15th largest metropolitan area in Canada (Statistics Canada, 2011) and similar in makeup to other middle-sized metropolitan areas in Canada. By conducting my study in Greater Victoria, I had access to urban, suburban, and rural youth, as well as to Aboriginal youth living on and off reserves. I asked participants to narrate their experiences with citizenship, rights and responsibilities, and belonging and/or exclusion. The interviews began with close-ended background questions about participant experiences in government care and with parental and/or nonparental guardians in the home. Following this, I asked participants questions about rights, citizenship, and community in their daily lives. Throughout the interviews, expressions of home emerged from participant responses to questions about accessing rights and citizenship in home, about their care experiences, and implicitly through discussions of identity, belonging, and exclusion inside and outside the home.

To analyze the data, I used an analytical hierarchy strategy on transcripts of the interviews; this technique involves data management, indexing, and categorization of the material (Spencer, Ritchie & O'Connor, 2003a; 2003b). Spencer, Ritchie and O'Connor (2003a, p. 213) argue that this data-analysis technique is particularly useful for research analysis based on interpretations of meaning. An analytical hierarchy strategy allows for the identification of key descriptive dimensions and accounts, and encourages a move towards "patterns of association" in the data and looking for linkages between and across accounts (Spencer et al., 2003a, p. 215). In performing such analysis, I was able to ascertain associations and themes that are central to understanding expressions of home, which I explore in the results section below.

FINDINGS

For young people on the margins, home can be a place of belonging, but it can also be a place of exclusion, unrest, and alienation. For youth-in-care, home can be understood as a place, a feeling, a person, and/or an idea. Ambiguity in experiences with home were evident in participants' lives as citizens inside and outside the home. Moreover, state intervention in the private home, via social workers, the court system, the police, or others, affects how young people experience the home environment. Feelings of home for youth-in-care are also influenced by a transience that is not evident for many youth; these young people are coming and leaving a variety of homes, which means that their relationships with the home and the people in the home may be short term, temporary, and businesslike or long term, complicated, and familial. In discussing how they see home, participants describe it as everything from a place that they need to escape from, to a temporary holding place, to a safe haven or anchor. For some participants, therefore, practising citizenship in the home environment involves many opportunities for participation, unfettered access to rights and responsibilities, and experiences of belonging; conversely, for others, the home is not a place where it is easy or possible to regularly exercise citizenship. In understanding how participants practise citizenship, I found that one key feature in expressions of home was the participants' relationship with family (biological and otherwise). Relationships with family in the home are crucial to understanding which kinds of home environments are most conducive to citizenship practices in late modernity, when we see a downloading of responsibilities from the state to the family home (Hayward, 2012). In this section, I explore how these family relationships shape participants' citizenship practices within the home.

Practising citizenship in the home inevitably involves interactions with family members. If citizenship involves expressing one's rights and responsibilities, experiencing feelings of belonging, and having opportunities to participate (Beauvais et al., 2001), then the people with whom one lives play an important role in how one can actually participate in citizenship. Participants described family relationships that ran the gamut from unhealthy to ambivalent to supportive. These relationships offer insight into the challenges and opportunities of practising citizenship in the home. They tell us about the kinds of homes that are conducive to allowing for the full gambit of citizenship practices. I will first examine the unhealthy relationships, then the ones that expressed ambivalence about family, and then finally those that had supportive homes. These experiences with family can be seen in the context of citizenship practices described by Butler and Benoit (2015). Furthermore, these expressions of family life illustrate the complexities of citizenship for youth-in-care within the home.

Before discussing these features of home, I offer a few observations about the homes that participants lived in. The homes in question varied among participants; some had only one foster or group care home experience, while others had many: eight participants experienced only one care home or facility, four were in two to three care homes, four were in four to seven care homes, and four were in eight or more care homes. In terms of length of time in care, ten participants spent less than two years in care, five participants spent two to four years in care, and five spent longer than four years in care. As for age when entering care for the first time, three participants were ages two or under, two participants were ages three to nine, ten participants were ages ten to thirteen, and five were ages fourteen and over. The variety of care experiences are represented in each of the following expressions of relationships in the home.

Toxic relationships: "How am I ever going to be normal when I'm surrounded by so much crazy?" (Karina, age 19)

For a plurality of participants (N=9), relationships in the home were toxic: these relationships made participants want to leave home because of the difficulties they had with various people in the home environment. Home became a place that these young people wanted to leave immediately. Participants expressing this version of home felt detached from the home, in large part because of the parents or foster parents they had to deal with on a regular basis within the home.

For those who found their relationships in the home to be mainly toxic, their practices of citizenship are consistent with a reluctance towards the idea of being a citizen. Some participants indicated discomfort with the term citizenship and questioned many of the practices that may be associated with citizenship. Many youth, not just youth-in-care, express uncertainty with the term *citizenship* (Mortier, 2002). However, for youth-in-care, their already precarious position as outsiders navigating public and private realms makes this reluctance potentially more detrimental. Participants practising reluctant citizenship were hesitant in terms of identifying as citizens, but, more importantly, they were also hesitant in their actions as citizens. They expressed uncertainty, disinterest, and apathy towards their understandings of being a citizen: that is, they were not engaging in and with their communities in any sustained way.

In some ways, the reluctant citizen resembles Merton's (1957) "retreatist" who rejects cultural goals and institutional means—a positioning that involves a complete escape from the pressures and demands of organized society. Study participants who practised reluctant citizenship had no interest in being part of mainstream goals and were also not interested in dissenting citizenship practices that privileged alternative ways of being or expressing citizenship. Reluctant citizenship practices do not tend to challenge the status quo; rather these practices can be seen through expressions of exclusion and apathy. In terms of how this practice relates to the home, the reluctant citizen is unsure of his or her place within the home environment, and as a result he or she feels excluded. Home becomes a place to leave and is not a space from which to enact resilient citizenship practices.

For some young people, home was where abandonment and abuse occurred. Tyler, age 20, states, "My grandparents abandoned me with him out in Calgary, and my dad assaulted me, so that's when I got into foster care 'cause I didn't know where else to turn." Similarly, Ruby, age 22, notes: "My mom was doing lots of drugs, and this guy adopted me. My mom got married to him and left us with him, and he didn't want us, so he kicked us out on the street, and I ended up going into foster homes." For Tyler, Ruby, and others, the people who were supposed to take care of them clearly did not.

Abuse was also a common theme in participants' relationships in the home. Sophie, age 21, said she put herself in care when she was 13 in large part due to her abusive relationship with her father. As a toddler, she had been in temporary care before returning to live with her biological family, but at the age of 13 she made the choice to go back into temporary care, mainly because home was so unpalatable. Home as a place where bad things occurred can also be seen in the narrative of Robert, age 21: "I was abused, and nothing, nobody really helped me. It was basically either go into a foster home or staying at home and dealing with all the problems we had." Sophie and Robert's experiences with abuse were not unique: abuse and/or neglect were common themes in the stories that youth told about going into care. Of the 20 participants in my study, 19 said they had experienced some form of abuse at home, and that abuse was partly responsible for them going into care, running away from home, or ending up living with friends. Abuse also played a role in the relationships that participants continued to have with their families, even after they had left care or home.

Expressions of the home as a place that must be escaped or left illustrate the many challenges that youth-in-care face both while they are in the foster care system and after they leave it. The feelings of exclusion from the family environment may exacerbate their relationship to citizenship: how can they act as citizens if they feel like they do not truly belong in their own home? The home is a crucial site for practising citizenship; reluctant citizenship participants illustrate the problems experienced by those youth who do not have stable home environments.

Ambivalent relationships: "They were really nice, but ... I didn't really fit in [or] really feel like I belonged ... They were nice people [but] they weren't my mom and dad." (Shelly, age 14)

For some participants (N=6), the people they met in the home environment were not particularly helpful or harmful in their attempts to practise citizenship. For these individuals, the relationships they established in the home were perfunctory: the emotional connections we associate with the term *home* (see, for example, Lasch, 1977) were absent. These participants claimed that home was simply a place for sleeping and eating; relationships with family (foster or otherwise) were not necessarily central to their attempts to practise citizenship.

When practising citizenship in the home, those who expressed ambivalence about family relationships tended to practise self-responsible citizenship (Butler & Benoit, 2015). Citizenship for these young people is about self-responsibility: relationships with family inside the home are in some ways incidental to practising citizenship because they see citizenship as an individual pursuit. Maira (2009) observes self-responsible citizenship in her work on Muslim-American youth and claims that these young people strive for experiences in the labour market, volunteer out of their individual goodwill and virtue, and pursue education as a means to get ahead (pp. 136–137). In terms of how this self-responsibility relates to family members, it is clear that citizenship is something that occurs externally, away from the home. Self-responsible citizens emulate a kind of good citizenship that emphasizes personal responsibility at all times (Hayward, 2012, p. 12). Being a self-responsible citizen is about being accountable for one's personal choices. A self-responsible citizen, in his or her view, manages his or her own life without surveillance from social-service workers, parents, foster parents, or probation officers, and also without support from the state in the form of income and/or disability assistance. Relationships with family members are seen as separate from the pursuit of citizenship.

Lauren, age 16, exemplifies this ambivalence towards family in her citizenship practices. She has returned to her family after being in care, but has found her relationships with family members to be strained; home does not feel "like home." Her parents moved her to Canada to give her a fresh start, but she and her parents still do not really understand each other. She notes that she no longer feels like running away: "I just needed that independence and to be able to make decisions for myself, and now I'm, like, going to university in a couple years, and I know I'm moving out of my parents' house, so that's kind of motivation to get my stuff done and move out of there." Similarly, Shelly, age 14, has returned home after being in temporary care but says that it is uncomfortable because she feels as though her mom is not supportive: "It's kind of awkward ...'cause I'm overweight and it's obviously a challenge for me, so it's the pressure of being in a new place and starting over again, plus that it's, like, oh.'" Her mom has a new boyfriend who makes Shelly feel sick every time she is around him. Shelly still sees herself as responsible for making the situation work, though; she ends up leaving home for most of the day so she does not have to be around him. Richard, age 15, went back to his mom after being in temporary care because relations improved after a little while, and he has been getting along better with her since he returned home: "We have our ups and downs. She knows I'm struggling and helps me, though. That's it." In all these cases, the participants had moved back home after being in temporary care; they did not feel as though they had a stronger connection to the home than they did in the past. They talked about enacting citizenship separately from their relationships with the adults in their lives.

Participants saw their relationship with parents as one in which they were supposed to learn about responsibility. When youth did not learn individual responsibility at a young age, they saw this as a failure on the part of the government care system or parents. Blake, age 19, discusses his frustrations with his foster parents and biological parents for not teaching him to be responsible: "I think your parents should be able to show you how to survive later on in life.... They never taught me anything about getting a job, or how to save money, or pay rent, or where groceries went, or how to pay my bills— and so basically I was 18, and I didn't know what to do. I thought everything was free!" Blake thought parents should embrace a "good citizenship" so their children could also learn that this was the way to act. Richard, age 15, says he did not learn about personal responsibility as a child and has only recently learned about this:

I didn't really realize what life was like until I was, like, 14, 15, and then I actually realized, like, what was going on and how it works.... When I was a little kid I had no worries and things—I thought I was invincible and that nothing could happen to me. But then stuff started happening, and I realized how, like, dangerous it really is out there ... getting involved with the wrong people and getting in trouble.

Rather than questioning why there is so little structural support for them or why parents should provide this, Blake and Richard both emphasize their roles as self-responsible citizens.

Finally, participants who expressed ambivalence about their family relationships often commented that they were "lucky" that they did not have worse experiences. Lauren, age 16, sees her body as inferior because it does not look the same as her stepmother's. However, she also resists the image that her stepmother is striving for: "And she'd be really, like—she'd make sure she looked, like, pristine, and her hair was perfect, and everything was, you know, perfect, and yet I didn't have money, you know. I'd go over there, and my hair would be messed up, I'd be wearing dirty clothes, and like, you know, it doesn't matter, like, she couldn't understand that she was really, like, shallow and stuff, I guess." Lauren acknowledges that appearances matter in how people are regarded, but that this is a rather surface concern, and goes on to say that her relationship with her stepmother "could have been worse." Participants espousing ambivalent relationships were often adamant that they had been lucky and had avoided the horror stories they had heard from friends or acquaintances. Such an individual focus is not uncommon for people who are vulnerable or marginalized (see, for example, Kennelly & Dillabough, 2008).

As Hayward (2012) illustrates, many young people are influenced by the neoliberal ideal of citizenship as personal responsibility, which places a great priority on the role of the individual in determining their life course. Ambivalent citizenship practices are congruent with downloading responsibilities onto family members (foster and biological). It appears that this emphasis on personal responsibility removes the social-contract element of citizenship for youth: responsibility for citizenship lies with the individual and family in the private sphere.

Supportive relationships: "You need your own space, but you also need to be able to turn to someone." (Ruby, age 22)

For a minority of participants (N=5), the home was a place where citizenship could be explored and expressed, due in large part to positive relationships with family members. The third expression of family relationships in the home includes those who found home to be a place of refuge and support. For these youth, home—and the people they meet there—can be a place of resiliency. Home is not always an ideal living environment, but in general these participants note that their relationships at home involve safe spaces, understanding adults, some flexibility in terms of rules and expectations, and structure.

This third kind of expression of home relationships is consistent with dissenting citizenship (Butler & Benoit, 2015). Dissenting citizenship concerns not disagreement but dissent with mainstream notions of self-responsible citizenship. When expressing dissenting citizenship practices, participants mentioned knowing what "good" citizenship was supposed to be (in their opinion), but in practice they worked to act as citizens in different ways. This subgroup appeared to be more aware of the structural constraints that exclude some people from being considered citizens: that is, they mentioned the various ways that systemic issues shaped their daily lives. They also discussed how they were able to build relationships with people who were not their parents or siblings; this acceptance of an inclusive version of home and family were key.

Understanding the role of supportive adults means recognizing what a good home looks like: "[A] good home [is] not get kicked out on the streets, get your education, and go to the college or something. Maybe your parents can help you with some rent when you're doing that to start you off as a boost. When you don't have that boost, it's going to be really hard" (Robert, age 21). In this comment, Robert shows that he recognizes that there are ways that structural and contextual factors shape understandings of home.

For participants espousing home relationships as supportive, developing strong relationships with nonbiological family members was key to expressing citizenship in different kinds of homes. Ella, age 16, contrasted community with family: "I'm just friends with people that are nice to me and people that I'm nice to, and my family—well, I don't really have a choice." Molly, age 24, was taken in by a foster family at age two and remained with them until she aged out of care. She says that her "now" family made her feel like she actually fit in. She was not formally adopted by the family, but she took their last name and considers herself to be an aunt to her foster parents' grandchildren. Molly was very comfortable with the idea of having more than one parent: "I have seven or eight moms running around the city right now and Jewish Auntie. … Some of them are my ex-boyfriends' mothers who loved me so much to bits that I call them mom still to this day." Molly goes on to say that she has lived with some of them and not with others, but she feels comfortable and supported inside these women's homes.

Participants who express this certain iteration of home emphasize collective responsibilities and the role of youth as social agents in practising citizenship within the home. The home becomes a place to resist neoliberal regimes' emphasis on individual responsibility. Instead, it can be a place to carve out a new way of embracing and enacting citizenship. Dissenting citizenship illustrates that resiliency within the home comes from strong relationships, safe environments, consistent but flexible rules, and supportive family members. Youth citizenship in the home involves a reframing of self as an actor in the home environment and as a participant in one's own citizenship narrative.

CONCLUSION

For young people in care, the home is a fluid cultural construction: they may have certain experiences with home at various times that cause them to embrace particular images of home, and then later these expressions or images may change. Consistent across all three expressions is the notion that belonging and exclusion are not exclusive: one can experience both in a particular home, from the same individuals, in the same place. Across narratives, then, there are discussions of abuse, neglect, discrimination, but also of support and inclusion. Nevertheless, it is clear that some expressions of home are more congruent with enacting citizenship than others. My findings indicate that a safe home, with a supportive family (biological, foster, or otherwise), flexible rules, and consistency, is the ideal for youth-in-care, and perhaps for marginalized youth more generally, when it comes to practising citizenship.

Like other youth, the youth-in-care in my study were navigating challenges, such as family and peer relations, the school system, and questions about belonging. However, unlike many other youth in Greater Victoria, the position that participants occupied as wards of the state in an era of self-responsibility has meant that they are asked to negotiate their own citizenship within a context of changing care homes, transient living situations, and relations with social workers, judges, and other youth workers. The challenges facing these youth are numerous, and yet, in many cases, the diversity in experiences with home and in expressions of citizenship highlight varied experiences with the care system across individual narratives, as well as broader social inequalities. By drawing attention to practices of citizenship, we gain further insight into the home experience for marginalized youth.

NOTES

1. I use the term *youth-in-care* to refer to youth who either have been in government care at some point in their lives or have been on youth agreements (Smith et al., 2011, p. 10).
2. In terms of numbers, approximately 3% of British Columbia youth in grades 7–12 have been in government care at some point in their lives (Smith et al., 2011), and 1% have been in care in the past year (MCFD, 2010, p. 1). Besides the 8,000 children and youth currently in care, there were also almost 7,000 young people living in other care arrangements in 2009, including 4,500 children living with relatives under the Child in the Home of a Relative program; 300 children living in "kith and kin" arrangements and out-of-care placements; another 1,500 First Nations children living in the home of a relative in the federally administered Guardianship Financial Assistance program on reserves; and over 600 youth per year living independently on youth agreements (RCY, 2009, p. 13).

3. While *youth* is a contested term, the age range of 14–24 reflects the terminology used by youth-serving organizations in Greater Victoria, as well as by government agencies such as the British Columbia Representative for Children and Youth [RCY].

REFERENCES

Andrews, Y. (2008). *FBCYICN Member Engagement Consultation Project Report*. Federation of BC Youth in Care Network. Retrieved from http://fbcyicn.ca/wp-content/uploads/2009/08/member-engagement-report.pdf

Beauvais, C., McKay, L. & Seddon, A. (2001). *A Literature Review on Youth and Citizenship*. Ottawa: Canadian Policy Research Networks.

Beck, U. (1992). *Risk Society: Towards a New Modernity*. London: Sage.

Butler, K. & Benoit, C. (2015). Citizenship practices among youth who have experienced government care. *Canadian Journal of Sociology*, 40(1), 25–50.

Callahan, M. & Swift, J. (2007). Great expectations and unintended consequences: Risk assessment in child welfare in British Columbia. In L. T. Foster and B. Wharf (Eds.), *People, Politics and Child Welfare in British Columbia* (pp. 158–183). Vancouver: UBC Press.

Child and Youth Officer for British Columbia. (2005). *Executive Summary Joint Special Report: Health and Well-Being of Children in Care in British Columbia: Report 1 on Health Services Utilisation and Mortality*. Ministry of Health Office of the Provincial Health Officer. Retrieved from http://www2.gov.bc.ca/assets/gov/health/about-bc-s-health-care-system/office-of-the-provincial-health-officer/reports-publications/special-reports/exec_summary.pdf

Duyvendak, J. W. (2011). *The Politics of Home: Belonging and Nostalgia in Western Europe and the United States*. Houndmills, UK: Palgrave Macmillan.

Fisher, M., Marsh, P., Phillips, D. & Sainsbury, E. (1986). *In and Out of Care: The Experiences of Children, Parents and Social Workers*. London: Batsford in association with British Agencies for Adoption and Fostering.

Giddens, A. (1992). *The Transformation of Intimacy*. Cambridge, UK: Polity Press.

Hall, T., Coffey, A. & Williamson, H. (1999). Self, space and place: Youth identities and citizenship. *British Journal of Sociology of Education*, 20(4), 501–513.

Hare, F. G. (2007). Transition without status: The experience of youth leaving care without Canadian citizenship. *New Directions for Youth Development*, 113, 77–88.

Hayward, B. (2012). *Children, Citizenship and Environment: Nurturing a Democratic Imagination in a Changing World*. New York: Routledge.

Howe, B. (2005). Canadian education for child citizens. *Canadian and International Education*, 34(1), 41–49.

Kasinitz, P. (2013). Book review: Towards a sociology of home. *Sociological Forum*, 28(4), 881–884.

Kennelly, J. & Dillabough, J. (2008). Young people mobilizing the language of citizenship: Struggles for classification and new meaning in an uncertain world. *British Journal of Sociology of Education*, 29(5), 493–508.

Lasch, C. (1977). *Haven in a Heartless World: The Family Besieged*. New York: Basic Books.

Lister, R. (2007). Why citizenship: Where, when and how children? *Theoretical Inquiries in Law*, 8(2): Article 13.

Maira, S. (2009). *Missing: Youth, Citizenship, and Empire After 9/11*. Durham, NC: Duke University Press.

Marshall, T. H. (1964). Citizenship and social class. In T. Marshall (Ed.), *Class, Citizenship and Social Development* (pp. 70–118). New York: Doubleday.

Masten, A. S. (2006). Promoting resilience in development: A general framework for systems of care. In R. J. Flynn, P. M. Dudding, and J. G. Barber (Eds.), *Promoting Resilience in Child Welfare* (pp. 3–17). Ottawa: University of Ottawa Press.

Merton, R. K. (1957). *Social Theory and Social Structure*. New York: Free Press of Glencoe.

[MCFD] Ministry of Children and Family Development. (n.d.). *Agreements with Young Adults*. Retrieved from www.mcf.gov.bc.ca/youth/aya.htm, March 9, 2013.

[MCFD] Ministry of Children and Family Development. (2010). *Third Annual Progress Report on Children in Care in the North*. Retrieved from http://www.mcf.gov.bc.ca/foster/pdf/Northern_CIC_2010.pdf

Mortier, F. (2002). The meaning of individualization for children's citizenship. In F. Mouritsen and J. Qvortrup (Eds.), *Childhood and Children's Culture* (pp. 79–102). Odense, DK: University Press of Southern Denmark.

Munson, M., Lee, B. R., Miller, D., Cole, A. & Nedelcu, C. (2013). Emerging adulthood among former system youth: The ideal versus the real. *Children and Youth Services Review*, 35, 923–929.

Parton, N. (2006). *Safeguarding Childhood: Early Intervention and Surveillance in Late Modern Society*. Basingstoke, UK: Palgrave Macmillan.

Parton, N., Thorpe, D. & Wattam, C. (1997). *Child Protection: Risk and the Moral Order*. Basingstoke, UK: Palgrave MacMillan.

Ragg, D. M., Patrick, D. & Ziefert, M. (2006). Slamming the closet door: Working with gay and lesbian youth in care. *Child Welfare League of America*, 85(2), 243–265.

[RCY] Representative for Children and Youth and B.C. Office of the Provincial Health Officer. (2009). *Kids, Crime and Care: Health and Well-Being of Children in Care: Youth Justice Experiences and Outcomes*. Victoria, BC: British Columbia Representative for Children and Youth.

Shaw, M. & McCulloch, K. (2009). Hooligans or rebels: Thinking more critically about citizenship and young people. *Youth and Policy*, 101, 5–14.

Smith, A., Stewart, D., Poon, C., Saewyc, E. & the McCreary Centre Society. (2011). *Fostering Potential: The Lives of BC Youth with Government Care Experience*. Vancouver: McCreary Centre Society.

Smith, N., Lister, R., Middleton, S. & Cox, L. (2005). Young people as real citizens: Towards an inclusionary understanding of citizenship. *Journal of Youth Studies*, 8(4), 425–443.

Spencer, L., Ritchie, J. & O'Connor, W. (2003a). Analysis: Practices, principles and processes. In J. Ritchie and J. Lewis (Eds.), *Qualitative Research Practice* (pp. 199–218). Thousand Oaks, CA: Sage Publications.

Spencer, L., Ritchie, J. & O'Connor, W. (2003b). Carrying out qualitative analysis. In J. Ritchie and J. Lewis (Eds.), *Qualitative Research Practice* (pp. 219–262). Thousand Oaks, CA: Sage Publications.

Statistics Canada. (2011). *National Household Survey: Income and Housing.* Government of Canada. Retrieved from https://www12.statcan.gc.ca/nhs-enm/2011/dp-pd/dt-td/Lp-eng.cfm?LANG=E&APATH=3&DETAIL=0&DIM=0&FL=A&FREE=0&GC=0&GID=0&GK=0&GRP=0&PID=0&PRID=0&PTYPE=105277&S=0&SHOWALL=0&SUB=0&Temporal=2013&THEME=98&VID=0&VNAMEE=&VNAMEF=

Ungar, M. (2004). *Nurturing Hidden Resilience in Troubled Youth.* Toronto: University of Toronto Press.

Woolley, P. (2013, April 8). "Aging out": Tough road for teens too old to be "in care." *The Tyee.* Retrieved from www.thetyee.ca/News/2013/04/08/Aging-Out/, April 25, 2013.

CHAPTER 7

LOW-INCOME LONE MOTHERS AND "HOME": THE IMPORTANCE OF SOCIAL RELATIONS

Amber Gazso

Many of us will define the concept of home as the residence we live in, the place where we grew up, or perhaps even the country where we were born. These, we may agree, seem to be common-sense definitions of home. If one task of sociology is to unpack how our lived experiences can be taken for granted, it makes sense that we may have to revisit these definitions.

In feminist scholarship, the concept of home has always had a place. Many feminist sociologists either explicitly or implicitly reference the meaning of home in their research. That is, any feminists who study family and gender relations through topics such as the division of paid and unpaid work, or mothering and parenting, can make the experience of home relevant. Moreover, some recent and largely interdisciplinary scholarship encourages us to consider the importance of recognizing the more abstract meanings of home: home as associated with emotions and not necessarily equated with residence.

In this chapter, I take on the challenge of this edited collection to contribute to the sociology of home. I assume a feminist political economy perspective to analyze interviews that were completed with 30 lone mothers about their management of low income and of their own and their family's needs through networks of social support. More specifically, I undertake a narrative analysis of mothers' stories for what they implicitly reveal about the meaning of home when in a position of low income. I analyze mothers' stories in connection to life-course events and relations, and how their lives are linked to the lives of others. Another key assumption of my narrative analysis is that mothers' stories reflect and contrast the norms and values of the wider political and economic context.

The remainder of this chapter is organized as follows. To begin, I review how the study of the meaning of home invites a focus on low-income lone mothers. In the next section, I review some of the ways lone mothers' daily lives are understood in the current academic literature. Following a description of my methods, I then share my findings about what mothers' stories of managing low income imply about how they conceptualize and experience home. In the final section, I substantiate the main argument of this chapter: for lone mothers, home is a place, a social construct, and a feeling constituted by support relations over the life course.

CONCEPTUALIZING "HOME"

While the meaning of home has begun to garner considerable research attention, Parsell (2012) reminds us that this meaning can still be quite ambiguous. In my reading of the literature on home in the discipline of sociology and others, I observe that there are three conceptualizations of home most relevant to this chapter's focus on the stories of low-income lone mothers.

First, there has been considerable discussion about the place of home. Home can be defined as a place in terms of where you live, whether this is a residence, a community, or even a nation (Bigonnesse, Beaulieu, & Garon, 2014; Duyvendak, 2011). Mallet (2004) observes that, particularly in Western thought, there is a tendency to privilege a house as a home; home in this sense can be taken for granted (Gorman-Murray, 2007). Indeed, Parsell's (2012) study offers the important reminder that for people who are unhoused, home is desirable and seen as possible through the experience of becoming housed. Among adults aged 75 years and older, Bigonnesse et al. (2014) also found that the challenge of accessing affordable housing was associated with the definition of a physical place as a home.

Second, there has been growing attention to the emotional dimension of home. Through a comparative analysis of Western European and American societies, Duyvendak (2011) aimed to deconstruct the meaning of "feeling at home." Duyvendak encourages us to move away from the tendency to link "feeling at home" with only a material place, a neighbourhood, or a country. One of Duyvendak's central contributions is his argument that "feeling at home" is also symbolic and emotional. "Feeling at home" can be understood through the perspective of theories of emotions; a person can feel at home much like a person can feel sad. Individuals "feel at home" largely through their interactions with others (Duyvendak, 2011, p. 30).

Gorman-Murray (2007) offers additional support for this idea that the affective meaning of home need not be tied to place alone. In his study of gay men and lesbians, he found that they associated the meaning of home with their interactions with those they felt were emotionally close. Feelings of support and social connection, however, can also inform older adults' perceptions of their place of residence as a home (Bigonnesse et al., 2014).

What we glean thus far from the existing literature is that the meaning and feeling of home can be materially based, can involve social relations and social context, and can also have an element of social construction (Parsell, 2012; Tester & Wingfield, 2013). Home can be a private space, a residence, or perceived through relations with others in the public sphere, such as when individuals feel belonging to a group. For Duyvendak (2011), individuals can feel at home in private life, such as within their residence, or in public through their relations with others.

This last point of Duyvendak's has relevance for the third insight in the literature, that there is a social and familial dimension to home. Specifically, there is a keen awareness among scholars that home is intertwined with conceptualization of family and roles within it (Bigonnesse et al., 2014), and there can even be a tendency to conflate the meaning of home with family (Gorman-Murray 2007; Mallet 2004; Parsell, 2012). Home has been thought to be the centre of family life (Somerville, 1997).

For feminists, the home or place where people live together has always been one site of the practice of family life, of social relations, of caregiving and nurturing, which are mostly performed by women. Home tends to continue to be conceptualized as women's space (Quin, 2010). In the industrial revolution, the private sphere or the home was thought to be reserved for women, and men's place was in the public sphere or in the workplace and/or wider economy (Mallet, 2004). Nancy Cott (1977) reminds us that the powerful ideology of the cult of domesticity, emergent in the period of industrialization and the apparent separation of paid work from home work, rested on central principles to which women should ascribe. These principles included "home as a haven" and the idea that women's values were attached to their caregiving ability and creation of this haven.

While this idea of home as a place of refuge or safety has been retained in meanings of home, particularly for women (Duyvendak, 2011; Mallet, 2004), feminist scholarship has since squashed the middle- and upper-class idea of separate spheres of social life, revealing that some women, especially racialized women, have always worked for pay (Ghorayshi, 2002). Moreover, what women were and are doing in the home has been recognized as *work* that reproduces families, including members' relationships with the labour market. In an often-cited definition, Laslett and Brenner (1989, p. 382) use the term *social reproduction* to refer to "activities and attitudes, behaviours and emotions, responsibilities and relationships directly involved in the maintenance of life on a daily basis and intergenerationally."

Feminist political economists study the interactions of various institutions—the state (and therefore politics), the market, the family/household, and the voluntary sector—and how women achieve mental, manual, and emotional social reproduction in relation to them (Bezanson & Luxton, 2006; Laslett & Brenner, 1989); meeting the daily and generational needs of families includes both paid and unpaid work and assumes involvement of communities and the state (Adkins & Dever, 2014). Considerable attention is also given to how political, economic, and cultural processes create societal conditions of inequality for women (Gazso, 2009). Women within families are understood to have greater responsibility for social reproduction relations than the state (Picchio, 1992), with the state understood as exacerbating women's unpaid work through restructuring and downloading responsibility onto families (Bezanson, 2006; Kunz, 2010). There are also differences in the experiences of social reproduction performed by women that cut across race and class. For example, immigrant women who are paid caregivers for affluent families contribute to the social reproduction of these same families but are often not fairly paid in the process (Romero, 2013).

Connecting the three conceptualizations of home with a feminist political economy perspective, I come to the following outlook: in performing social reproduction—housework, child care, and emotional labour (i.e., the management of feeling) (Hochschild, [1983] 2003), and often alongside paid work—women are constituting home in all its dimensions. If social reproduction includes everyday activities to sustain generations and is not limited to a physical site, this social reproduction and the meaning making and practice of home that are intertwined with it therefore transcend both private and public spheres. This perspective, as we will see below, informs how I analyzed the stories of low-income lone mothers.

To summarize, current research on home acknowledges that home does not simply refer to the place where one lives. The meaning of home can have physical, individual, and social dimensions, thus giving home emotional, psychological, and social significance (Biggonnesse et al. 2014; Parsell, 2012; Somerville, 1997). The site of social interaction can be in a home, but so too can social interactions feel like home. Feminists have also made important contributions that can inform how we think of the activities and practices in relation to home. From feminists, especially via feminist political economy, we learn of the importance of understanding how social reproduction occurs within and outside a place of home and begin to grasp the significance of social reproduction as constitutive of home.

LOW-INCOME LONE MOTHER FAMILIES

In Canada, there are more women than men that head lone-parent families (Statistics Canada, 2012). Many lone-mother families have incomes that fall below Statistics Canada's Low Income Cut-Offs (LICOs); this happens even despite their receipt of Ontario Works, a social assistance (or welfare) benefit, and other child benefits to support them in the everyday costs of living. In 2013, the average welfare income of a lone-parent family in Ontario was

$18,854; this was $5,212 below the after-tax low-income threshold (Tweddle, Battle, & Torjman, 2014). Feminist criticisms have been levelled against social assistance programs for years with regards to how they may permit mothers to achieve a semblance of survival but may not improve mothers' economic opportunities in the long term (see, for example, Breitkreuz, Williamson, & Raine, 2010).

The inadequacy of social assistance benefits for lone mothers is connected to their design and administration, especially the changes to these created by restructuring. Social assistance programs across Canada are designed as programs of "last resort" for families in economic need. From the political right, the concern has been primarily with correcting mothers' perceived dependency on these programs. Still other neoliberal-infused concerns have rested on the sheer cost of social assistance programs in times of economic challenge, such as government deficit or debt or employment recessions (Rice & Prince, 2013). The political response has been the restructuring of social assistance programs, notably in Ontario the Common Sense Revolution of 1997 onward. Social assistance programs have been redesigned as welfare-to-work programs that require mothers with school-age children to attend work and/or education programs or complete voluntary work placements under the assumption that such experience will provide them the skills and resources necessary to enter into the job market (Gazso, 2012).

From a feminist political economy perspective, the restructuring of social assistance and other family policies is seen to impact women's structural positions and their everyday experiences negatively. Lone mothers' economic security and access to affordable housing and, subsequently, their social re-production are shaped by the decisions of social actors like policy makers and politicians. However, these decisions are made in response to the conditions of the larger economy and not necessarily the everyday life experiences of lone mothers. Indeed, the difficulty for many mothers on social assistance is that their participation in welfare-to-work-oriented programming inhibits their desires to be "good" or perhaps even full-time caregivers to children (Gazso, 2007a). The administration of social assistance regulations around welfare-to-work can come at the cost of ignoring shortages of available day-care in communities, among other things. Since social assistance incomes are so low, further economic challenges are created for mothers if they cannot additionally access housing or daycare subsidies.

Canadian research reveals the ways in which lone-mother families cope with low income and these challenges (Bezanson, 2006; Breitkreuz et al., 2010; Gazso, 2007b; Hanson & Hanson, 2010; Pulkingham, Fuller, & Kershaw, 2010). Lone mothers may share child transportation and/or borrow and lend money or food or other goods with family and friends. Indeed, the development of networks of social support including not just family and friends but community organizations and multiple government benefits is integral to their own and their children's daily existence (Gazso & McDaniel, 2015). Neysmith and Reitsma-Street (2005) call mothers' actual work of securing resources by networking with community centres (resources that I would argue facilitate social reproduction) "provisioning."

Lone-mother families in Canada that experience low income face daily challenges in achieving their own and their children's survival. Undoubtedly, these mothers are engaged in social reproduction that intermeshes their home lives with their communities and the state. While the state provides mothers a semblance of income security, their social reproduction is exacerbated because this income is not sufficient to meet all of their daily needs. In the remainder of this paper, I examine how mothers' stories of managing low income can actually be read as much more than management and additionally understood as implicitly revealing meanings and experiences of home.

METHODS

In this chapter, I draw on interviews that were completed with 30 lone mothers as part of a larger project about family's management of poverty through networks of social support in 2009 and 2010. This larger project included 70 participants that comprised 20 one-to-three generation families. As part of this project, the 30 lone mothers I use as my sample were recruited for participation through non-profit community organizations in the city of Toronto.

I interviewed lone mothers who identified as Aboriginal, Caucasian (born and raised in Canada or immigrants from Eastern and Northern Europe), of mixed race/ethnicity, or immigrants of East Asian, Caribbean, Latin American, and Middle Eastern racial and ethnic backgrounds. Mothers' ages ranged from 18 to 50, and they had anywhere from one to five children in their care. The children of two mothers were in the care of others. All but six mothers received Ontario Works as their main source of income; the six mothers who worked for pay did so for low wages. Twelve mothers had some post-secondary education or a university degree. The remaining 18 mothers had high-school education or less. Fourteen of the mothers had immigrated to Canada.

I analyzed these 30 mothers' stories from the perspective of home developed from my review of the literature: home has material, emotional, and social dimensions interwoven with family and gender relations and shaped by the social-policy manoeuvrings of the welfare state. My reading was guided by a desire to explore how mothers' stories of managing poverty, and in turn social reproduction, implicitly reference home. I framed my analysis through the following additional questions: How do mothers explicitly speak of home? What are mothers' experiences of feeling at home? What are the meanings of home conveyed in mothers' stories?

Narrative analysis was most suitable to answer these questions. Narrative analysis treats individuals' stories as the recounting of experiences that are perceived to have meaning to themselves and others (Bischoping & Gazso, 2016). My narrative analysis was directed strategically by a few assumptions. Drawing on how stories can be understood from a life-course perspective, I saw mothers' stories as experiences of events and transitions over their lives that were determined by not only their agency but also their family and wider social relations and sociohistorical context (Elder, 1994). My interest was in interpreting their stories of their lives for how they referenced home, whether this was explicit or implicit. I was also attuned to how their stories were about a key period of their lives—the raising of children while economically inse-cure—and how their social reproduction seemed to be linked to the lives of others. Finally, I saw mothers' stories as socially contextualized, as reflecting and contrasting the norms and values of the wider political economy. Within feminist political economy itself, there has been emerging awareness that the broader structures, institutions, and relations of a capitalist political economy are understood to be revealed through the experiences and perspectives of women (Bezanson & Luxton, 2006; Vosko, 2002).

FINDINGS

My analysis revealed three interconnected themes about home, whether insinuated or obvious, in mothers' stories: Life Happens—and This Is My "Home"; Practising "Home," Creating "Home"; and "Home" Is Supportive Relationships. Due to limitations of space, I present only mothers' stories that are most exemplary of each theme.

Life Happens—and This Is My "Home"

Lone mothers' stories reveal how the place of home is shaped by events over their life course. These events can inform perceptions of home as temporary or as stable, with varying emotions attached therein.

Eleven of the mothers I interviewed were taking part in an unnamed non-profit program (XXXX program)[1] that transitioned them out of the shelter system, housed and educated them for four years, and then aimed to transition them into stable employment with a reasonable income and subsi-dized housing.[2] Christine (age 25) moved into her current residence with her daughter after they lived in a shelter, before which she lost her residence when her own parents separated. She implied that she is proud of her current place of home by her reference to what home was like before:

> Christine: I lived with my parents. About a year and a half ago they split up. They had a house and mortgage and stuff. My mom took off, and she had handled a lot of the financials.... So, like, my dad couldn't really afford to, like, start paying it. And so they sold the house. I really had no choice left but to come to a shelter.... It's a blessing. I did have to struggle to get here [XXXX program].

Interviewer: How so?

Christine: Just like everyone else here. We all have to struggle, but I did stay in a shelter for four months with my daughter.... Everybody was just in front of everybody. There was no own space. Like, a room was even shared by a mother and another daughter. So, there was no privacy. There is nothing. There was no locks on the doors.

For Christine, a home can be a place, but not all places are home. And given her experiences, for a house to be a home, it should be connected with all the trappings of an economically secure life: "I want to own my own modelling agency ... for short women on the runway.... That's my drive and knowing that in doing that I'd be a boss. And in doing that I would be boss and have lots of money and have nice things, like a Mercedes Benz, a nice house, and give my daughter more than what she gets now."

The XXXX program exposed Kyla to new experiences of a place of home. Kyla, like two other mothers, experienced homelessness when she was a young adolescent and before she had her first child. She was 25 and the mother of two children when I interviewed her. Different events in her life suggest that home has never been a place of permanence. Moreover, her story suggests a home does not always feel safe or unconditionally available:

Interviewer: When you were saying your teen years and you were kind of moving around doing things, would you ever consider that you were homeless at any point in time?

Kyla: Well, yeah. You know, when somebody says get out of my house, then you are—officially do not have a home anymore. [laughs]

Interviewer: Yeah, exactly, and then you were in shelters.

Kyla: Oh yeah. I lived on the street, Nathan Phillips Square. So I did that too. So yeah, I guess you can call me well rounded. [laughs]

Latisha is an undocumented lone mother. Her place of residence was her sister's apartment. Her children, twins, were born in Canada and so were entitled to government benefits like the Canada Child Tax Benefit through Latisha's sister. But Latisha's lack of citizenship made her dependent on the financial and other instrumental and expressive support her sister provided. For Latisha, home is a place that both shelters her and constrains her movement:

Latisha: Yeah, and, like, when the babies, when they get their money, like, for the month from the government. I will use it to buy clothes for them, food and formula and stuff like that.

Interviewer: Oh what, so you have a government benefit for the kids?

Latisha: Through my sister, 'cause they're Canadian, they were born here, so they don't have a problem, like, doing anything. It's just, like, with me. Because if they want to go to daycare now, they can go to daycare. But if they go to daycare, I'm going to be home doing nothing, so I just let them stay home with me…. They can get whatever they want, what treatment and stuff like that.

Practising "Home," Creating "Home"

Lone mothers' stories are also about the experiences of home. Specifically, mothers' stories are about practising social reproduction and thereby creating home in the midst of poverty.

Macy (age 21) and her two children under age three joined the XXXX program after Macy left her ex-partner. For Macy, the social reproduction she engaged in to raise her children was a source of security and comfort in the midst of the other challenges of the program, like completing her education:

> Yeah, I was talking, me and Sharon [director of XXXX program] had a meeting the other day, and we were talking. She asked me sort of, ah, we were talking about a lot of things, and she asked me how do I deal with the stress of parenting and stuff. And I said, "Well, Sharon, you know, but I just—parenting is my escape." When things start to stress me out, and I've got meetings I've missed or I have homework to do, like things are piling up, and I feel like they're really getting to me, I just play with my kids all day, you know. It's good, and it's bad. Because I haven't got those organizational skills for … other business too. I'm working on it. But, yeah, when I realized that I was, I was like, "Oh, I didn't really realize I did that." I don't really get stressed out with the kids. Like, I have my moments, when I get irritated, but there's not, it's not a burden at all, like, so I don't know. It's neat.

Mothers often engaged in social reproduction with the assistance of several others. Kendra (age 36) raised her son by pooling resources and networking outward. That is, she lived with her sister, who was also a single mother of Larissa (age 16), to share costs of housing and raising children. She created a home for her son by endorsing the support he received from his father and her ex-partner, and the much-needed caregiving support from her niece Larissa.

> He [ex-partner] has a relationship with his son. He comes by every other weekend, he picks his son up … he takes him, picks him up Saturday morning, brings him back Sunday night…. Yes, and even my niece, the one that lives with me … sometimes she would pass by son's school, she would pick him up from school, bring him home, and the two of them gets to be in the apartment until I get home from school.

Darlene (age 31) was raising her three children on Ontario Works and support from her kin and community. She considered her family of origin's residence as home but also indicated the importance of her creation and practice of home elsewhere:

> Darlene: I am "Daddy's little girl." So it was, like, you know, that I was taken away from him. So that was kind of hard for him to deal with, you know, me getting married and having my own family. My own house, my own everything. So that went kinda hard, and the only two people that live with my parents are my sisters, but it is not the same. And my Dad has been asking me, a couple of times, move in, move back in. Move back in. I'm like, no …
> Interviewer: Oh, like, come with the boys?
> Darlene: Yeah. Yeah.
> Interviewer: What do you think about that idea?
> Darlene: Hmm, no, I'm like 31 already [laughs], and I'm away from home already 13 years. So to go back again, I'll feel like I'm 15 again [laughs]. So, I'm like, no, no no.

If we read Darlene's statements through our perspective on home, we can understand that one of the reasons she cannot go back to her parents, even though they are implicitly offering her more support, is because she has developed her own practices of social reproduction to sustain her two boys and so has created her own sense of home.

"Home" Is Supportive Relationships

The preceding theme focused on mothers' social reproduction and how it enabled them to practise and create home as a place. The emphasis was also on the actions and doings that constitute home. My emphasis here is on interpreting mothers' "family" relations of support as symbolic and emotive of home, with the physical location of home subordinate to these meanings. The key to this theme, and how it is connected to the others but different, is to understand that for many mothers I interviewed, their families included fictive kin or people who feel like family. For example, Kyla told of how her friends are her family more than actual kin:

> I guess I'm a sucker for the lost sheep … I can help you, I can do it, you know, a little stranded, that's basically all the people in my life that have come to be, you know, the friends that are like family,… so that's basically where my family that I have created kind of comes around—we've all been the black sheep of our family.… If I have an issue, I don't call her [her sister]. She would be one of the last people I would call.

What I extrapolate from her story is that Kyla has established a feeling of home with her fictive kin, thereby disturbing the ideas that family is performed at a home and only blood relations feel like home. This finding in particular echoes Duyvendak's (2011) argument that people can feel at home through their interactions with others. Indeed, other mothers' stories of how people close to them support their social reproduction imply feelings of home. Sheila's (age 34, mother of two children) story of her relationship with Leyla (age 43, mother of one child), both of whom are participating in the XXXX program, suggests this:

> But another friend here, Leyla, I'm so close to her, and we are helping each other too. Like, last night, before last night, my kids were so sick, you know, I don't have a car, so she took me.... She was there for a couple of hours.... Yeah, you know, like, she's nice, and if she doesn't have nothing, I mean if she's not busy, so she help me too. Even me, in the return, I do as much as I can to help her. She's kind of my best friend here, we are so close here. I mean, so our two exes—and you know, because she has the same situation, so yes.

In making reference to how Leyla shares a past of domestic violence too, Sheila's story echoes the earlier theme of how events in one's life can lead to a current place of home.

DISCUSSION AND CONCLUSION

> Darlene: There was one time ... this was after my husband left. There was a one time that we didn't have nothing to eat ... I mean nothing. And I was crying, crying, and crying, and my kids didn't know why. And suddenly, somebody knocks on my door. Okay, that's strange, I wasn't expecting anybody. And we were living above two restaurants. And so, I opened the door.... "Yeah, the chef cooked something for you—here it is." And she's like, "Let me know if this is enough." I'm like, "Okay, how do I pay you? I don't have anything right now to give you." And she's like, "No, no, don't worry—he just wants to give it to you."
> Interviewer: And then you, you were friendly, neighbours?
> Darlene: Yeah. Yeah! I was really surprised because you don't find this in Canada! [laughs] Especially here in Toronto. You know what I mean? Yeah. You would find that back home. You know what I mean? Like a cake, or a cup of sugar, or bread, or whatever, back home ...
> Interviewer: Whatever they got?
> Darlene: Exactly. But not here. So that was a very big surprise for me.

Darlene's telling of one important story of her life wraps up the central contributions of this chapter. In this brief story, Darlene powerfully highlights the level of complexity with which we need to think about home for low-income lone mothers. Here, I take up this final quote of Darlene's to discuss how it represents the three themes and can be understood through a feminist political economy perspective. While I present the themes separately, I do so only for reasons of clarity, as they are often intertwined.

Among the mothers I interviewed, a mother's sense of home as a place was rooted in events that have happened. In Darlene's case, her current home is the result of the breakup of a marriage. There can also be multiple emotions that filter into one's perception of a place as home, seen here in Darlene's reference to crying and repeated earlier in other mothers' stories too. Moreover, from a feminist perspective, the events that have happened in mothers' lives, such as divorce and a new-found experience of income insecurity, are not their fault alone. Lone mothers in Ontario experience a political and economic climate that is ill prepared for their poverty, with a lack of affordable and quality housing and child care, and a social assistance program designed only to provide assistance once extreme need is demonstrated and to push mothers off of benefits as soon as possible.

Embedded within Darlene's story is also confirmation that home as place can indeed lie at several levels of abstraction, just as the existing scholarship documents. Mothers can have many homes. Darlene spoke to the idea of a nation as home, as well as of her country of origin as home. Moving from a local perspective on the political economy to a global one, this meaning of home has resounding implications. If home is place and nation, no matter the processes of migration, we may be witnessing the lesser value attached to state boundaries of citizenship and family lives in mothers' stories too.

Home is also socially constructed. When mothers' social reproduction can occur anywhere and despite their poverty, an experience of home is perceived. Thus, the work that mothers do to raise their children indeed constitutes home. Darlene was in a position of not being able to feed her children—and, possibly, not achieve social reproduction—which is telling of the importance of these acts (of social reproduction) to what is seen as home. As well, Darlene's crisis position signals deep holes in the existing social-policy safety nets. It also speaks to a core assumption of the feminist political economy lens: private and public spheres are inseparable and are instead permeable, making social reproduction possible or not—as in the case of this crisis.

Finally, social interactions with others can represent feelings of home. Darlene's neighbours' support implicitly created for her a feeling of home. But again, mothers' receipt of support from others in their communities—from neighbours and friends—is also telling of the wider political economy. As Bakker (2003) observes, the restructuring of government programs, such as lessening their benefit amounts, has the consequence of re-privatizing social reproduction. Pushing responsibility for assisting mothers in economic need onto the shoulders of their neighbouring citizens is of benefit to neoliberal governments worried about achieving cost efficiency in a competitive global marketplace.

In conclusion, for low-income lone mothers, home has many meanings. Home is a place that is derived through a variety of transitions, a construct grounded in acts or relations of social reproduction and in a feeling of comfort and belonging created by relations of support. Most profoundly, I learned from mothers that support relations that feel like home are, indeed, home. If home is where the heart is, the heart need not be tied to a place. Feeling at home can emerge simply in mothers' social relations with others.

NOTES

1. For reasons of confidentiality, I have not named the program in which the mothers participated. I have also used pseudonyms to protect mothers' identities.
2. Mothers had to complete an extensive application process to be part of this program, and one of the eligibility criteria was their previous experience of domestic violence. Mothers who were deemed eligible to participate in the program then received Ontario Works and the Canada Child Tax Benefit as their main source of income. Their continued eligibility was dependent on their remaining committed to the goals of completing some post-secondary education and transitioning back into their communities. This program was administered out of the same apartment building in which these mothers also resided.

REFERENCES

Adkins, L. & Dever, M. (2014). Housework, wages, and money: The category of female principle breadwinner in financial capitalism. *Australian Feminist Studies, 29*(79), 50–66.

Bakker, I. (2003). Neo-liberal governance and the reprivatization of social reproduction: Social provisioning and shifting gender orders. In I. Bakker & S. Gill (Eds.), *Power, Production and Social Reproduction* (pp. 66–82). New York: Palgrave-Macmillan.

Bezanson, K. (2006). *Gender, the State, and Social Reproduction: Household Insecurity in Neo-Liberal Times.* Toronto: University of Toronto Press.

Bezanson, K. & Luxton, M. (2006). Introduction: Social reproduction and feminist political economy. In K. Bezanson & M. Luxton (Eds.), *Social Reproduction: Feminist Political Economy Challenges Neo-Liberalism* (pp. 3–10). Montreal: McGill-Queen's University Press.

Bigonnesse, C., Beaulieu, M., & Garon, S. (2014). Meaning of home in later life as a concept to understand older adults' housing needs: Results from the 7 age-friendly cities pilot project in Québec. *Journal of Housing for the Elderly, 28*(4), 357–382.

Bischoping, K. & Gazso, A. (2016). *Analyzing Talk in the Social Sciences: Narrative, Conversation, and Discourse Strategies.* London: Sage.

Breitkreuz, R. S., Williamson, D., & Raine, K. D. (2010). Dis-integrated: Welfare-to-work participants' experiences of integrating paid work and unpaid family work. *Community, Work and Family, 13*(1), 43–69.

Cott, N. F. (1977). *The Bonds of Womanhood: "Woman's Sphere" in New England, 1780–1835*. New Haven: Yale University Press.

Duyvendak, J. W. (2011). *The Politics of Home: Belonging and Nostalgia in Western Europe and the United States*. New York: Palgrave Macmillan.

Elder, G. H. Jr. (1994). Time, human agency, and social change: Perspectives on the life course. *Social Psychology Quarterly, 57*(1), 4–15.

Gazso, A. (2007a). Balancing expectations for employability and family responsibilities while on social assistance: Low income mothers' experiences in three Canadian provinces. *Family Relations, 56*, 454–466.

Gazso, A. (2007b). Staying afloat on social assistance: Parents' strategies of balancing work and family. *Socialist Studies, 3*(2), 31–63.

Gazso, A. (2009). Mothers' maintenance of families through market and family care relations. In N. Mandell (Ed.), *Feminist Issues: Race, Class, and Sexuality* (5th ed.). Toronto: Pearson/Prentice Hall.

Gazso, A. (2012). Moral codes of mothering and the introduction of welfare-to-work in Ontario. *Canadian Review of Sociology, 49*(1), 26–49.

Gazso, A. & McDaniel, S. (2015). Families by choice and the management of low income through social supports. *Journal of Family Issues, 36*(3), 371–395.

Ghorayshi, P. (2002). Working Canadian women: Continuity despite change. In V. Dhruvaraja & J. Vickers (Eds.), *Gender, Race, and Nation: A Global Perspective* (pp. 123–146). Toronto: University of Toronto Press.

Gorman-Murray, A. (2007). Reconfiguring domestic values: Meanings of home for gay men and lesbians. *Housing, Theory and Society, 24*(3), 229–246.

Hanson, C. & Hanson, L. (2010). Unpaid work and social policy: Engaging research with mothers on social assistance. *Action Research, 9*(2), 179–198.

Hochschild, A. [1983] (2003). *The Managed Heart: Commercialization of Human Feeling*. Berkeley: University of California Press.

Kunz, R. (2010). The crisis of social reproduction in rural Mexico: Challenging the "re-privatization of social reproduction" thesis. *Review of International Political Economy, 17*(5), 913–945.

Laslett, B. & Brenner, J. (1989). Gender and social reproduction: Historical perspectives. *Annual Review of Sociology, 15*, 381–404.

Mallet, S. (2004). Understanding home: A critical review of the literature. *The Sociological Review, 52*(1), 62–89.

Neysmith, S. M. & Reitsma-Street, M. (2005). "Provisioning": Conceptualizing the work of women for 21st century social policy. *Women's Studies International Forum, 28*, 381–391.

Parsell, C. (2012). Home is where the house is: The meaning of home for people sleeping rough. *Housing Studies, 27*(2), 159–173.

Picchio, A. (1992). *Social Reproduction: The Political Economy of the Labour Market*. New York: Cambridge University Press.

Pulkingham, J., Fuller, S., & Kershaw, P. (2010). Lone motherhood, welfare reform and active citizen subjectivity. *Critical Social Policy, 30*(2), 267–291.

Quin, B. (2010). Care-givers, leisure, and meanings of home: a case study of low income women in Dublin. *Gender, Place and Culture, 17*(6), 759–774.

Rice, M. J. & Prince, J. J. (2013). *Changing Politics of Canadian Social Policy* (2nd ed.). Toronto: University of Toronto Press.

Romero, M. (2013). Nanny diaries and other stories: Immigrant women's labor in the social reproduction of American families. *Revista de Estudios Sociales, 45,* 186–197.

Somerville, P. (1997). The social construction of home. *Journal of Architectural and Planning Research, 14*(3), 226–245.

Statistics Canada. (2012). *Fifty Years of Families in Canada: 1961–2001.* Retrieved from www12.statcan.gc.ca/census-recensement/2011/as-sa/98-312-x/98-312x2011003_1eng.cfm

Tester, G. & Wingfield, A. H. (2013). Moving past picket fences: The meaning of "home" for public housing residents. *Sociological Forum, 28*(1), 70–84.

Tweddle, A., Battle, K., & Torjman, S. (2014). *Welfare in Canada: 2013.* Retrieved from www.caledoninst.org/Publications/Detail/?ID=1057

Vosko, L. F. (2002). The pasts (and futures) of feminist political economy in Canada: Reviving the debate. *Studies in Political Economy, 68,* 55–83.

CHAPTER 8

LACKING THE SAFEGUARDS OF HOME: EXPERIENCES OF YOUTH HOMELESSNESS

Jennifer L. Robinson

Idealized notions of childhood, youth, and growing up at home denote home as a caring, safe space that facilitates and encourages positive transitions from youth to adulthood. These idealized notions presume that *home* functions in ways that are inclusive in the production of active and engaged citizens. Such ideas also suggest that youth are protected in the private sphere, while being prepared for engagement in the public sphere. As Mallett (2004) notes, the home is often constructed as a privileged structure and a place "where space and time are controlled and structured function-ally, economically, aesthetically, and morally" (p. 65). In the public/private divide, home is often constructed as a haven connected to the private sphere, which is comfortable, secure, and safe. The outside, the public sphere, is space that is threatening, imposing, and potentially dangerous. Home as "haven" signifies control over space, freedom to engage in private activities, and is characterized by caring relationships (Mallett, 2004, pp. 71–72). However, this idealized notion of home often does not reflect reality. For some, the private sphere of the home is a dangerous and imposing space, an unsafe space. Home as an unsafe space is particularly poignant for youth, as this may hinder their transitions to adulthood or expedite this complicated transition.

In contemporary North America, home is "characterized as a place where children are nurtured and reared, and finally depart when they come of age" (Mallett, 2004, p. 74). Giroux (2003) notes that youth are granted restricted privacy and personal liberties as determined by various adults and agencies.

Certainly, youth have a diminished role in the public sphere and, as citizens, are often denied agency solely as a consequence of their youthful status. Accordingly, the voices of youth are rarely included in the debates regarding the policies and practices that are created for their needs (Giroux, 2003). In an age-stratified society, youth is a transitional status that straddles the categories of childhood and adulthood. The in-between nature of this age category is evinced by the fact that its occupants are denied full citizenship rights, as they are presumed to be protected and cared for in a home environment. However, this is not always the case.

To be *homeless* implies the absence of physical and socio-emotional comforts and supports, and is particularly poignant for youth. Youth homelessness occurs for a host of reasons, including, but not limited to, abuse and neglect; family violence; substance abuse; mental-health issues; poverty; bullying; homophobia; learning disabilities and school failure; and residency in foster-care settings and institutional-care facilities (Collins, 2007; Fowler, Toro & Miles, 2009; Gaetz, O'Grady & Buccieri, 2010; Karabanow, 2006; Laird, 2007). Other researchers have emphasized that the backgrounds of homeless youth are frequently characterized by violence, mistrust, and physical, sexual, and/or emotional abuse (e.g., Buccieri, 2010; Collins, 2007; Tyler & Bersani, 2008). Karabanow (2010, p. 145) observes that even though homelessness may not be an ideal solution to any and all of its precipitating causes, some youth perceive their lives on the streets, in the public sphere, to be safer and healthier than their prehomeless lives. For many youth who experience homelessness, home was not a safe space.

Although youths who experience abuse or neglect in a home or care setting are commonly understood as deserving of empathy and assistance, those who leave these types of situations and, in doing so, become homeless, may evoke sentiments of fear, apprehension, and disdain. As Karabanow (2010) observes, homeless youth are understood as "public nuisances, or worse, criminals that warrant increased control and punishment" (p. 146); these perceptions, he charges, evince a lack of "understanding of the root causes of homelessness." Similarly, Schissel (2009) maintains that "experts" who lay emphasis upon, for example, the prevalence of mental illness, "risky sexual behavior," or substance abuse among homeless youth may, perhaps unwittingly, contribute to the demonization of this group (p. 28). These social stereotypes, Schissel charges, operate as an "oppressive mechanism" and further entrench the stigmatization of an already marginalized group. Such treatment of homelessness does not facilitate its treatment as a social issue.

Understanding homelessness as a broader social issue is facilitated by the work of C. Wright Mills (1959), as his concept of the "sociological imagination" invites researchers to work between "the personal troubles of milieu," located in individual biographies, and "the public issues of social structure," located in the institutional and historical possibilities of social structure (p. 8).

Homelessness is a private trouble embedded in public issues. It is a personal identity and a lived experience shaped by social structures, including, but not limited to, social supports, housing, education, employment, and citizenship.

On an individual level, those who experience homelessness, an extreme form of marginalization rooted in poverty, are often treated as though homelessness is a personal trouble. Individuals who experience homelessness are often constructed as blameworthy for their social location and/or treated as *other*: as deviant, dangerous, or a nuisance. In Canada, from a policy standpoint, few social investments are made to prevent homelessness or to intervene quickly and effectively when it occurs. However, Canadian governments have generally taken a reactive approach; individuals are forced to rely on emergency services, such as shelters and food banks, once all other resources are depleted.

Despite pronouncements that paradoxically declare children to be our country's greatest national resource, homeless youth are sometimes described less as a population to be treasured than as an unruly and dangerous mob that requires care and control. In this context, the term *care* is a euphemism for "discipline" and the favouring of a correctional or law-and-order approach (Karabanow, 2010, p. 140). Claiming that adult society is generally fearful of the young, Schissel (2009) pointedly notes that if "the public views youth as dangerous and criminal they are less likely to be sympathetic to the increasingly dire economic situation that today's youth face, and are more likely to favour law-and-order" approaches to youth misconduct rather than "social investment" programs (p. 32). In like fashion, Karabanow (2010) charges that street youth are commonly viewed by politicians, along with law enforcement and child-protection agencies, as "menaces in need of punishment and correction" (p. 140). Youth homelessness, much like homelessness in general, is cast as a private trouble based on individual choice, rather than as a public issue with structural roots. Understanding the pathways that led one to become homeless may add clarity to the discussion of homelessness as a public issue and of homeless youth as socially excluded.

To be without a home is impactful for youth, as when they leave, by choice or by force, they leave space that not only impacts shelter but also often their family ties, friendships, education, and support systems. Youth who leave home may face extreme poverty and marginalization, and might also experience social exclusion (Silver & Miller, 2003). Social exclusion is a multidimensional phenomenon that can include the denial of participation in social, economic, civil, or cultural aspects of society. Social exclusion is linked to social citizenship: the rights of an individual to social safeguards, such as having access to the basic needs of life in times of need and to have access to protections from the state. Those who are socially excluded may have limited access to the rights of social citizenship; such experiences are perpetuated in a neoliberal state.

Those who experience homelessness constitute one of the most destitute populations in Canadian society. Yet, as Lyon-Callo (2004) observes, the current neoliberal climate encourages limited supports from the state for those who are impoverished and offers little support for the consideration of systemic inequalities. Rather, neoliberalism encourages individuals to view social inequities as the inevitable by-product of a social world in which certain groups deserve rewards and others do not. According to Morris (1994, p. 60), neoliberalism works to direct attention away from structural inequalities and towards the putative failings of individuals who experience homelessness.

Neoliberal ideologies encourage the entrenchment into the public con- sciousness of the twinned constructs of the *deserving* and *undeserving poor*. The former term refers to those who are not viewed as culpable for their own impoverishment and who are thus considered deserving of state assistance (e.g., elderly widows, young children). The undeserving poor, on the other hand, are thought to cause their own impoverishment through their "lazi- ness," "sloth," "irresponsibility," and/or "dissipated" lifestyles. In examining the constructs of the deserving and undeserving poor, Cortese (2003, p. 67) emphasizes that political meanings permeate this language. The way these ideas are framed impacts public understandings of the homeless as legitimate or illegitimate claimants of state assistance and other forms of social justice. These understandings may reflect social-policy responses to homelessness that provide for assistance to those deemed to be deserving and for the disci- pline of the undeserving (Feldman, 2004).

Youth who are homeless do not readily fit into conventional understand- ings of social citizenship. Most people who experience extreme poverty—cer- tainly youth who are homeless—are left on the margins of society, blamed for the social and economic positions they inhabit. When people are both poor and young, they are doubly marginalized. The social safeguards of the state are generally intended to provide for adults and/or their dependants. Youth who "remove themselves" from home—from families—and absent themselves from schools may not be guaranteed the same social safeguards, as they may be cast as a nuisance and undeserving users of public space (Cooper, 2004). What follows in this chapter is an excerpt of a larger participatory study with 30 youth who experienced homelessness in Southwestern Ontario. The youth participants discuss the consequential aspects of lacking home via limited protections from the state, stigma, and discrimination. This work highlights the connections between homelessness and social exclusion, as framed in a neoliberal state.

THE PROJECT: YOUTH HOMELESSNESS AND SOCIAL EXCLUSION

Using a "methods from the margins" approach, this project represents an effort to work *with* youth in exploring the applicability of a social exclu- sion framework to their lived experiences of homelessness and to privilege marginal voices in the production of knowledge (Kirby & McKenna, 1989). This work builds on the perspectives of youth (ages 16–25) who have experienced homelessness and who participated in a pilot project of focus groups (N=12) and in individual interviews (N=30), the main data collection method, which were conducted at three shelters for homeless youth in the "Tri-Cities" (Kitchener-Waterloo-Cambridge, Ontario). This project was facilitated by my 10 years of direct community work experience with marginalized populations.

Eight females and 22 males were interviewed. The average age was 20.4 years. The amount of time that these youths had spent homeless ranged from 3 months to 11 years (average 3.95 years). Indicative of the range of the educational attainment, the lowest level of education attained by the sample of respondents was grade 8 and the highest a college diploma. At the time of my one-on-one interviews, 10 had recently obtained housing; 12 were staying at a shelter; and 8 noted that they were "couch surfing" or living on the street. Further, 10 youths were employed at the time of the one-on-one interview. Youth were provided with a $20 gift card for Tim Hortons or bus tickets as compensation for participation. All youths' names are pseudonyms, and identifiers were removed.

THE VOICES OF YOUTH: LACKING SAFEGUARDS, EXPERIENCING STIGMAS

The experiences of social exclusion are important considerations in discussions of age and housing, as we explore youths' knowledge of access to safeguards, including rights and formal protections. Canada is a democratic society, but one that is guided by neoliberal ideologies. We have rights and responsibilities as citizens and, reciprocally, should expect safeguards and protections from the state. Being young and being without a home complicates this relationship. What follows is a discussion of youths' understanding of their rights, the obstacles homelessness adds to their lived experiences, and the limited access they have to formal protections that are offered to most domiciled individuals. Following this, the youths' views on stigmas, the negative social constructions of homelessness, are unpacked.

Participants expressed that as youth, and as youth who are homeless, they have a limited voice in political and legal systems. In linking rights to recognition and having "proper place" in the social order, youth also conveyed that they are constructed as deviant, dangerous, and a nuisance, extending social exclusion and restricting social citizenship. The youth perceived that being homeless limited their ability to exercise the rights they possessed as citizens. For example:

> If you're homeless, you don't have access to all your rights, in my opinion. 'Cause you have the right to basic essential needs ... where's your basic essential needs then? There isn't any.... They tell you to go to the

soup kitchen.... People who try to sleep and don't sleep because they can't because they're on a park bench. There's no rights there. And you don't even have a name tag, because you don't have any other ID, but in order to get ID you really need to do something. Because people don't know who you are, ... what they're doing isn't enough. We don't have a social networking system. They say we do. But there's not—also not as safeguarded as they say. (Elaine, age 21)

And when you're homeless, because you always have the harassment by police, the biasness of the landlords, and the full weight of the judicial system coming down on you. So there's been instances where youth who are, have a history of being homeless and interaction with the law—because they go hand in hand—where they get in trouble. And maybe it was for, like, selling drugs, but what the judge doesn't know is that they were selling drugs so they could pay their rent, because they're on welfare and they're trying to cover this and make food, so it's a crime of poverty as opposed to somebody trying to make a multibillion-dollar industry off it. And where they'll actually lose their housing, get into jail, and then start from square one again. (Randy, age 23)

Elaine's comments suggest that she believes that the rights of Canadians include the right to having their basic essential needs provided for by the state. However, while parents are charged with providing the necessaries of life to their young children in the private sphere of home, youth who are older confront the realities of a restricted social safety net under neo-liberalism. Randy's comments suggest a nascent awareness of the divide between the law in the books—the formal protections that are contained in federal/provincial/territorial human-rights codes—and the law in action. His comments also direct attention to the stigma of homelessness and how the poverty that underlies it can result in various forms of social exclusion. While housing is a basic need, it is not considered a fundamental human right in Canada, leaving many in precarious positions when it pertains to having a home. According to Laird (2007), "Canada's lack of national strategy on housing and homelessness is one of Canada's greatest economic and cultural liabilities" (p. 5). As Randy's comments above suggest, being without housing is not only a form of social exclusion in itself but also works to perpetuate additional forms of exclusion.

Persons who experience homelessness live a substantial portion of their private lives in public spaces, altering their relationships to state-controlled safeguards. This situation increases the likelihood that their conduct will be subject to police scrutiny and social control. Allen (2004) charges that this situation dampens the likelihood that the citizenship rights of the homeless will be respected: "When one can no longer inhabit public space, be arrested for one's status rather than a crime, and only exercise political power with extreme difficulty, one cannot be said to be a citizen" (p. 1). Correspondingly, many youth reported negative interactions with the police:

> They [the police] just look at you, and they're like, "Oh, this stupid street kid, right, he's not good," so they fuck with us all the time ... for no reason.... Oh yeah. They're very bad. There's this one cop, every time he sees me, 10 people could jaywalk with me, you know ... but he'll pick me out of everybody ... to come and give me a ticket. (Nathan, age 17)

> I think they [the police] need to have an exercise where they have nothing but the clothes on their back and you can stay out on the streets for a few days. Tell me, how'd you get by? You have no access to your bank card, your bank accounts—anything—your ID all gone. You're not allowed to touch anything else, you just have to stay out there and do where you're wet, you have holes in your shoes, and it's really bad weather or something. You have to keep warm, and you have to stay warm, and you have to find a place—and then tell me why we find, then you try to tell me why it's wrong for me to break into an apartment building and sleep in their laundry room. And then we get charged for it. Yes, it's wrong, but they don't understand the reasonable factor of death. (Elaine, age 21)

> And the police just kind of interpret youth who are homeless as people who don't like rules, who feign an authority and just kinda wanna fight authority whenever they have the chance. So they kinda take it personally as an attack against them, like, "Oh, you're just a youth, so you don't know what you're doing, because if you did know, you wouldn't be homeless right now." They don't look at it as, like, a social issue but more as an issue of that individual, with whoever they were. There, like, the belief is there, I feel, from the police that it's just like, "Youth don't—you didn't like the rules your parents gave you so you left. And now you're going to follow my rules." (Randy, age 23)

The overwhelming majority of the youth in this project felt that, due to their homelessness, they had been treated unfairly by the police. They perceived that the police lacked empathy for those who were homeless and stereotyped homeless youth as problem kids, very much treating homelessness as an individual, private trouble. The youth in this project did not, in general, perceive the police as guardians and protectors of *their* rights. As Heisler (2005) notes, while citizenship "figures in the assurance or denial of rights, economic benefits, social services, education, due process of the law and opportunities to affect political decisions ... it does not guarantee equal fairness, justice, economic well-being, dignity or the respect of public officials or fellow citizens" (p. 667). The comments of the youth suggest a similar divide between the "rights" that they possessed in theory and in practice.

Experiencing homelessness impacts social exclusion and limits one's access to rights and formal protections from the state. Furthermore, being without a home can end "youth" and force young Canadians to take on adult-like social roles and responsibilities (O'Grady, Gaetz, & Buccieri, 2011). Nevertheless, recognition of the struggles that these young people face might be overshadowed by a variety of negative stereotypes that suggest that they are in general deviant (Schissel, 2009) and dangerous individuals who refuse to abide by the norms of "civil" society, as they live private lives in public spaces (Mitchell, 2003; Gharabaghi & Stuart, 2010, p. 1685).

Moving forward, the following discussion addresses the youths' understandings of power, stigma, social order, and social exclusion. The youth recognize that others may view them as deviant, threatening, and/or a nuisance, since they are without home, and discuss how these perceptions impact them in their daily lives. The youth were also aware that they lacked institutional and social power, and spoke of how their powerlessness influenced their interactions with agents and agencies of social control. Feldman (2004) has noted that those who are constructed as a nuisance are often viewed as disposable and/or treated disrespectfully as non-persons, without concern for preserving their dignity. Part of being included as a member of society and a citizen is recognition: recognition of one's rightful place or positioning within the social order. Unfortunately, this recognition is something that is often denied to those who are young and without home.

Mosher (2002) explains that homeless individuals are constructed as "others" who constitute a threat (p. 52). These negative social constructions are fateful. The youth in this project voiced their perceptions of how they are viewed by their peers and by the larger social order. Their sense of how others view them can have tremendous influence on their own sense of self. It also guides their perceptions of themselves as members of society and as being socially included or excluded. In general, the respondents felt that homeless youth were not well understood by society. They continuously reported that those without personal experience of homelessness did not understand the reality of homelessness and how this social location impacted the daily lives of those who experienced it.

In our discussions, many youth noted the negative stereotypes and ideologies that impact understandings of youth homelessness. For example:

> Like, you see people stereotype, like, what a homeless person should look like, and they are bummy and stuff and do drugs and everything— but it's not always like that. It's not. I don't think I look totally like a druggie or a bum. I don't. I try not to. I don't know. (Fiona, age 18)

Just a lot of people won't give you the time of day if you are homeless. You're asking for spare change, and they tell you to go fuck yourselves. They tell you to go get a job. But you apply for a job being homeless, half the people don't want to give it to you because they think you're not reliable, right? So it's harder to find jobs than these people make it out to be. No one willing to give you a chance. You get really pissed off at society. (Ogden, age 22)

The comments of these youth illustrate the active component of social exclusion and the relational side of rejection, isolation, and humiliation (Silver & Miller, 2003). Youth are well aware of social stereotypes of the homeless and the stigma of homelessness. Fiona is aware of what *homeless* looks like in the eyes of the public. She works to conceal this identity by not falling into stereotypes of what a person experiencing homelessness *should* look like. Ogden also acknowledges these negative perceptions of homeless youth and shows his awareness of neoliberalism's preferred response to society's have-nots. However, he also emphasizes the difficulties that homeless people face when they attempt to find employment. Other respondents signalled their awareness of the get-a-job response to the homeless that is championed under neoliberalism by pointing to additional difficulties. For example: "Some other people just think of it as, 'This person doesn't want to get a job, blah, blah, blah, they're just bums,' 'They can't get a house because they don't want to hold a job' or whatever. So ... but some people can't hold a job because of said mental disabilities and whatnot. And maybe addictions of certain kinds" (Ken, age 25). Ken suggested that while the general public may think that homeless people should go get a job, their lack of employment is not always a choice or a personal trouble. Rather, unemployment can also signify a public issue and a lack of necessary social supports for those who confront mental-health problems and substance-abuse issues, and that the youth unemployment rate is double the adult rate. Mosher (2002) and Gaetz, O'Grady, and Buccieri (2010) have also urged that attention be paid to the structural components of homelessness. Based upon my respondents' comments, it would seem that homeless youths are often treated as non-persons with restricted social citizenship rights.

Fraser (2010) notes that misrecognition, the denial of dignity and respect, is integral to social exclusion. The treatment homeless youth receive from others may incur or intensify a perception of themselves as deviant, socially marginal, worthless—a legitimate object of social exclusion. The youth reported that they were excluded from society in a variety of ways. They perceived that they were often treated as non-persons—as if they simply did not matter:

There's nothing I like about being homeless. I've stayed at [adult shelter] just down the road, which is filled with homeless people. It's not ... I don't know, the greatest feeling. When you're homeless, you gotta get used to the disappointment. That's what you are feeling. (Tom, age 22)

I guess by society you're seen somehow less of a human being. (Miles, age 22)

Once you're in a shelter, you're the lowest of the low, no matter who's looking at you, you know? Just having, like, people looking down on you all the time when there's not a necessary need to be doing it. They should be helping you, not looking down on you. (Josh, age 22)

There is much pathos in Tom's comment. It would seem tragic that in a country as rich as Canada, youth who are homeless should perceive that their only option is to "get used to the disappointment." Nevertheless, Miles also perceives that Canadians view the homeless as "somehow less of a human being" or as legitimate objects of exclusion. His comment records his perception that among members of Canadian society, an absence of housing also diminishes one's humanity. Further, Josh perceives that those who experience homelessness are positioned at the very bottom of Canadian society. However, he charges that Canadians "should be helping you, not looking down on you." Youths repeatedly directed attention to the experiences that they had endured while homeless. Given that Canada has consistently ranked high when measured by the United Nations on the Human Development Index, these situations they describe are almost unfathomable. Nevertheless, their comments make evident that some young Canadians suffer extreme deprivation in the new millennium and feel that their sufferings are ignored.

A number of youths believed that if Canadians had a better understanding of homelessness and the homeless, their situation would be less bleak:

I just wish everybody would stop being so judgmental. Like, I wish they would just, like honestly, what I said earlier, just step in our shoes for a day and see how it is. Like, it's not fun. Not at all. (Ian, age 23)

I would tell them, maybe instead of just prejudging people, that you should get to know them and get to know their back story, then make a judgment on them. And keep in mind, what would happen, what would you do if that happened to you, like, you know, how would you react if you had to leave home when you were, like, sixteen or fifteen years old. How would you react? Would you be able to stay strong and keep your focus on school? And keep your focus on work? When the government is taking half of your money, you have practically no time to do school, because your mind is, you know, where, how am I gonna afford this, how am I gonna afford that? Or would you get sucked into the whole, "Screw it. Everyone thinks I'm a reject of society, no one believes in me—I'm just gonna act like they want me to"? Would you be able to rise above that? No? (Gayle, age 17)

Several of the youths questioned, to varying degrees, the extent to which those who have not experienced homelessness could understand what this situation entails and/or understand those who are homeless. Can one understand homelessness without having experienced it? Perhaps not fully, but many of my respondents believed that interacting with homeless youth would be quite productive in altering preconceived notions and stereotypes about this group and in lessening the degree of marginalization and social exclusion they experience.

Ian and Gayle, like many others in this project, believed that the general public does not understand and does not empathize with youth experiencing homelessness. These youths also suggested a need for people to consider both the background and social factors that led to homelessness before assuming that homeless youth choose to be homeless. Gayle, for example, challenged those who criticize homeless youth to consider the challenges youth face and to acknowledge the strength and resilience of those who persevere in the face of adversity.

For my respondents, being subjected to the negative judgments of others was obviously a constant reminder of their social exclusion. For example:

Some adults treat me differently. They look at me with disgust. (Flynn, age 18)

If I don't have, like, a shower or clean clothes on, and I feel like shit, and I'm like, "Oh my God, everyone is staring at me"—they know I'm homeless. I remember me and [partner] were just sitting on the ground one day, and this girl, drunk, coming out of a bar, she's like, "Oh look, homeless people!" and I was so embarrassed. Like, so embarrassed, like, I wanted to fuckin' just hide. But we were just sitting there because we had nothing to do, right? And she's like—no, it wasn't, it wasn't "homeless people"— shit—oh, it's "street people," like, meaning homeless. But whatever she said, I was just like, "Oh my God!" I wanted to die. It's embarrassing. I think it's more embarrassing than anything. (Betty, age 22)

These comments are poignant reminders of the human costs of social exclusion. They also suggest how being the target of stigma and the negative judgments of others can be internalized into the self. For example, Betty's comments make clear that when passersby treat the homeless as objects of mirth, their comments can be deeply hurtful to those who are their targets. Betty possesses post-secondary education and did not experience homelessness until her early 20s. Unlike many of the youth who were involved in my study, Betty described herself as having had a generally positive home life. She also admitted that prior to becoming homeless herself, she had negatively stereotyped those who were homeless. For Betty, *homelessness* was clearly a stigma label, and she actively attempted to pass as a person who was not homeless. As her comments note, she was terribly embarrassed when people identified her as being homeless. Betty maintained that being homeless has given her a completely different perspective on those who are homeless.

This work examined, first, youths' views on their limited access to the basic rights of a citizen, including feeling protected by the police. Instead of feeling like they could access formal protections, they felt as though they were the targets of front-line police officers. Further, this work outlined the stigma and discrimination the youth faced through discussions of how they have been constructed as dangerous, deviant, and/or a nuisance. Rather than having support systems to assist youth in poverty and without a home, they are socially excluded with limited access to rights and resources. The limitations on the freedoms and powers of youth are severe for youth who experience homelessness. They are viewed as *out of place,* in two senses of the phrase: i.e., not engaged in normal youthful activities and not living as they should be (De Benetiz, 2003). As voiced by the youth, social exclusion as tied to their age and living situations limits and restricts their ability to claim the rights that are associated with social citizenship.

CONCLUDING REMARKS AND MOVING FORWARD

Canada's approach to governing and social policy is informed by neoliberal ideologies that emphasize individual responsiblity and self-sufficiency. Canadian social policies are reactive in their responses to homelessness, offering, at best, minimal assistance and then only when an individual has exhausted all other resources. Further, neoliberal social policies and responses to homelessness work to regulate the behaviour of individuals. As Sommers (2013) explains, such policies, including municipal bylaws that regulate the location of shelters, safe-streets acts, and the practices of private-sector shelters, aim to reinforce socially and economically responsible behaviours of youth who are homeless (pp. 369–380). This individualized and minimalist approach, I argue, is harmful to many, especially youth who experience homelessness.

Rather than an individualistic approach, we should adopt a collective responsibility to respond to social injustices such as extreme poverty and exclusion. To address such inequalities, I turn to Young's (2011) position, where she states, "My responsibility is essentially shared with others because the harms are produced by many of us acting together within accepted institutions and practices, and because it is not possible for any of us to identify just what in our own actions results in which aspect of the injustice that particular individuals suffer" (p. 110). The causes of homelessness do not rest entirely or even primarily at an individual level. The causes of homelessness are largely structural, and the harms of homelessness are perpetuated by neoliberal social policies. Blaming individuals for homelessness does not offer solutions. Telling those who are homeless to be responsible and self-sufficient while criminalizing their actions or use of space through legislation, such as safe-streets acts, does little to reduce or minimize their exclusion from many aspects of mainstream society. Such actions merely perpetuate social exclusion, as they have serious consequences for the individual and can be taxing on systems, including the criminal justice system (Chesnay, Bellot & Sylvestre, 2013). Through my work, I hope to, as Young (2011) notes, "persuade others that this threat to well-being is a matter of injustice rather than misfortune" (p. 112) and to encourage a collective effort to address the social exclusion of youth who experience homelessness.

For youth who experience homelessness, home was often not a safe space. Youth left home because of abuse, neglect, and/or violence. On the streets, youth may form fictive families or find provisional space, though these constructs are often temporary. Youth find themselves in marginalized positions, with limited access to resources and restricted social citizenship rights. Further, because *home* holds such normative assumptions of the safe and proper place for youth, once removed from this environment, they are too often constructed as deviant, dangerous, and a nuisance. Instead of people in need of assistance and support, they are constructed as a group to be feared and controlled. The human impacts of lack of home are consequential.

Youth homelessness is a complex topic. The needs of homeless Canadians in general, and homeless youth in particular, are many. Yet recognition of their right to receive social assistance and support has been slow in coming. It would seem that many Canadians feel that the homeless are culturally legitimate victims (Weis & Borges, 1973), people who deserve ill treatment. As documented throughout this project and reported in a number of other Canadian-based studies (for example, see work by Kidd and Carroll, 2007), youth who experience homelessness are often treated unkindly by the general public because of some combination of misunderstanding, fear, or general disdain. Governmental responses to homeless youth, such as Ontario's Safe Streets Act, are equally unkind and suggest that homeless youth are less often seen as victims than as young-offenders-in-training. In addition, youth who are homeless lack social safeguards. They may be dispossessed of the rights of social citizenship, however limited they may be in a neoliberal state. Canada's treatment of youth who experience homelessness would seem to contradict its claims of being committed to equality and inclusivity. The reports of my respondents suggest that Canada must still travel some distance in order to achieve equality and inclusivity for homeless persons.

REFERENCES

Allen, T. C. (2004). *Someone to Talk To: Care and Control of the Homeless*. Halifax: Fernwood Publishing.

Buccieri, K. (2010). Harm reduction as practice: Perspectives from a community of street youth and social service providers. *Social Development Issues, 32,* 3, 1–15.

Chesnay, C., Bellot, C. & Sylvestre, M. S. (2013). Taming disorderly people one ticket at a time: The penalization of homelessness in Ontario and British Columbia. *Canadian Journal of Criminology and Criminal Justice, 55,* 2, 161–185.

Collins, T. (2007). Youth homelessness: Facts and beliefs. In Child Welfare League of Canada (Ed.), *The Welfare of Canadian Children: It's Our Business: A Collection of Research Papers for a Healthy Future for Canadian Children and Families* (pp. 92–95). Saint-Lazare, Quebec: Child Welfare League of Canada.

Cooper, D. (2004). *Challenging Diversity: Rethinking Equality and the Value of Difference.* Cambridge: Cambridge University Press.

Cortese, A. J. (2003). *Walls and Bridges: Social Justice and Public Policy.* Albany: State University of New York Press.

De Benetiz, S. T. (2003). Reactive, protective and rights-based approaches in work with homeless street youth. *Children, Youth and Environments 13,* 1, n.p.

Feldman, L. C. (2004). *Citizens Without Shelter: Homelessness, Democracy and Political Exclusion.* Ithaca: Cornell University.

Fowler, P. J., Toro, P. A. & Miles, B. (2009). Pathways to and from homelessness and associated psychosocial outcomes among adolescents leaving the foster care system. *American Journal of Public Health, 99,* 1453–1458.

Fraser, N. (2010). Injustice at intersecting scales: On "social exclusion" and the "global poor." *European Journal of Social Theory, 13,* 3, 363–371.

Gaetz, S., O'Grady, B. & Buccieri, K. (2010). *Surviving Crime and Violence: Street Youth and Victimization in Toronto.* The Homeless Hub. Retrieved from www.homelesshub.ca/(S(ubjrf455ekxl3d555pnuio2n))/Library/Surviving-Crime-and-Violence-Street-Youth-and-Victimization-in-Toronto-48609.aspx

Gharabaghi, K. & Stuart, C. (2010). Voices from the periphery: Prospects and challenges for the homeless youth service sector. *Children and Youth Services Review, 32,* 12, 1683–1689.

Giroux, H. A. (2003). Racial injustice and disposable youth in the age of zero tolerance. *Qualitative Studies in Education, 16,* 4, 553–565.

Karabanow, J. (2010). Street kids as delinquents, menaces and criminals: Another example of the criminalization of poverty. In D. Crocker & V. M. Johnson (Eds.), *Poverty, Regulation and Social Exclusion: Readings on the Criminalization of Poverty* (pp. 138–147). Halifax: Fernwood Publishing.

Karabanow, J. (2006). Becoming a street kid: Exploring the stages of street life. *Journal of Human Behavior in the Social Environment, 13,* 2, 49–72.

Kidd, S. & Carroll, M. (2007). Coping and suicidality among homeless youth. *Journal of Adolescence, 30,* 2, 283–296.

Kirby, S. & McKenna, K. (1989). *Experience, Research, Social Change: Methods from the Margins.* Toronto: Garamond Press.

Laird, G. (2007). *Homelessness in a Growth Economy: Canada's 21st Century Paradox.* A Report for the Sheldon Chumir Foundation for Ethics in Leadership. Calgary: Sheldon Chumir Foundation for Ethics in Leadership.

Lyon-Callo, V. (2004). *Inequality, Poverty and Neoliberal Governance: Activist Ethnography in the Homeless Sheltering Industry.* Peterborough: Broadview Press.

Mallett, S. (2004). Understanding home: A critical review of the literature. *The Sociological Review, 52,* 1, 62–89.

Mills, C. W. (1959). The professional ideology of social pathologists. *The American Journal of Sociology, 49,* 2, 165–180.

Mitchell, D. (2003). *The Right to the City: Social Justice and the Fight for Public Space.* New York: Guilford Press.

Morris, L. (1994). *Dangerous Classes: The Underclass and Social Citizenship.* London: Routledge.

Mosher, J. (2002). The shrinking of the public and private spaces for the poor. In J. Hermer & J. Mosher (Eds.), *Disorderly People: Law and the Politics of Exclusion in Ontario* (pp. 41–53). Halifax: Fernwood Publishing.

O'Grady, B., Gaetz, S. & Buccieri, K. (2011). *Can I See Your ID? The Policing of Youth Homelessness in Toronto.* Toronto: JFCY & The Homeless Hub.

Schissel, B. (2009). *Still Blaming Children: Youth Conduct and the Politics of Child Hating.* Halifax: Fernwood Publishing.

Silver, H. & Miller, S. (2003). Social exclusion: The European approach to social disadvantage. *Indicators, 2,* 5–21.

Sommers, R. (2013). Governing the streets: The legal, social and moral regulation of homeless youth. In S. Gaetz, B. O'Grady, K. Buccieri, J. Karabanow & A. Marsolais (Eds.), *Youth Homelessness in Canada: Implications for Policy and Practice* (pp. 369–386). Toronto: Canadian Homelessness Research Network Press. Retrieved from www.homelesshub.ca/ResourceFiles/Documents/YouthHomelessnessweb.pdf

Tyler, K. A. & Bersani, B. E. (2008). A longitudinal study of early adolescent precursors to running away. *The Journal of Early Adolescence, 28,* 2, 230–235.

Weis, K. & Borges, S. (1973). Victimology and rape: The case of the legitimate victim. *Issues in Criminology, 8,* 2, 71–115.

Young, I. M. (2011). *Responsibility for Justice.* New York: Oxford University Press.

PART THREE
HOME BEYOND HOME: NEIGHBOURHOOD AND COMMUNITY

E ach of the chapters in this section explores the way that homemaking and home feeling extend from domestic spaces into streets, neighbourhoods, and communities. Renaud Goyer, in vividly tracing the challenges faced by working-class, largely immigrant populations in a Montreal suburb, argues that secure, healthy housing is needed for urban residents to be included in wider communities. John Phyne and Christine Knott remember an inner-city neighbourhood of substandard houses that nonetheless was more of a home than the "improved" housing offered by governments and planning professionals whose modernist gaze could only see houses. Joseph Moore reflects on how street festivals might reclaim roadways as public spaces available for homemaking and home feeling, underscoring the message that the sorts of community resiliencies to which Phyne and Knott refer might need to be remade. Closing the section, Tracey Harris draws upon the experience of the owners of seasonal tiny homes to reveal that the material limits of small living spaces shape the experience of home in community and in nature.

Goyer's chapter reminds us that, by and large, Canadian cities defied the American experience of the concentration of poverty and racialized exclusion in inner cities. Instead, new immigrants and the least advantaged of the working class have increasingly found themselves pushed to the suburban margins. The challenge of home in these margins is not the middle-class anomie of single-family housing in monocultural settings that our cultural imagery of suburbia prepares us for, but rather struggles with landlords and the problems of mobility that come with dispersed settlement.

The respondents' conflicted discourse speaks to the continued role of home as a haven: a space that one can bring under control, in a world where such control is elusive and concentrated in the hands of the few.

Even when faced with structural and spatial inadequacies that threaten their physical or mental health, their apartments offer respite and a place of retreat. Goyner makes the case that the struggle for healthy and comfortable domestic space is not a retreat into the home but rather the shoring up of a base from which inclusion into the neighbourhood and community can be launched.

Indeed, it is most telling that for these respondents the search for better accommodations is constrained not simply by economic or cultural disadvantage but also by the attachment to a home in community. The respondents acknowledge that their well-being rests not only on the quality of their domestic home space but also on the physical, cultural, and social aspects of the wider community. If home is a haven, these respondents suggest that neighbourhoods and their communities are havenly places as well.

As Phyne and Knott's chapter demonstrates, governments and the planning community have often missed this insight. The modernist gaze of these powers, enamoured with the rearranging of urban space for predictability and efficiency, have seen right past the places, the social connections, and community resiliencies they are given charge of improving.

In a neoliberal context, where the growth machine of urban capital tears through neighbourhoods with abandon, and where both elite and working classes are increasingly rootless, there is the distinct danger of unrestrained nostalgia for a bygone world where homes, communities, and families were more solid. Staying true to the voices and experiences of their respondents, Phyne and Knott avoid this sentiment by acknowledging that these neighbourhood homes were also places of racism, classism, and sexism. Men, for instance, created home spaces in pubs that excluded women. These men and boys were afforded greater mobility, extending their home range further afield than wives and daughters. Meanwhile, women and girls found themselves tightly bound to the physical and emotional demands of homemaking in domestic spaces.

With such caveats acknowledged, Phyne and Knott echo a truth that also is apparent in the other chapters in this section: that people can make home and feel at home in public spaces. The respondents recall with affection the fluid flow of children through neighbourhood homes and streetscapes alive with activity and the social connection of community. One can only speculate that middle-class reformist planners were not simply blind to such homemaking in the streets but fearful of it. Whatever the motive, many of the residents of the St. John's "slum" referenced in this chapter got better housing but lost a home.

Joseph Moore's chapter picks up this thread and suggests that there exists a concerted effort by some (he hesitantly refers to this as a social movement) to promote homemaking and home feeling in public spaces. While Moore centres his argument on a street festival, he suggests that community gardening, urban homesteading, Critical Mass rides, and other urban projects are bringing streets and neighbourhoods under some control, building social solidarity, and encouraging inhabitants to extend their home into their neighbourhood.

Moore also calls attention to the dark side of community hinted at by Phyne and Knott: that feeling at home in a neighbourhood can come at the expense of other groups who also wish to claim this space for their home-making. The argument is made that public spaces demand an appropriate and limited form of homemaking, one rooted in "light" and multiple social connections and the trust of strangers. As Moore notes, this is not the village-like solidarity that existed in central St. John's, but in a diverse urban context, this is probably a "good thing."

In her consideration of the Tiny Home Movement, Harris employs a sociological eye attuned to the emplacement of our lives. The interviewees are keenly aware of a point often lost on sociologists, that their social interaction, their community possibility, and their relations with natural and built environments are entangled in the immediate and material context of their homes. Bricks and mortar and square footage are products and producers of emotion and patterns of sociability.

The respondents speak passionately of their personal agency in building and choosing physically constrained seasonal small homes as a response and challenge to a neoliberal context of hyperconsumption and enforced busy-ness. But once their homes are constructed, respondents also grant them a hand in their community engagement and in their relation to the natural world. The interviews make clear that, as for many who are so lucky, home is a place of emotional attachment. However, there is also the distinct impression that the physical space of these homes is a propelling force, deeply implicated in a new-found sociability and engagement with community.

Taken together, these chapters speak to the neoliberal crisis of home noted in our introduction. The more interventionist state of the 1960s and 1970s promoted sprawl, bisected neighbourhoods with highway projects, and cleared vibrant low-income neighbourhoods in the name of redevelopment. Under neoliberal regimes in the 1980s to the present, income and wealth inequality grew, speculative housing markets drove up housing costs, and the state, especially at the federal level, abandoned programs that supported housing and families. The costs of social reproduction were pushed into domestic spaces just as traditional community supports withered. One response, for those with the means, was the retreat into the private spaces of homes whose girth, continuous renovation, and shortened product cycle mirrored the cultural economic demands of neoliberal times.

Many, as Harris and Moore acknowledge, have come to question the social and ecological consequences of all of these shifts, yet it remains unclear where resistance will come from. Harris suggests that conscious retreats to small vacation homes, in rural and semirural areas, may entail a distancing from home lives scarred by the intensity of neoliberal social relations. These are in no way, however, retreats from the social itself; rather, these small homes serve as springboards into less alienated, joyful, and sustainable homemaking and self-realization in community and nature. In speaking to the role of urban spaces as an infrastructure of dissent, Moore reminds us that cities and their neighbourhoods have been the place of revolution, and that extensions of home into the streets (and parks and coffee shops) can offer resources for progressive politics. In each case, what seems at first blush to be a rather mundane defensive struggle for a good home is understood as pregnant with political possibility. For those looking for an ecologically responsible way to rebuild a social fabric worn bare, the struggle to secure space for public homemaking and to provide individuals and families with safe and healthy domestic space—Occupy Home, if you will—might indeed be a place to start.

CHAPTER 9

HOME IS MORE THAN A SHELTER: THE EXPERIENCE OF HOUSING SPACE AND THE PROCESSES OF EXCLUSION

Renaud Goyer

Each February in Quebec, many tenants receive a rent increase notification from their landlords. Most leases are due on June 30, and tenants need to confirm their renewal by April 1, which also means that landlords are required to send in the new lease conditions (including the rental amount) by March 1. This simple notice raises tough questions for tenants, for even though they can refuse the increase and continue living in the same place, for many it means having to choose between staying or leaving. In this assessment, tenants *analyze* their situation and *evaluate* their mobility options. In doing so, they review their own experience of housing through time and space, as well as compare it with experiences of people they know. This paper seeks, on the one hand, to present these events as they are analyzed by tenants themselves and, on the other, to illustrate how their experiences of housing relate to space, revealing possible processes of exclusion through and in space.

HOUSE, HOUSING, AND HOME: A CONCEPTUALIZATION

The concept of a house is complex and multidimensional, comprising a number of means and purposes. The first meaning of *house* is very clear: it is a building allowing one or more individuals to find accommodation (Havel, 1985). However, its means and the purposes begin to diverge in the attainment of the need to find accommodation. A priori, housing is considered to be a fundamental human need, but it is also a consumer good, a property, and an investment, an asset inscribed in space, creating a locus for those who inhabit it (Authier, Bonvalet & Lévy, 2010). It is therefore also defined by its financial dimension. A house, then, means property, distinguishable by its inhabitants or residents, by its localization and the geographic space it occupies—whether urban or rural—or by its architectural form or material components (Segaud, Bonvalet & Brun, 1998). Additionally, it is possessed of a somewhat more symbolic nature, however, originating from the same source as its material qualities. It provides a sense of pride, a foundation for family life, a cultural and collective identity, a social network, and social support and security to its inhabitants, thus undeniably acquiring a psychosocial and interactional dimension (Carter & Polevychok, 2004). Lastly, the localization and space it occupies, including the immediate neighbourhood and access to services—its spatial dimension—also represents an important function of the social, professional, and residential standing of its inhabitants (Lazarotti, 2012; Grafmeyer, 1998). In effect, a house integrates individuals by anchoring them spatially, personally, socially, and institutionally, and in doing do, it reassures and stabilizes them (Boucher, 2008; Bernard, 1998; Tardieu, Oré & Frenette, 1992).

Therefore, a house is central to our lives. More than just a shelter, protecting us from the elements and providing a place to rest, it is also our link to the world around us, particularly because it gives us an address. In this respect, it personalizes and socializes individuals, integrating them into society (Butler & Hamnett, 2012). Our houses are intimately linked to a universal need for reference points and security; they are our pride, identity, and family base, anchoring us in the neighbourhood and beyond. Once this base is weakened, either by financial, interactional, or spatial problems—including poor sanitary conditions—the risk of exclusion increases for the tenant and her family. All individuals, employed and unemployed alike, put their house or dwelling at the centre of their social existence and their relationship to the outside world (Morin & Dorvil, 2008; Hay, 2005; Grémion, 1996). According to McAll (1995), exclusion through housing represents one of the most visible and straightforward expressions of social inequality, notably because of the symbols it evokes (closed doors, no anchor). In effect, exclusion from housing combines two losses: loss of control over one's life space and the ensuing incapacity of fully enjoying one's citizenship rights (Somerville, 1998).

In Quebec, studies of housing conditions generally make use of two distinct but complementary approaches: they focus either on the economic dimension or on sanitary conditions. The first one, known as "housing economics" (Segaud, Bonvalet & Brun, 1998), postulates a typology of tenants and accommodations according to their availability, quality, and "affordability," in the goal of preventing or explaining housing-related issues. Studies of this type accentuate economic inequalities created by the housing market (Ball, 2012; Clark, 2012). The second approach concentrates on the consequences of poor housing conditions to human health, that is, on everything related to health and safety. Based on the notion of "social determinants of health," these studies emphasize the importance of good housing conditions to an individual's health. Their goal is to assess inadequate housing conditions and account for the number of people affected (Moret, 1998).

Using statistics to demonstrate the importance of housing problems, whether in terms of accessibility and/or health, these studies point to a potential process of exclusion occurring in the housing context. However, they do not permit others to understand the lived experience of tenants and consequently to act to implement efficient measures for empowerment and inclusion. In contrast, research presented in this paper is intended to report on the reality of substandard housing—its lived experience—and the possible exclusions it might entail. Consequently, the research question that guided our study was: How do tenants analyze the processes of exclusion, based on their housing experiences? In answering it, we focus first on tenants' individual experiences of housing and then present them as constructed in relation to space, revealing the possible processes of exclusion through and in space.

RESEARCH METHOD

This research was carried out in the summer of 2013 among the tenants of Montreal's Saint-Laurent borough, in collaboration with the local Comité logement (Housing Committee). Data was obtained from 10 semistructured interviews, each approximately one hour long, and from 60 hours of observation conducted in the course of house visits, meetings with tenants, and Housing Forum discussions. Subsequently, the data was transcribed and thematically coded to reconstruct the housing experience of tenants by using an inductive method. Before reporting our research results, however, it seems pertinent to describe briefly the Saint-Laurent borough, followed by the definition of social experience as proposed by Dubet (1994), which served as our theoretical framework.

Measured in square kilometres, Saint-Laurent is the second largest borough in the city of Montreal, and the second least densely populated. Within the vast territory it occupies, some zones are very densely populated, while others (industrial parks) remain practically uninhabited. Housing infrastructure is more recent than in Montreal's older boroughs, although in some sectors it is already aging rapidly. A significant proportion of all households in the area are rentals, although this percentage is still below that of the city of Montreal. Finally, the borough of Saint-Laurent is an area that receives many newcomers, who have become a central element of its sociodemographic reality. As a case in point, in the 2006 census over 57% of tenant households indicated persons born outside of Canada as primary breadwinner (18% for recent immigrants). For many tenants we met, this was their first housing experience in Canada, which illustrates how housing experience overlaps with the experiences of migration (Ville de Montréal, 2009).

Regarding our theoretical approach, we adopted the notion of "social experience" developed by Dubet (1994) to highlight the mechanisms of inclusion and exclusion central to tenants' experiences. Inspired by phenomenology, Dubet (1994) argues that social experience is constructed through life challenges and/or ordeals, and that it is through the latter that social reality takes form:

> Social experience is a product of a double mechanism. On the one hand, it is a way of coping with the social world, of receiving and defining it through a range of situations, images, and preimposed constraints. It is a subjective version of social life. On the other hand, because the social world has neither unity nor coherence, social experience is a way of constructing this world, as well as oneself. (Dubet & Martuccelli, 1998, p. 57)

In this definition, the social experience is the "society" lived by individuals, through challenges or trials. However, this "social" is no longer unique or universal; it is the experience of it that produces our understanding of the social and thereby "constructs" the reality (Berger & Luckmann, 1966). Thus, we turn to the representation of housing problems by the individuals affected (challenges) in order to understand the individual and collective realities of housing (experience) and the processes of exclusion they potentially entail. The following section presents an account of challenges that constitute the experience of housing.

THE HOUSING EXPERIENCE

As we have seen, housing is a multifaceted concept, but the housing experience—and the experience of exclusion in particular—is constructed primarily in its spatial dimension. Butler and Hamnett (2012) remind us that

> cities are divided, socially and spatially, into an often complex mosaic of social groups and residential areas differentiated by social class, income, race and ethnicity and religion…. Place of residence is a very important social marker for many people. Not only is it very important in terms of quality of life (or the lack of it) but also it tells others a great deal about the sort of person that lives in an area. (p. 147)

Indeed, housing experience is an experience of space (Paquot, 2007), with its embedded social relations that can involve processes of inequality, discrimination, and exclusion—thus sometimes creating housing classes (Rex & Moore, 1967). The tenants' relationship to space is twofold: (a) geographic, as it links individuals to society; and (b) intimate or psychological, as it separates and distinguishes one from others (MacLennan, 2012; Paquot, 2007, Pezeu-Massabau, 1983). A house, in its material form, exists at a specific location. Therefore, it is geographically located, but it also locates its residents in space, constituting our most significant spatial point of reference and providing anchorage. A house is more than an address associated with a building: it materializes as a roof, a shelter from the elements, and finally a source of security and intimacy that separates and distinguishes us from the collectivity of society. This space is a foundation on which we build our personal and family life. Linked together, these relationships make the experience of space a social experience (Lévy, 1994; Cox, 1991) from which we construct our citizenship (Paquot, 2007). The following section illustrates how housing experience is marked by space, or rather how housing becomes the point of departure for the experience of space.

Anchored in Space: The Geography of Housing

All tenants interviewed in our study appreciated their neighbourhood and a majority expressed no wish to move to another part of the city. One of the most frequently raised points was the belief that Saint-Laurent in general—and their block in particular—was safe, as compared to other areas of Montreal, even though some petty crimes were committed nearby. It was described as a good place to raise children, where residents do not have to worry about them coming home late in the evening: "They found us a house in [borough name]. You know, there, it's a bit, it's not that—it's not that safe. They offered us a house there, but because of children. They come home late because sometimes, when they go play basketball, it ends late. So we couldn't take that house. It was far and also because of safety reasons. Because there, it's really dangerous [door creaking] because of children." In addition, many residents explain their choice of Saint-Laurent by its proximity to their affective network, and especially the presence of friends:

> R: I came here because I had friends here. Maybe, if by some chance my friends were in another place, maybe ...
> I: You would have been somewhere else.
> R: I would have gone there. But it, it would maybe come with, with experience.

Furthermore, they believe that proximity to services—and commerce in particular—makes their lives easier. They appreciate being able to do their shopping on foot, especially since few of them own cars. Availability of child care, quality of schools, and other government services is deemed advantageous as well: "But unfortunately we are looking for something nearby, because we have child care here, etc. And also we don't want to leave this place, that's it." Some of our interviewees, especially those working evenings and nights, talked about the challenges of commuting to distant workplaces by public transit. However, it was not perceived as a problem by residents who said they liked their neighbourhood, because of a good bus connection to work:

> I: Because you are still a bit far from all services here.
> R: Yes. Look, when I leave the Hôtel-Dieu [hospital], I go to Sherbrooke [station], ride up to Crémazie, then take the 100 [bus], which drops me off by … there is this Dodge car dealership, and then I walk. In winter it's not fun.
> I: It's long.
> R: Yes, it's long, it's long. If not, I have to wait for the 124. 124 passes by Plamondon [station] at one thirty. So I leave at quarter past midnight. Well, arriving here at a quarter to two is not … with the other one, I have to run a little bit, because it's the last bus. I take it at forty-seven minutes past midnight, and at least I arrive here at home at one o'clock in the morning. But I'm calm about it.

For some residents, especially those who live on the borough's outskirts, noise represents a major problem. For instance, a tenant who lives close to the highway and a busy boulevard reported trouble sleeping at night and wished to find a quieter place. To others, it was proximity to the bus terminal and the metro and the constant coming and going of passengers that was the biggest source of noise: "Because again, the house, the building is not far from the highway, the 15. So there is always noise. There is also the Côte Vertu Avenue, so day and night, so there's noise."

Many private-housing tenants that we met found that the amount of rent they paid was too high for the quality of their apartments. Although this kind of criticism seems obvious, many tenants considered that it was the best they could do cost-wise, regardless of the value-for-money factor. There is little or no truly cheaper accommodation, and they already live in the cheapest housing available: "My apartment is small, compared to other, to other apartments, but it's cheaper. Even if these days for me, according to my revenues, it's still expensive." This situation puts them on hold. To many, happiness seems to be elsewhere, thus they are always ready to move in search of a more affordable dwelling: "As I told you, I have actually looked before. Even my wife, every day she's on Kijiji, seeing appartments.… But we haven't found anything within our reach, that's it."

Housing and Living Environment: The Intimacy of Space

Beyond its physical existence, a dwelling is also a life space, a home base for the construction of our lives. The interviewed tenants believed it to be the only place where one could truly relax, comfortable and unperturbed. An additional important quality of a house is that it comes with an address, which gives us a social existence, shared with family, friends, and institutions.

Houses, it's, it's our life, eh. When we leave and then come back, we are home then, we are more relaxed. We relax when we are home. And we spend a lot of time here. It's our house, you see. First, there is night, and then there's daytime. So we are [here] all the time, so it's the big twenty-four hours.... Sometimes we can stay twenty-four hours inside.... So this house is my shelter, and it's very important to me.

However, the dwellings occupied by tenants we met did not allow them to create such a life space. The biggest obstacle preventing our interviewees from building a safe environment, a roof over their heads, is poor sanitary conditions. Whether the problem is structural issues or vermin, substandard housing deprives residents of any real control over their space. For example, mouse poison becomes a concern for tenants with children, while bedbugs make them repeatedly change mattresses and fear contact with the outside world (so as not to contaminate others).

I: There are no problems with cockroaches or anything like that here, are there?
R: We exterminated them, yes. We still get some, sometimes, but there are follow-ups often. I had bedbugs, too.
I: Did you have bedbugs here or there?
R: Here.
I: Here?
R: Yes.
I: That makes it harder to sleep, doesn't it?
R: I got rid of everything—my bed, my mattress—everything that was in my bedroom.

Furthermore, tenants cite problems with heating as an element compromising their quality of life. Some point out that it prevents them from sleeping; others report that low temperatures make their children sick. Lack of hot water, especially when it is supposed to be included in the rent, is also listed as a serious issue, as in certain cases this means not being able to shower:

So I'm telling you, you can never sit here, or here. You always have to sit there, you see, a bit farther from the windows, because there is a draft. So, we had to sit here to avoid the cold. Even my children became sick a few times because of that. Because if he sleeps here, the cold affects him. The next day, he has full-on flu, etc., it's because of that. And it's the same in the other bedroom.

Tenants living in unsanitary conditions are afraid, especially for their children, and do not feel safe in their dwellings:

R: Yes, it's discouraging, for sure. It's the kind of a thing that is wrong, wrong problems. We don't want to have these kinds of problems. It's obvious. Housing is everyone's right. Living in peace is everyone's right. Everybody has a right to live in peace. Because when I live these kinds of things, when I sleep, it's not a peaceful sleep. I am not at peace.
I: No, you don't feel safe.
R: Yes, I am not safe in my house. I don't feel like it's my home. You see what I'm trying to say? I don't feel like I'm home. Even though I pay my bills, I don't feel that this is home.

This relationship to intimate space, then, depends not only on tenants but also on the conditions of the lease they had signed. The lease sets out the rules for the use of a place, but it also implies frequent exchanges between tenants and landlords. The negotiation of space is a recurrent theme in the discussions and relations between these actors.

First, tenants noted that in the case of individual owners and small buildings (of less than four apartments), landlords felt that they had every right to the rented place. They entered apartments unabashed, sometimes without obtaining the tenants' permission. The latter felt bothered by this attitude, which they perceived as arrogant:

She came in the morning, she came in the middle of the month—I remember it was the twentieth, twentieth day of the month. Normally I give her a cheque on the first day of each month. She came, she knocked on the door in a disrespectful way for … [sobbing voice]. And my children are asleep. Without no respect, she knocked on the door inappropriately. I opened the door, "Hello, ma'am." Her: "You didn't answer," etc. She'd already entered, in her shoes and all.

Second, tenants reported that some landlords tried to control the way a dwelling was being used, for example by complaining about noisy children on behalf of the neighbours, or even by modifying lease terms midcontract or at a time of changing ownership (even if, in the latter case, the previous lease remained valid). This attitude has a negative impact on the tenants' efforts to create a life space and the sense of safety a dwelling should provide.

I'll give you examples. For example, at the beginning, when we were discussing with the mother-owner, I asked her, "Can I put up a Tempo shelter for my car?" She said, "No problem." Because she had had a Tempo for years and years, she told me: "It's not a problem." When the daughter-owner came, one of the first things she did was, no Tempo.…
I said, "Why, ma'am, does it bother you? Is it a problem for the neighbours?" And she told me, "First of all, because it's not allowed here in

Saint-Laurent." I was a bit surprised because it's been years since Mrs. owner had a Tempo shelter herself. Twenty or thirty years. But a year ago I put up this Tempo here, and there were no problems at all.

The contract (lease) between a tenant and a landlord stipulates that, in exchange for rent, the latter must ensure the quality of housing to the former. Therefore, it is the tenants' right to require that repairs be made. Housing quality, just as good relations with the landlord, is essential to be able to relax in one's place, yet, as it happens, the most common cause of tensions between landlords and tenants is repairs. Two typical situations frequently resurface in the data we collected: repair requests that are either not acknowledged or not carried out by the owners, and billing the performed repairs to tenants, which often results in a hearing at the Régie (Rental Board).

In situations of the first type, most tenants we met are not satisfied with the physical conditions of their housing (these issues will be addressed in more detail in the next section). A large majority asked the landlord or his representative (either an administrator or a janitor) to perform repairs, and the other party refused. Some owners propose less expensive alternatives, which quickly prove to be ineffective. For example, when a bath drain is blocked, instead of unclogging it, landlords advise tenants to purchase products that could dislodge a clog. In most cases, the problem returns, and so trust is undermined—at least on the tenants' side:

> The first problem that we had with the apartment had to do with gas; next there was the thing with the wash basin. Then the bathtub, that is the drain, because the tub drain is a small pipe at the bottom. And every time it's the same! So, again, I have to go see her. She tells me, "You have to buy, you have to use bleach, you have to buy products." I bought all products on Canadian Tire. Because at a time I was looking, that is, I was always waiting to be called in for work, etc.... So it's not even worth it bothering her, it just takes time, it's an old lady, etc.

In situations of the second type, the landlord agrees to carry out repairs but holds the tenant responsible for damages and charges her for the service. When this happens, the owner-tenant relations turn sour, and, in some cases, disputes end at the Régie du logement. Tenants do not really know how to react to such demands, which creates stress:

> R: She came to the house; no one was there. She went and just removed the door and put another door in. From the moment we renewed the lease with her, she began to change her behaviour. I don't know, a week or two, maybe a month [later] she comes to me with the bill, three hundred dollars for the door. I said, "Listen, ma'am, I didn't ask you to fix

the door. I asked you to fix the door handle." Because of that handle, I needed key duplicates, etc.

I: So every time there were repairs to do, she asked you to pay.

R: Exactly.

I: And then she sent you the bill.

R: She brings the bill herself. That's her, she brings it, she says, "Here, this is for the bill to pay." I said no.

Renting an apartment implies sharing a life space, whether with neighbours living in the same building or with the family in the same apartment. Almost all our interviewees expressed appreciation for their neighbours. In some cases, they were friends, helping each other to get through difficult moments or months. For example, one tenant mentioned sharing food with her neighbours at the end of difficult months. Another resident talked of being accommodated by neighbours after a fire in the building, which forced her to leave her apartment for the time of cleanup. This closeness reassures her and reaffirms her commitment to the building, the borough, and even her apartment. However, in one particular case, a tenant shared a story of a neighbour who made his life unbearable. Noises coming from his apartment at night prevented our interviewee from sleeping and eventually poisoned his relations with his neighbour. After months of sleep deprivation, he knew he had to move: "You're asleep, and then, at one moment, you suddenly sense the noise. You get up—it's like a nightmare. I sleep here [in the living room]. I sleep a bit with sleeping pills." Tenants rarely criticize their family members. Nonetheless, some residents mention the impact of family on their life space. Some admit that the size of their family makes it difficult to find adequate housing at a price they can afford. In one case, children, tired of moving, refused to leave the apartment, and so the mother agreed to sleep in the living room in order not to exasperate her children.

EXCLUSION IN AND THROUGH SPACE

While relational and financial dimensions may create barriers to one's full participation in city life, exclusion through housing materializes in the dimension of space.

The problem causing the most distress to tenants we met and/or interviewed was unquestionably poor sanitary conditions. Whether it be vermin (cockroaches, bedbugs, mice), mould, or structural deterioration, these housing problems deprive tenants of a safe living and make them live in fear under their own roof. Many have not had a good night's sleep in months; others had to change their furniture more than once. One family reported sleeping with the lights on to keep cockroaches at bay. This situation has great effects on their mental health. One father looked at us during an apartment visit, weeping, saying that he was on the brink of depression. "I can't take it anymore," he said. Another woman, who lived in an apartment with cockroaches a few years ago, said: "I was always afraid. I was afraid when I opened the door of the kitchen at night. I was afraid to look into my bag when I was outside the house. It is like it follows everywhere."

In a case involving mould, part of a ceiling collapsed in the middle of the night, exposing frightened tenants to cold air entering through the roof. The family, recent immigrants, had nowhere to go because they had no relatives or friends in Montreal. The following morning, the Comité logement called the Red Cross to relocate them. We met the family a week later; they mentioned that they were still not sleeping well, and the mother mentioned having nightmares of the event. These tenants are isolated. Most of them are newcomers who do not know how to exercise their rights or find recourse, nor do they have a network that could help them leave substandard housing.

In addition, our interviewees often live in shame, which only isolates them more, as they refuse to welcome friends or family to their place, either because it is in deplorable condition or because it is overrun by pests. One father of a family residing in an apartment infested by cockroaches stated that he did not dare invite friends, even in the daytime when cockroaches hide away. He also reported scrupulously checking his clothes and his daughter's school bag for cockroaches every morning. The feeling of shame was overwhelming, and he could not see a way out of his situation. These problems add to the difficulties tenants might already be facing in their integration process. According to our immigrant interviewees, housing issues hinder them from making themselves at home, which is exactly what they need. Without this possibility of turning a house into a home, finding firm social footing or using a dwelling as a stepping stone towards integration becomes a much harder task.

On the issue of control exercised over space, some tenants we met reported discrimination on the part of their landlords. In certain cases, tenants felt that the arguments used by landlords to justify their behaviours and decisions were unacceptable, if not outright false. In others, tenants reported not being given any explanation for changes in lease conditions, rent increases, repair bills, or even repairs themselves. This "symbolic violence" (Bourdieu, 1994) designates them as being incapable of thinking or choosing, and some newcomers interpret these behaviours on the part of landlords as xenophobic. Some emphasize that this kind of conduct is forbidden in Canada, and that it should not be acceptable for owners to engage in it just because they are dealing with immigrants.

However, exclusion in relation to space can be expressed not only in a dwelling's interiors but also in its in anchorage in space, that is, its locus within the city. The majority of people we have encountered through our interviews and observations did not choose to live in Saint-Laurent: they were either born there, or they had friends or family members find them apartments before they arrived in the new country. This nonchoice aside, the tenants of Saint-

Laurent do not have very many options to change neighbourhoods within the same borough, as houses for rent are concentrated in but a few areas, rather similar in terms of available services and street safety. Leaving Saint-Laurent for another borough also seems quite difficult, since rents in other, more central areas of the city remain expensive, while affordable housing tends to be located even further into the peripheries and away from the workplaces. Several renters mentioned having felt "stuck" for many years. However, leaving Saint-Laurent is for many tenants not an option. They appreciate their neighbourhood and its services, the proximity of family, friends, and neighbours, and the quality of schools and health services, and therefore would prefer to move into another apartment still in Saint-Laurent.

To many, family represents the heart of their social relations. However, in the case of housing-related family relations, some women experience difficult situations, mentioned only reluctantly. In many cases, not being able to afford apartments big enough for all children to have their own bedroom, mothers prefer to sleep in the living room. They describe this situation as difficult, but they have no means to move. And even when something cheaper becomes available in other boroughs, they refuse to relocate, even when offered subsidized, low-rent housing, because their children do not want to leave.

CONCLUSION

The processes of exclusion discussed in this paper limit the opportunities for tenants' mobility. Many renters, stuck in their homes, experience intolerable situations, yet are unable to find other affordable housing in seemingly safe neighbourhoods. These same situations are the reasons that other tenants move, either by choice or by obligation. In our study, these strains appear to be central to renters' housing experiences. Tenants in difficult situations are often told to leave, but their mobility does not just happen by itself. Whether they move or stay, the processes of exclusion marking their housing experience seem to remain. In that regard, agency exists; they recognize the necessity to move, but the structure of the housing market limits the possibility to encounter a better dwelling.

First, the realm of housing possibility is much more limited if you are an immigrant, a woman, a family, and/or a member of a visible minority. Many studies show that these populations are much more vulnerable to discrimination from possible future landlords (Clapham, Clark & Gibb, 2012). In our case, the financial restrictions associated with moving were mentioned most. People felt they could not move, and when some did, because they could not bear living in their dwellings anymore, they did not find a better home. For others, social housing was the solution for which they had waited for years. However, in only one case did the tenant evaluate that his housing situation got better. When tenants move, they rarely find a quality dwelling to live in.

Second, if they were to move, the tenants in our study would rather stay in Saint-Laurent: the borough is their home. In fact, even though their dwelling situation makes it difficult to create a home, many of the tenants greatly appreciate living in Saint-Laurent. They find its location in the city relatively central, easily accessible by public transit, well connected to the transportation system, and it has many good health and education services. They also feel their neighbourhood is secure, and they fear they would have to move to other parts of the city with cheaper housing possibilities but with a bad reputation. Many tenants estimate that these neighbourhoods are the only ones with dwellings whose rent they can afford.

In conclusion, our research conceptualized the housing experience as having two relations with space: a geographical dimension linking individuals (tenants in our study) with space and to society; and an intimate dimension that enables individuals to protect themselves from the environment and society in order to better construct their relation to society. Home, in this view, is more than a shelter. It is our harbour, where we can resource ourselves, and it is also our habitat, where we relate to the territory and to society. In this sense, our housing experience leads to inclusion/exclusion processes.

REFERENCES

Authier, J.-Y., Bonvalet, C. & Lévy, J.-P. (Eds.) (2010). Élire domicile: *La construction des choix résidentiels*. Lyon: Presses universitaires de Lyon.

Ball, M. (2012). Housing building and housing supply. In D. Clapham, W. Clarke & K. Gibb (Eds.), *The SAGE Handbook of Housing Studies* (pp. 27–46). London: Sage.

Berger, P. & Luckmann, T. (1966). *The Social Construction of Reality*. Garden City, NY: Anchor Books.

Bernard, Y. (1998). Du logement au chez-soi. In M. Segaud, C. Bonvalet & J. Brun (Eds.), *Logement et habitat: L'état des savoirs* (pp. 374–381). Paris: La Découverte.

Boucher, J. L. (2008). Habitat et santé mentale: Le particularisme outaouais. In P. Morin & E. Baillergeau (Eds.), *L'habitation comme vecteur de lien social* (pp. 95–120). Québec: Les Presses de l'Université du Québec.

Bourdieu, P. (1994). Rethinking the state: Genesis and the structure of the bureaucratic field. *Sociological Theory*, 12, 1, 1-18.

Butler, T. & Hamnett, C. (2012). Social geographic interpretations of housing spaces. In D. F.

Carter, T. & Polevychok, C. (2004). *Housing Policy Is Good Social Policy*. Ottawa: Canadian Policy Research Networks.

Clapham, D., Clark, W. & Gibb, K. (Eds.) (2012). *The SAGE Handbook of Housing Studies*. London: Sage.

Clark W. (2012). Residential mobility and the housing market. In D. Clapham, W. Clarke & K. Gibb (Eds.), *The SAGE Handbook of Housing Studies* (pp. 66–83). London: Sage.

Cox, K. R. (1991). Classes, localisation et territoire. In J. Lévy (Ed.), *Géographies du politique* (pp. 161–173). Paris: Presses de la Fondation Nationale de Sciences Politiques.

Dubet, F. (1994). *Sociologie de l'expérience*. Paris: Seuil.

Dubet, F. & D. Martuccelli (1998). *Dans quelle société virons-nous?* Paris: Seuil.

Grafmeyer, Y. (1998). Logement, quartier, sociabilité. In M. Segaud, C. Bonvalet & J. Brun (Eds.), *Logement et habitat: L'état des savoirs* (pp. 409–417). Paris: La Découverte.

Grémion, C. (1996). L'accès au logement social. In S. Paugam (Ed.), *L'exclusion: L'état des savoirs* (pp. 519–529). Paris: La Découverte.

Havel, J.-E. (1985). *Habitat et logement.* Paris: Presses Universitaires de France.

Hay, D. (2005). *Housing, Horizontality and Social Policy.* Ottawa: Canadian Policy Research Networks.

Lazarotti, O. (2012). Habiter: Le moment venu, un moment donné. In B. Frelat-Kahn & O. Lazzarotti (Eds.), *Habiter: Vers un nouveau concept?* (pp. 11–24). Paris: Armand Collin.

Lévy, J. (1994). *L'espace légitime.* Paris: Presses de la Fondation Nationale des Sciences Politiques.

MacLennan, D. (2012). Understanding housing markets: Real progress or stalled agendas. In D. Clapham, W. Clarke & K. Gibb (Eds.), *The Sage Handbook of Housing Studies* (pp. 5-26). London: Sage.

McAll, C. (1995). Les murs de la cité: Territoires d'exclusion et espaces de citoyenneté. *Lien social et politiques*, 35, 81–92.

Moret, F. (1998). Le logement et la question sociale (1830–1870). In M. Segaud, C. Bonvalet & J. Brun (Eds.), *Logement et habitat: L'état des savoirs* (pp. 19–26). Paris: La Découverte.

Morin, P. & Dorvil, H. (2008). Le logement comme déterminant de la santé pour les personnes ayant des problèmes sévères de santé mentale. In P. Morin & E. Baillergeau (Eds.), *L'habitation comme vecteur de lien social* (pp. 23–40). Québec: Les Presses de L'Université du Québec.

Paquot, T. (Ed.) (2007). Introduction. "Habitat", "Habitation", "Habiter", précisions sur trois termes parents. In *Habiter, le propre de l'humain* (pp. 7–16). Paris: La Découverte.

Pezeu-Massabau, J. (1983). *La maison: Espace social.* Paris: Presses Universitaires de France.

Rex, J. & Moore, R. S. (1967). *Race, Community and Conflict: A Study of Sparkbrook.* New York: Oxford University Press.

Segaud, M., Bonvalet, C. & Brun, J. (Eds.). (1998). *Logement et habitat: L'état des savoirs.* Paris: La Découverte.

Somerville, P. (1998). Explanations of social exclusion: Where does housing fit in? *Housing studies*, 13, 761–780.

Tardieu, C., Oré, M. & Frenette, Y. (1992). *Le logement et les communautés culturelles: Analyse de la situation.* Montréal: Conseil des communautés culturelles et de l'immigration.

Ville de Montréal (2009). *Profil statistique en habitation de la ville de Montréal.* Direction de l'habitation, Service de la mise en valeur du territoire et du patrimoine. Montréal. Retrieved from http://ville.montreal.qc.ca/pls/portal/docs/page/habiter_v2_fr/media/documents/Profil_Ville_Montreal_Mai_2009.pdf

CHAPTER 10

OUTSIDE OF THE PLANNERS' GAZE: COMMUNITY AND SPACE IN THE CENTRE OF ST. JOHN'S, NEWFOUNDLAND, 1945–1966

John Phyne and Christine Knott

The lead author of this paper grew up in downtown St. John's in the late 1960s and early 1970s. He witnessed the building of the new City Hall. City Hall stood alone in the midst of vacant land that spread from Carter's Hill in the east to Barron Street in the west (less than one kilometre), and from New Gower Street in the south to Livingstone and Central Streets in the north (less than two hundred metres). No other structure appeared in this area until the Radisson Hotel (now Delta) opened in 1987. His paternal great-grandparents once lived in a dwelling close to where the current City Hall stands.

The 1945 nominal census for Newfoundland showed approximately 1,500 inhabitants in the area discussed above (Government of Newfoundland, 1945). The area was on a steep hillside. Many homes lacked plumbing and were in poor structural condition. It was referred to as a *slum*. By the early 1940s, plans were initiated that over the next 20 years resulted in the resettlement of this population elsewhere in St. John's. By the end of the twentieth century, this area was commercialized.

This paper deals with the slum that existed in the city centre of St. John's. First, we analyze the assumptions of planners, who held a modernist gaze along the lines of their counterparts in other older industrial cities in the North Atlantic. This gaze looked to better housing and urban renewal. Second, we draw from interview data and other sources to argue that, while the city centre was replete with poor housing conditions, its residents possessed resilience that lay outside of the gaze of planners.

In the remainder of this paper, we outline the plans from 1942 to 1966 that eventually led to the clearance of the city centre. Such plans reflected the gaze of modernity and assumed that better living conditions provided a better community. Next, we discuss the methods used to investigate the nature of the community that occupied the slum. This is followed by a demographic breakdown of the population, work, schooling, leisure, food sourcing, and community ties. We then provide an overview of the attitudes community members had after relocation between 1950 and 1966. By the 1960s, some people resisted being removed in hope that better financial compensation would be offered. We conclude with a discussion of the wider implications of urban planning that does not consider the views of people who are being removed to "better conditions."

THE PLANNERS' GAZE: SLUM CLEARANCE AND URBAN RENEWAL, 1942 TO 1966

In the middle decades of the twentieth century, urban planning in Britain, Canada, and the United States developed as a "scientific discipline" devoted to improving the living conditions of the urban poor, who largely lived in congested inner cities. Poor housing and disease caught the attention of "scientific planners" and the public health movement. In the early postwar period, planners moved the urban poor from the centres of many cities to public-housing developments. Moreover, "slum areas" in inner cities were razed for private commercial development projects (see Guay and Hamel, 2014).

In poor areas of Boston (Gans, 1962), New York (Jacobs, 1961), and Halifax (Clairmont and Magill, 1999), residents opposed relocation and the redevelopment of their former community for other purposes. While there was some resistance in the 1960s, there was no concerted protest by residents over their removal from the slum area in the centre of St. John's from 1950 to 1966. Nevertheless, the planning rationale here reflected the modernist vision of new housing developments and urban renewal.[1]

The slums north of New Gower Street drew the attention of St. John's Municipal Council in the early twentieth century. In the early 1930s, Newfoundland was in the midst of a financial crisis, and rule over the country reverted to Great Britain until it joined Canada in 1949.[2] While Newfoundland was under rule from Great Britain (called the Commission of Government), St. John's Council was offered a loan for new housing, but the commission wanted financial jurisdiction until the loan was repaid. The Municipal Council refused this offer. In 1939, councillor John Meaney called upon the city and the commission to build homes. In 1942, Eric Cook, the deputy mayor, moved to have the newly elected council act on housing. A committee consisting of 13 members under the leadership of Justice Brian Dunfield was appointed to the Commission of Enquiry on Housing and Town Planning (CEHTP). Dunfield rapidly exercised control over the CEHTP (Sharpe, 2005). As we shall see, the CEHTP did not solve the "slum problem" but prepared the groundwork for post-Confederation projects that did so (Collier, 2011; Sharpe, 2005).

The CEHTP (1943) did a survey of 6,500 homes in St. John's to assess the overall quality of homes, the desire for better housing, and the willingness to pay for such housing. It received 5,700 survey responses that covered 4,613 homes. While data were not provided by street name, a substantial portion of the dwellings that needed to be replaced (1,000), condemned soon (525), or immediately condemned (225) were located in the city centre. Most homes in the latter two categories lacked water or sewer facilities. Many city-centre households collected water from public tanks. Waste water was dumped into open drains that ran downhill, and at night a horse-drawn wagon collected "night soil" that was dumped into a collection tank at the top of Adelaide Street (see figure 10.1).[3]

FIGURE 10.1: ST. JOHN'S IN 1932. THE BOTTOM PORTION OF THE CIRCLED AREA ON THE MAP ROUGHLY CORRESPONDS TO THE SPACE CLEARED AND COMMERCIALIZED FROM 1964 TO 1987. MUCH OF THIS AREA WAS RESETTLED FROM 1950 TO 1966. MATTHEW SCHUMACHER, DEPARTMENT OF EARTH SCIENCES, ST. FRANCIS XAVIER UNIVERSITY, ASSISTED WITH THE ALTERATION OF THE ORIGINAL IN ORDER TO PROVIDE THE DETAIL SEEN HERE.

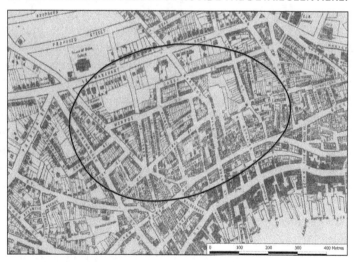

Source: Digital Archives Initiative, courtesy of the Centre for Newfoundland Studies, Memorial University Libraries. www.collections.mun.ca/cdm4/item_viewer.php?CISOROOT=/maproom &CISOPTR=13&CISOBOX=1&REC=7. Retrieved May 30, 2012.

Following British and Canadian planners, the CEHTP advocated market-based solutions. CEHTP established the St. John's Housing Corporation to build housing on land north of St. John's. The objective was a "filtering up" process to relocate the "better off" in the city centre to new housing and to free up better housing in the city centre for those in more destitute conditions (Sharpe, 2012). Nevertheless, the housing development known as Churchill Park became a middle-class suburb beyond the means of homeowners in the city centre. It was part of eight hundred acres of expropriated land that became the basis for housing developments after Newfoundland became a Canadian province in 1949.

Prior to 1949, the only social-housing development in St. John's occurred on acquired property (Ebsary Estates) northwest of the city centre. This was cofinanced by the Municipal Council and Commission of Government. The development known as the Widows' Mansions consisted of 17 properties with four apartments each; some residents from the slum area were rehoused here.

Six federal-provincial housing developments existed from 1950 to 1956, consisting of 584 units: 408 were in the area acquired for Churchill Park; 140 units were built near the Widows' Mansions. This project, known as Westmount, was the first public-housing scheme after Confederation and resulted in the removal of 98 homes from the city centre. The first project in the Churchill Park assemblage consisted of 152 units; 24 homes were taken down in the city centre as part of this project. Thirty-six units were also built on Livingstone and Goodview Streets in the city centre.

In 1959, Municipal Council contracted with Project Planning Associates (1961) of Toronto for an urban-renewal study. This study included housing development for the city centre; despite owning two-thirds of the land in the slum area, the municipality did not consider this option. Taxation earnings were meagre, and business was declining in the downtown core. The municipality opted for urban renewal and the potential revenue from new commercial properties. At this time, 186 new housing units were slated for Buckmaster's Field (a former military base) to the north of the city centre, and 400 in an area northeast of the city centre. From 1964 to 1966, Municipal Council removed remaining residents from the slum area in an urban-renewal process that included a new City Hall, commercial development, and the widening of New Gower Street as part of an arterial road system linking the city centre to the Trans-Canada Highway.[4] The cleared slum area, with the exception of the new City Hall, lay vacant for nearly two decades.

Outside of living in slum conditions, we know little about the community that lived above New Gower Street. Who were these people? How did they secure their livelihood? What meaning did the area have for this population? How did they feel about their removal between 1950 and 1966? These questions are the subject of the remainder of this paper.

METHODS AND DATA SOURCES

The remainder of this paper is based upon evidence from semistructured interviews with former residents of the city centre, the 1945 census of Newfoundland, and the regular and special minutes from the City Council of St. John's (1964–1966).

We draw from an availability sample of those who resided in the old city centre and departed from 1950 to 1966 during one of the relocation periods. To find former residents of the city centre, an advertisement was placed in the Saturday, November 1, 2014, edition of the *Evening Telegram*, the newspaper with the largest circulation in Newfoundland and Labrador. As a result of this advertisement and contacts provided by early interviewees, 21 interviews were held from early November 2014 to the end of April 2015.[5] The interviews averaged from one to two hours. Our respondents consisted of 11 females and 10 males from 59 to 90 years in age at the time of our interviews. The respondents lived in the area cleared from 1950 to 1966 (N=15) or on streets directly adjacent to the area (N=6). Since the latter individuals interacted with residents in the area from 1950 to 1966, their views are recorded. Although the 1945 nominal census shows that the area was 65% Catholic and 35% Protestant, our sample to date is 90% Catholic.[6] As we shall see, religious affiliation proved important to school and church membership, and divided the neighbourhoods that existed in the city centre.

Our interviewees were asked to discuss their experiences growing up, the employment of their parents, any work they did to earn money as children and/or young adults, the sourcing of food from nearby stores and farmers, relations with neighbours, leisure activities, schooling, and the attitudes their families had over relocation. To elicit memories, old photographs and a 1932 map of St. John's were used as interview aids. The overall objective was to see if there was a sense of community in the area.

We use the 1945 statistical census for Newfoundland to provide an overview of St. John's (Government of Newfoundland, 1949). The nominal census for 1945 is also used (Government of Newfoundland, 1945), which consists of the census details for approximately 1,500 individuals who lived in the "slum area." From this, we provide a brief assessment for 500 individuals who lived in the area near the current City Hall.

Finally, special and regular minutes of St. John's City Council from 1964 to 1966 (especially the special minutes held in camera) reveal details on the final removal of the population from the city centre. These include information on those who accepted compensation and those who had their properties expropriated.

LIVING ON THE CITY CENTRE'S HILLSIDE, 1945 TO 1966

The Population of the City-Centre "Slum"

Approximately 1,500 individuals lived in the slum area in 1945 (see figure 10.1; calculated from Government of Newfoundland, 1945). Catholics constituted over 65% of this population, which exceeded the percentage of Catholics that lived in St. John's (just over 46%; calculated from Government of Newfoundland, 1949). This population likely descended from early nineteenth-century Irish immigrants and from those who moved to the area after the 1846 and 1892 fires.[7] From this population, we have data for those (500) who occupied an area near the current City Hall.[8] In 1945, over 19% (96) of this population was born elsewhere in Newfoundland. Only three individuals were born in another country. The population in this area was also 80% (400) Catholic.[9]

FIGURE 10.2: THIS IS DUGGAN STREET. SOME OF THE WORST HOMES IN THE CITY CENTRE WERE IN THIS AREA.

Source: Photo 11-02-105, courtesy of City of St. John's Archives.

FIGURE 10.3: THIS IS ADELAIDE STREET. SOME OF THE BETTER HOMES IN THE CITY CENTRE WERE LOCATED HERE. MOST HAD PLUMBING. THE CURRENT CITY HALL IS IN THIS AREA.

Source: Photo 01-13-060, courtesy of City of St. John's Archives.

New Gower Street formed the southern boundary of the *entire city centre* (circled portion in figure 10.1). Over 20% (72) of its population in 1945 was born elsewhere in Newfoundland. New Gower Street had immigrants from China (12), Syria (4), and Canada (3) (calculated from Government of Newfoundland, 1945). The Chinese and Syrians operated businesses. The term *Syrian* was an official census category; our respondents sometimes referred to them as Lebanese.

The Chinese owned laundries and restaurants. Some informants commented that in the 1940s Chinese launderers picked up shirts in horse-drawn carts from "better off" homes. One informant, whose mother was a Lebanese grocer, provided a hand-drawn map for 97 stores along both sides of New Gower Street for the period from 1958 to 1962. These included 11 Lebanese and 7 Chinese stores. He commented on the history of his family and the Lebanese community:

> My mother's family—Lebanese came in 1895, five brothers and one sister … the sister was my mother's grandmother. My great-grandmother was only 27 in Lebanon with four children. They all pooled their money and came over…. There was [also] a man called Kaleem Noah—he had a wholesale business … and he fit people out with things you could put on your back or in a knapsack … needles and pins … things that people around the bay could not buy. They would go as far as the train would go and sell what they had and go on the coastal boats and when they come back, they pay for what they had and get another lot and go on … Newfoundland people resented them … they said, "No Tally is going to be in my family." Why [the term] "Tally"? I suppose Italians? Look what they could buy after 15 years, places like that [reference to a photo of a building being demolished]. (Interview no. 4, 10/11/14)

Tally was a derogatory term used towards the Syrian/Lebanese community in the period before World War II. Due to their darker skin complexion, they were confused with Italians (Bassler, 1992). This community experienced some assimilation (Ashton, 1999).[10] Our respondents indicated that while the Chinese were accepted, they experienced occasional harassment and were rarely befriended.[11] With the exception of purchasing goods or eating in restaurants, most respondents had little interaction with the Lebanese or Chinese communities. In the remainder of this paper, we focus upon the largely Catholic community that lived in the "slum area" in the city centre.

Work

By 1945, 11,361 males and 4,853 females were employed as wage earners in St. John's. For males, the service (2,869), transportation and communication (1,936), and manufacturing industries (1,887) were the main employers. The service sector (2,664) was the main employment for females, with many receiving work as domestics (1,084). Males had average earnings of $26.56 per week, and females had average earnings of $13.28 per week. Female domestics had average earnings of $5.76 per week (Government of Newfoundland, 1949; see Cullum, 2014). Females worked fewer hours and earned less per hour, which likely reflects the fact that women mostly worked the interval period between school completion and marriage (see Forestell, 1989).

These patterns were reflected in the city-centre area cleared for the new City Hall. Males were employed more than females.[12] The weekly average earnings for males ($23.59) were higher than those for females ($13.28). Males worked for the Newfoundland Railway, in the armed forces, as truck drivers, as checkers in factories, and as general labourers (Government of Newfoundland, 1945). General labourers often sought longshore work in daily queues for employment on the St. John's waterfront (Horwood, 1997). In addition to domestic work, females worked in manufacturing and as sales clerks in grocery and department stores (Government of Newfoundland, 1945).

Our 21 respondents noted that their fathers, more so than their mothers, were involved in the paid labour force and/or operated their own business. Six were grocers, and six worked on the longshore or as seamen.[13] Other employment included customs work, health care, security, baker, typesetter, council work, telephone company supervisor, and tailor. One respondent's father never had steady work. We have no information for the work of the father of one respondent. Six mothers served as grocers with their husbands, one did secretarial work for a lawyer, and another held two part-time jobs as a cleaner. Thirteen mothers worked at home.

The harbour was close to the city centre, and males gathered there to seek work off-loading vessels in port. One male indicated:

> My father worked down on longshore, which meant, if a coal boat came in, he'd have to unload the coal boat—he would come home looking like Nat King Cole. All you can see was teeth. That meant we were going to have fabulous meals for another while…. If Dad came home with a black face, you know what I mean? Yeah, that meant money. If he came home and looked like he was when he left, that meant he wasn't chosen to unload the boat. (Interview no. 1, 05/11/14)

He also referred to the role of the Longshoremen's Protective Union (LSPU):

> Now the LSPU Hall—what those letters represent is the Longshoreman's Protective Union. So, nobody could show up down there to get chosen without a badge in their hat. So my father used to have a pepper and salt hat, with a little top that snapped with the bottom. And on the front of that, it had to be visible; so the person that was picking, they'd look and

say, "You, Hanlon, Smith, Jones."... I asked Dad many times, "How did you get picked?" And he said, "Well, you know, they just picked me." I don't know, I think they picked because of your reputation and you would do a day's work and they don't have to keep after you, right.

Some mothers worked outside of the home prior to marriage, but this was largely discontinued unless they worked as grocers with their husbands. Some exceptions are noted. One interviewee who grew up in the 1950s and early 1960s indicated that her mother worked two part-time cleaning jobs after her father became ill with tuberculosis. Her mother hired a woman and gave her free rent in exchange for looking after the children (Interview no. 3, 10/11/14).

The home was their "mother's turf." Given the absence of running water and sewage for many households, women made daily trips with buckets to the public taps in the city centre in order to secure water for cooking and cleaning (see Fitzgerald, 1997). One male often helped his mother bring the water to the household: "I didn't want Mom to do it; Mom didn't want me.... It was a chore, and it wasn't very [pleasant] ... oh, it was heavy; yes, it was heavy" (Interview no. 1, 05/11/14).

Respondents recognized their mothers' hardships. Mothers were dependent on the earnings their fathers brought home. In some cases, this did not happen. One woman's father was an alcoholic who withheld money. Her mother had to seek employment (Interview no. 9, 17/11/14). Several indicated that children would be sent to seek out fathers in one of the taverns near the city centre in order to "come home for supper."

Schooling

Prior to the 1997 plebiscite that ushered in secular education, Newfoundland had a denominational school system that dated back to the mid-nineteenth century (see Greene, 1999). Since 19 out of our 21 respondents are Catholic, we focus upon the gender, class, and spatial divisions within this population.

Barter's Hill (centre of the circled area in figure 10.1) divided the parishes of the Basilica of St. John the Baptist (east of the line) and St. Patrick's (west of the line).[14] Catholic children west of Barter's Hill attended St. Patrick's (for girls) and Holy Cross Schools (for boys). The Presentation Sisters operated St. Patrick's, and the Christian Brothers operated Holy Cross.[15] Catholic children east of Barter's Hill attended St. Bon's or St. Patrick's Hall (for boys) and the Academy of Our Lady of Mercy or Presentation Convent (for girls). The Christian Brothers operated the boys' schools, the Sisters of Mercy ran the Academy of Our Lady of Mercy, and the Presentation Sisters presided over Presentation Convent.

Catholic boys paid higher fees to go to St. Bon's, and Catholic girls paid higher fees to go to the Academy of Our Lady of Mercy.[16] None of our 10 male respondents went to St. Bon's, but 3 of our 11 female respondents went to the

Academy of Our Lady of Mercy; two of these women were the daughters of shopkeepers.

One woman, a daughter of shopkeepers, reflected on her experiences at "Mercy":

> Mercy Convent ... College of Our Lady of Mercy ... CLM used to be on our school ring. We wore a full uniform, and your knuckles would be cracked if you did not wear it. I went there until grade 8 ... went to Holy Heart until grade 11.... School fees [at] Mercy, fifteen dollars every three months. If you had a hard time [did not have the money], you went to Presentation ... paid a dollar a year or something like that. (Interview no. 10, 18/11/14)

While there was a rivalry, another informant felt "Mercy" girls did not feel they were better than "Presentation" girls (Interview no. 9, 17/11/14). A woman who attended Presentation offered an alternative interpretation:

> Most of the poor Catholic girls went to Presentation ... the ones with more went to Mercy ... always the divide between the two schools ... still lingers.... The nuns let you know who was better than you ... the Presentation Sisters and the Mercy Sisters, they were the ones who in-stilled it.... The richer kids got more attention ... free music lessons be-cause their families were giving money to the church and the school.... The poorer kids who wanted music lessons did not get them. I am still bitter. (Interview no. 14, 26/11/14)

This limited evidence shows that children were aware of a class divide. Porter (2014) argues that elite Catholic and Protestant girls' schools not only perpetuated class divisions but also schooled the girls to be good citizens and mothers.[17]

Supervising Children

Barter's Hill not only spatially separated Catholic children in their schooling, but it also governed their interaction. This was apparent when respondents were asked if they frequented certain stores on the hillside. A common refrain was that "we did not go into that area." Our informants indicated gender divi-sions in their "freedom" to move around. Lorenzkowski (2010) argues that this was the case for children in St. John's during World War II. Her female informants reported greater restrictions than their male counterparts.

Our respondents from Holy Cross stated that the area east of Barter's Hill was for "St. Pat's boys" (St. Patrick's Hall). Yet boys, more so than girls, moved around the area in their leisure pursuits, as well as looked for "odd jobs" that would provide them money for treats or for the Majestic or Star Hall movie theatres located just outside of the area. Some males frequented the finger piers along the waterfront (see Fitzgerald, 1997; Lorenzkowski, 2010). Most male respondents went to Water Street (just above the waterfront) in order to buy fish weekly for their families. The fish was purchased from fish harvesters along one of the streets (called coves) that connected Water Street to the finger piers along the waterfront (see the bottom right corner of figure 10.1).

Girls largely "stayed in their area." One exception included trips to Bowring Park, which lay approximately three to four miles to the west of the city centre. Other female and male children would accompany them. A common practice was to walk along the sides of the railway tracks that connected the centre of St. John's to its urban periphery and beyond. As girls entered their midteens, they moved further afield, largely to find work in the retail sector that was concentrated along Water Street.

Sourcing Food

Despite poor housing in the city centre, evidence shows that this was a resilient community, apparent in the sourcing of food. Our respondents referred to grocery stores, confectionaries, butchers, farmers, and fish from the coves connecting Water Street to the harbour below it. Some grocers gave away food during "hard times," and food was often shared across households.

Forward (1957) shows a cluster of food stores on New Gower and Water Streets and the streets between these two main thoroughfares. In 1955, food stores in the city totalled 379 (just over 52%) out of the 722 retail establishments (calculated from Forward, 1957). Forward (1957) argues that "it is likely that the owners of many of these stores operate them with the aim of supplementing their income from other sources. With the appearance of more supermarkets a decrease in the number of confectionaries may follow" (p. 38). In 1955, there were five supermarkets in St. John's, all owned by the same company (Ayre's) and with locations north of the city centre.

Polk's (1961) directory for St. John's for 1960 to 1961 shows 22 grocery, confectionary, butcher, and bakery stores on New Gower Street and in the area cleared from 1950 to 1966. Our respondents frequented stores in the area (including two bakeries) and nearby stores. Some of the stores that they mentioned from the 1940s and 1950s were no longer in business at the time of the publication of Polk's directory (1961).

Respondents distinguished between grocery stores that sometimes had owners residing above the store, and smaller confectionaries with a "sheet over a doorway" that separated the store from the family quarters. Their views show that these firms, unlike "modern establishments," were embedded in the community (cf. Bedore, 2013). Respondents' parents shopped frequently during the week, since homes lacked refrigeration. The stores were nearby, which suited most people since they lacked an automobile. Most families used credit; credit was more common in grocery stores but was also used in some smaller confectionary stores (also see Fitzgerald, 1997; Hunt, 2011).

Some businesses were lenient when it came to collecting. One informant pointed to a store on New Gower Street that went out of business in the 1940s:

> Opposite the [name of store] was a grocery store run by [name of owners] … we had an account there. I think they went out of business because they never collected … anyone of us could go there and say Mom wanted a pound of butter or a pound of sugar and say, "Put that on the 'tick,'" whatever "tick" meant…. My mom figured out every week what she could afford because my dad got twenty-five dollars per week, and there was five of us. (Interview no. 13, 24/11/14)

A female informant indicated that store owners (some to their detriment) helped people get by on a regular basis so they could remain proud, no matter their circumstance (Interview no. 15, 26/11/14).

Many respondents referred to farmers from outlying areas coming in to the city centre on a weekly basis. Some families purchased only vegetables, whereas others also purchased meat. In addition, some farmers sold "splits" or bundles of wood used for heating.[18] Many meat markets in the city owned their own cattle stocks, which grazed in fields in or outside of the city (Fitzgerald, 1997; Murray, 2002).

Most families purchased fish from fish harvesters (usually on Friday) located along one of the coves connecting Water Street to the finger piers along the wharf. The fish would be either wrapped in newspaper or taken by hand to the home. Our male respondents stated that you would not buy a fish (usually cod) too big for you to carry.

Families also shared with neighbours. Two respondents, whose parents operated grocery stores, stated that food was given away in the area during "hard times." One pointed to the Depression, when her parents gave food to a family renting from them (Interview no. 21, 19/04/15). Another respondent's parents gave food away just after the war (Interview no. 10, 18/11/14). One man who grew up in the 1940s stated, "People were always sharing with everybody … that was the only way to go … if you had a pot of soup or some cakes, you brought some over [to your neighbours]" (Interview no. 11, 19/11/14). One woman who grew up in the 1950s and 1960s, and had a father with a secure job and a mother who rented one of the household's rooms to travellers from rural Newfoundland, discussed how her family provided money to help poor family that lived across the street from them (Interview no. 8, 17/11/14). While many, in looking back, referred to themselves as being poor, they noted that dealing with hunger was a collective issue. People looked out for their neighbours.

The Dynamics of Community: Home without Housing

A feature of looking back from the present is the way respondents discussed the "togetherness" in the city centre (cf. Halbwachs, 1992). One woman stated:

> It was almost like a bay community; everyone took care of everyone else. My father was the neighbourhood grocer—tough times—it was just after the war, I remember, and people were hungry and Dad would go with little boxes of food. There was so much he gave away … Mom as well. Anything that happened to anyone, everyone was there. When there was a funeral in the house … always someone there with them [family of the deceased] … never alone. No one had anything, but they had everything. We were the richest because we had a store. I had a slice of boiled ham when my friend could only have bologna. (Interview no. 10, 18/11/14)

A woman who grew up in the 1950s stated: "One big family there … everyone knew everyone else's business … I am sure there was abuse and that, but people did share … a lot of kids. Everyone in and out of everyone else's houses.… It was a slum area but had really tight bonds of family and friendship" (Interview no. 14, 26/11/14).

A male respondent discussed positive features of growing up in the 1960s:

> I mean there was a real community, and everybody looked after one another and the parents looked after everybody else's kids.… It was a real social thing; everybody used to sit out in the evenings or sit out in the summertime on the back steps. You know, if you were doing something and [adult female neighbour] was up here, she seen you, she would give you a scolding just as much as your mother, right. So there was a whole bunch of mothers there looking after all these kids. It was a real social place, everybody looked after one another. (Interview no. 5, 12/11/14)

One respondent who did not have a happy childhood while growing up in the 1930s and 1940s even recognized the area as a "close-knit community" where people helped each other "get by" (Interview no. 18, 04/12/14).

AFTER RELOCATION: 1950 TO 1966

Mixed Attitudes towards Relocation: 1950 to 1961

Although most respondents (with the exception of some who lived just outside of the cleared area) moved before 1966, we focus here on those who moved into public housing. Four individuals moved into public housing on Livingstone and Goodview Streets, adjacent to the cleared area.[19] These individuals still lived in the city centre, and their experiences differed from those relocated to public housing outside of the city centre. In terms of a sense of community, they never moved. It is among the five respondents who moved into public housing that we see mixed attitudes towards relocation.

One respondent who moved into the Westmount area in 1951 remarked how relocation proved positive for his family:

> It was out of the world for us. We moved into a house with a bathroom in it, hot and cold water ... all hardwood floors, believe it or not ... except kitchen and bathroom ... which had tiles ... a four-bedroom house, we moved in—still a lot of us there.... Everything [our belongings] had to be fumigated before we moved in ... don't forget, everything was full of cockroaches [our home in the city centre] ... never saw a bug on Cashin Avenue ... it was like going from a horse's stable to a palace ... big difference. (Interview no. 11, 19/11/14)

This individual preferred the "atmosphere" of downtown. People from the "central city" were moving into Westmount because the "central city was going," but the place had a "different atmosphere altogether. People from different areas up on Cashin Avenue" (Interview no. 11, 19/11/14).

Another man whose family moved to the Westmount area in 1951 recounted: "There was low-income housing built in the Cashin Avenue area ... we moved to Vicker's Avenue just off of Cashin Avenue. We were the fifth family to move in ... you were moving from a small cramped house to a brand new apartment." While his experiences in the former city centre were positive, he enjoyed the area around Vicker's Avenue because there were more children to play with (Interview no. 12, 24/11/14).

One woman whose family moved into the Westmount area in 1954 stated that the area eventually deteriorated:

> My mother and father lived there for over fifty years ... it was a housing project ... he was a foreman on the waterfront, and he made scads of money—you had to pay one-third of that for rent. But he wouldn't [leave] because he loved it there ... he lived to be ninety ... his housing was subsidized ... kind of balanced out. The place turned into crack houses all around, but he was oblivious to that. (Interview no. 9, 17/11/14)

The two individuals who moved to public housing northeast of the city centre had different experiences. One woman who felt a strong sense of community in the city centre stated that, in addition to the benefits of a new home her family moved to in 1960, a strong sense of community was replicated (Interview no. 14, 26/11/14). The son of single mother on social assistance considered his move in 1962 as stigmatizing. His family's poverty did not matter as much in the city centre: "Even though we were on social services, we were kind of in a house that wasn't—like our whole community wasn't on social services [reference to his home in the city centre]" (Interview no. 7, 14/11/14).

Resisting Relocation in the 1960s[20]

There was some controversy over relocation in the 1960s. Municipal Council passed a bylaw in 1952 that prevented repairs to homes in the central area of the city outside of basic maintenance to keep structures "wind and airtight." For some, this had the effect of devaluing their properties. A committee was formed in May 1964 that included the Progressive Conservative member of the Provincial House of Assembly for the area. The objective was to secure better compensation. In June 1964, the provincial Liberal government passed City Council's Central Area Redevelopment Act, which included wide powers of expropriation. In 1964, 130 properties (residential, commercial, and estate) were identified by City Council. The regular and special minutes of City Council from 1964 to 1966 provide data on 89 of these properties, 55 of which were residential. For residential properties, 40 homeowners accepted the offer from City Council, and 15 were expropriated (City of St. John's, 1964–1966). These latter individuals "held out" for better compensation. All expropriations occurred after the Central Area Redevelopment Act received royal assent.

Commercializing the City Centre

In 1966, City Council announced plans for a new City Hall and commercial towers backed by the St. John's Commercial Centre Company Limited. City Hall was built, but the latter never transpired. In the early 1970s, the Trizec Company from Montreal had plans for a commercial development that also never emerged. In the meantime, New Gower Street was widened and connected to the Trans-Canada Highway. For nearly two decades, the area lay vacant, with the exception of City Hall. One respondent referred to his former home as the location of "the mayor's office" (Interview no. 12, 24/11/14). In the late 1970s and early 1980s, a local developer acquired properties west of the area and increased the vacant space in the city centre. In 1987, the Radisson Hotel (now Delta) was built. In the late 1990s, the area, with the exception of a low-income housing development (east of City Hall), was filled with commercial establishments.

DISCUSSION AND CONCLUSION

This paper assessed the last two decades of the community that lived in the slum area of the city centre of St. John's and the process behind their removal. Beginning in the 1940s and continuing with the final clearance in the mid-1960s, planners adopted a modernist approach. This began with improved housing for slum-area residents with the eventual objective of urban renewal. The majority had to be relocated due to the poor structure of many houses in the area. However, by the early 1960s, the City of St. John's owned two-thirds of the land in the city centre (Phyne, 2014). Remaining residents in the slum area could have been housed in new dwellings there (cf. UN-Habitat, 2011). Despite this, urban renewal was the development mantra in the 1960s (see Bacher, 1993).

Interview data with former residents of the slum area show a resilient community. Sharing food, looking out for neighbours, and collectively caring for children were some of the positive dimensions of this community. Nevertheless, women were largely dependent on the earnings of their husbands. Life was difficult, and the prospects for many women improved as they moved into new surroundings.

Rice (2002) conducted one of the few studies of public housing since its inception after Confederation and found that the Newfoundland and Labrador Housing Corporation indicated that the "block housing" projects of the 1950s and 1960s would not be repeated. Many housing developments received complaints over poor design, maintenance, and vandalism (see McGahan, 1984; Mellin, 2011; Sharpe, 1993).

This spatial separation of the poor arguably intensified their stigmatization by middle-class authorities. In contrast, the urban poor in the former slum area interacted with and lived close by middle-class shopkeepers on the streets adjacent to the area. It was a poverty connected to the enabling features of social diversity. As Young and Willmott (1957, pp. 198–199) noted in the conclusion of their ethnography of Bethnal Green in East London:

> When the town planners have set themselves to create communities anew as well as houses, they have still put their faith in buildings, sometimes speaking as though all that was necessary for neighbourliness was a neighbourhood unit, for community spirit a community centre. If this were so, then there would be no harm in shifting people around the country, for what is lost could be regained by skillful architecture and design. But there is surely more to a community than that.

They add that kinship and friendship connected the people of one household to another in Bethnal Green. In the case of the former inhabitants of the city centre of St. John's, relocation to public-housing blocks distant from the city centre may have resulted in better accommodation, but our respondents had a mixed reception to that removal. By contrast, none of our respondents felt that there was an absence of community in the city centre.

Many of the inhabitants in the slum area had to be relocated. Despite this, the City of St. John's had vacant land in the city centre and could have built new houses in this area in the 1960s to rehouse the remaining inhabitants. One can only wonder if the "community spirit" of the area would have been maintained if they did so (cf. Young and Willmott, 1957).

ACKNOWLEDGEMENTS

We acknowledge funding from the Social Sciences and Humanities Research Council Insight Development Grant program for the research project *Contesting Urban Space: Social Change in the Centre of St. John's, Newfoundland and Labrador, 1950 to 1966*. The University Council for Research and Centre for Regional Studies, St. Francis Xavier University, also provided funding. We thank Helen White, Neachel Keeping, and Alanna Wicks of the City of St. John's Archives for their assistance in accessing photographs and other materials. Phyllis Bartlett of the City of St. John's provided access to the Special Minutes of Council Meetings. Joan Ritcey and Linda White of the Centre for Newfoundland and Labrador Studies, Queen Elizabeth II Library, Memorial University of Newfoundland and Labrador, provided permission for the use of figure 10.1. Julia Reddy painstakingly took data from photocopies of the 1945 census of Newfoundland and typed these into a more readable Excel-file format. Rhonda MacDonald, Administrative Assistant for the Department of Sociology at St. Francis Xavier University, transcribed the interviews. We thank Dr. Nicole Power of the Department of Sociology at Memorial University for her assistance. The authors also thank those who took the time to be interviewed for this study.

NOTES

1. Unless otherwise noted, the material in this section is from Phyne (2014). Sharpe (2000; 2005; 2012) has systematically studied the planning process.

2. Although the official name of the province is Newfoundland and Labrador, we refer to Newfoundland in the remainder of this chapter, as this was the official name of the country, and later province, for the period in question.

3. There were also concerns over disease in the area. In 1942, St. John's had a tuberculosis rate of 145 per 1,000 (average from 1938 to 1942). This was much higher than the rate for any of Canada's maritime provinces.

4. We will discuss these developments in more detail later in this paper.

5. There were 26 interviewees in the 21 interviews. The numerical interview discussed in this paper only pertains to the 21 primary interviewees. Five interviews consisted of 2 individuals. With one exception, the second individual was a spouse who was not a resident of the area. Another 30 interviews were completed as this chapter was submitted for publication.

6. The 1945 nominal census shows approximately 1,500 inhabitants in the city centre that was cleared from 1950 to 1966 (Government of Newfoundland, 1945). The nominal census is discussed further later in this section.

7. There is no firm evidence of how many residents moved to the area after these fires. The area east of Carter's Hill (see figure 10.1) was devastated by the 1892 fire and contained many people of Irish descent (see Lambert, 2010); it is likely some of this population moved into the area.

8. This includes the following streets north of New Gower Street: Adelaide Street, Barter's Hill, Cuddihy Street, Dammeril's Lane, Finn Street, James Street, Lion Square, Notre

Dame Street, and Simm's Street (see the southeastern section of the circled area in figure 10.1). The New Gower Street data reported here are separate from these 500 individuals.

9. Only 129 St. John's residents (52 from Canada) resided in other countries in 1935 (calculated from Government of Newfoundland, 1949).

10. For example, the name Andrea became Andrews, and Khouri became Cory.

11. Chinese immigrants coming to Newfoundland after 1906 (similar to their counterparts in Canada) were charged a head tax of three hundred dollars (see Bassler, 1992). The lead author's Chinese grandfather paid this amount upon his arrival in Newfoundland in 1925. His grandfather married into an Irish Catholic family that lived in the slum area.

12. At this time, 111 out of 137 males over the age 14 were employed. The corresponding figure was 34 out of 155 females employed (Government of Newfoundland, 1945).

13. One father worked on the longshore and operated a grocery with his spouse.

14. This division was not overly rigid. In one case, a male who moved into social housing in the west end of the city in the 1950s continued his schooling at St. Patrick's Hall, although he moved into St. Patrick's Parish and was expected to attend Holy Cross.

15. The Sisters of Mercy and the Presentation Sisters came to Newfoundland from Ireland in the 1840s. The Christian Brothers came to Newfoundland from Ireland in the 1870s.

16. In the west end of St. John's, Littledale, a Catholic girls' school, catered to middle- and upper-class girls. This school was distant from Holy Cross and St. Patrick's (both located on Patrick Street).

17. The significance of class and gender divisions in schooling will be further explored in future work.

18. Coal was largely used as a heat source.

19. The public housing on Livingstone Street was part of an extension that eliminated Wickford Street. It was on the northern boundary of the area cleared from 1950 to 1966.

20. Unless otherwise indicated, the information in this subsection (and the next) is taken from Phyne (2014).

REFERENCES

Ashton, J. (1999). "They got the English hashed up a bit": Names, narratives and assimilation in Newfoundland's Syrian/Lebanese community. *Lore and Language*, 17(1–2), 67–79.

Bacher, J. (1993). *Keeping to the Marketplace: The Evolution of Canadian Housing Policy.* Montreal and Kingston: McGill-Queen's University Press.

Bassler, G. (1992). *Sanctuary Denied: Refugees from the Third Reich and Newfoundland Immigration Policy, 1906–1949.* St. John's: ISER.

Bedore, M. (2013). Geographies of capital formation and rescaling: A historical-geographical approach to the food desert problem. *The Canadian Geographer*, 57(2), 133–153.

Clairmont, D. and D. Magill. (1999). *Africville: The Life and Death of a Canadian Black Community.* Third Edition. Toronto: Canadian Scholar's Press and Women's Press.

City of St. John's. (1964–1966). *Regular and Special Meetings of St. John's City Council,* various dates. City of St. John's Archives.

Collier, K. (2011). Clearing the slums: The evolution of public housing in St. John's, 1910–1956: Part 2. *Newfoundland Quarterly*, 104 (2), 42–51.

[CEHTP] Commission of Enquiry on Housing and Town Planning in St. John's. (1943). *Third Interim Report*. St. John's: Government of Newfoundland.

Cullum, L. (2014). Below the stairs: Domestic service in twentieth-century St. John's. In L. Cullum and M. Porter (Eds.), *Creating This Place: Women, Family and Class in St. John's, 1900-1950* (pp. 89–113). Montreal and Kingston: McGill-Queen's University Press.

Fitzgerald, J. (1997). *Another Time, Another Place: A Nostalgic and Humorous Look at Life in St. John's During the 1940s and the 1950s*. St. John's: Creative Book Publishing.

Forestell, N. (1989). Times were hard: The patterns of women's paid labour in St. John's between the two world wars. *Labour/Le Travail*, Fall, 24, 47–166.

Forward, C. N. (1957). Distribution of commercial establishments in St. John's, Newfoundland. *The Canadian Geographer*, 9, 30–48.

Gans, H. (1962). *The Urban Villagers: Group and Class in the Life of Italian-Americans*. New York: The Free Press.

Government of Newfoundland (1945). *Eleventh Census of Newfoundland and Labrador*. GN 2/39/A, Nominal Census, Books 36 and 41, Provincial Archives of Newfoundland and Labrador. St. John's: The Rooms Corporation of Newfoundland and Labrador.

Government of Newfoundland (1949). *Eleventh Census of Newfoundland and Labrador: Volume 1: Population*. Ottawa: Dominion Bureau of Statistics.

Greene, J. P. (1999). *Between Damnation and Starvation: Priests and Merchants in Newfoundland Politics, 1745-1855*. Montreal and Kingston: McGill-Queen's University Press.

Guay, L. and P. Hamel. (2014). *Cities and Urban Sociology*. Don Mills: Oxford University Press.

Halbwachs, M. (1992). *On Collective Memory*. Chicago: The University of Chicago Press.

Horwood, H. (1997). *A Walk in the Dreamtime: Growing Up in Old St. John's*. St. John's: Killick Press.

Hunt, R. (2011). *Corner Boys*. St. John's: Flanker Press.

Jacobs, J. (1961). *The Death and Life of Great American Cities*. New York: Vintage.

Lambert, C. (2010). *Far From the Homes of Their Fathers: Irish Catholics in St. John's, Newfoundland, 1840-86* (Unpublished doctoral dissertation). Memorial University of Newfoundland, St. John's.

Lorenzkowski, B. (2010). The children's war. In S. High (Ed.), *Occupied St. John's: A Social History of a City at War, 1939-1955* (pp. 113–150). Montreal and Kingston: McGill-Queen's University Press.

McGahan, P. (1984). *Police Images of the City*. New York: Peter Lang Publishers.

Mellin, R. (2011). *Newfoundland Modern: Architecture in the Smallwood Years, 1949-1972*. Montreal and Kingston: McGill-Queen's University Press.

Murray, H. C. (2002). *Cows Don't Know It's Sunday: Agricultural Life in St. John's*. St. John's: ISER.

Phyne, J. (2014) On a hillside north of the harbour: Changes to the centre of St. John's, 1942-1987. *Newfoundland and Labrador Studies*, 29(1), 6–46.

Polk, R.L. (1961). *Classified Buyer Guide of the Directory of St. John's, 1960–61.* Quebec City: R.L. Polk and Company Ltd.

Porter, M. (2014). "She knows who she is?": Educating girls to their place in society. In L. Cullum and M. Porter (Eds.), *Creating This Place: Women, Family and Class in St. John's, 1900–1950* (pp. 146–178). Montreal and Kingston: McGill-Queen's University Press.

Project Planning Associates (1961). *City of St. John's Newfoundland: Urban Renewal Study.* Prepared for the Municipal Council. Toronto: MacLean-Hunter.

Rice, J.G. (2002). *"Community" and Contradictions: the Role of a Community Centre in a St. John's Housing Project* (Unpublished master's thesis). Memorial University of Newfoundland, St. John's.

Sharpe, C.A. (1993). *Preserving Inner City Residential Areas: The Planning Process in St. John's, Newfoundland 1983–1991.* ISER Report No. 7. St. John's: ISER.

Sharpe, C.A. (2000). "… to arouse our city from its deathlike apathy, from its reproachable lethargy, from its slumber of industrial and social death": The 1939 St. John's municipal housing scheme. *Newfoundland and Labrador Studies,* 16(1), 47–66.

Sharpe, C.A. (2005). Mr. Dunfield's folly: The development of Churchill Park Garden suburb in St. John's. In A. G. MacPherson (Ed.), *Four Centuries and the City: Perspectives on the Historical Geography of St. John's* (pp. 83–122). St. John's: Department of Geography, Memorial University of Newfoundland.

Sharpe, C.A. (2012). "… to prevent confused or over-optimistic thinking and possible disappointment": Brian Dunfield and the slum clearance problem in St. John's, Newfoundland, 1944. *Newfoundland and Labrador Studies,* 27(1), 99–129.

UN-Habitat. (2011). Key findings and messages. In R.T. LeGates and F. Stout (Eds.), *The City Reader,* Fifth Edition (pp. 583–589). London and New York: Routledge.

Young, M. and P. Willmott. (1957). *Family and Kinship in East London.* Middlesex: Penguin Books Ltd.

CHAPTER 11

Car Free Day! Urban Homemaking Projects and the Neighbourhood Politics of Home

Joseph G. Moore

What would democracy be like if Occupy extended the multiple inheritances of its many progenitors into a politics of reclamation of space, housing, cities, and all aspects of living? What if Occupy Homes and its affiliates asked: how, with and on whom do we build our homes? (Jaleel, n.d.)

A coherent, progressive, and inclusive politics of home starts at home, or at least by reflecting upon the places and spaces we engage in, could engage in, or should engage in homemaking and home feeling. These include domestic spaces, our workplaces, our streetscapes, our pubs, and alleyways. An activist scholarship of home, moreover, will necessarily be reflexive, asking tough questions not simply of others but of ourselves as teachers, scholars, and homemakers. How often are we and our institutions complicit in the gentrification of neighbourhoods? In the reproduction of auto-dependent sprawl? How does our socialization in the academy that increasingly demands mobility throughout one's career shape our homemaking practice?

Here I address some of these questions by acknowledging that my own homemaking practices have been profoundly shaped by my work, my colleagues, and most of all by my students. I reflect upon how my dialogue with undergraduate students in social movement, environmental sociology, and urban sociology courses has shaped my engagement with urban spaces and involvement in an annual urban festival. I will argue here that my joyful frustrations in the classroom and similar experiences in neighbourhood politics reflect a growing cry for meso-level experiences of home, and that urban projects such as Car Free Day, but also community gardening, Critical Mass, and urban placemaking projects, help forge a space for this neighbourhood homemaking and home feeling. Finally, I will reflect on just what all this might mean for those looking for ecological alternatives to neoliberal triumphalism.

First let me turn to the classroom. For over a dozen years, I have been teaching upper-level undergraduate courses in social movements, urban sociology, work, and environmental sociology. During this time, student participation has taken two tacks that I initially took as contradictory. On the one hand, students have come to these courses ever more concerned about social and ecological problems. Moreover, they have been ever more eager to link these problems, including their own personal troubles, to dominant economic and political forms. On the other hand, however, these same students have become increasingly detached from or downright skeptical of the very movements that I have built my courses around. While most true of labour and feminist movements, this tendency also holds true for many environmental, peace, and LGBT movements.

I would like to be able to say that I found my way out of this conundrum. I did not. What I have done is come to listen closer to the shift in interest from what one student called "the old, new movements" to the "newer, new movements"—from traditional environmental movements (antitoxin, wilderness), women's, LGBT, and alter-globalization movements to an interest in cycling, community gardening, co-housing, and urban food production. Until recently, though, I was reluctant to centre many of these activities in our study of social movements—they were interests, hobbies, social gatherings, entertainment. My students, however, saw these as central ways in which they are questioning the world around them. These were *their* counterhegemonic projects. Reflecting on my own homemaking, I have come around.

Though tempted to situate the following as autoethnography, the purpose is not formal empirical study but rather to call upon my experience as a participant and organizer, public documents, and everyday conversations in the streets and classroom to develop theoretical insight into the political possibilities of urban homemaking projects. Or, as Sears (2014) describes, to invoke "conscious learning processes to understand the big-picture context that frames experience as the basis for processes of effective change" (26).

MAKING HOME IN A LIQUID CITY

Before moving to Vancouver in 1994, I had spent the previous nine years as a graduate student, and during that time had lived in nine different homes. Academic study and work, it seems, attracts, demands, and cultivates a rootlessness, and my own case reflects Jasper's (2000) suspicion that part and parcel of this mobility is a distrust of those more grounded. Growing up in a small mining town in Northern Ontario and a slightly larger working-class community "down south," the move to studies in Toronto, Montreal, and Hamilton reflected and reinforced a discomfort with the experience of rigid gender roles, xenophobia, and conservatism of my hometowns. My moves during university were not, in the main, triggered by unhappiness with my residential situation but by the seizing of economic, academic, and cultural opportunity. As leases came up for renewal, a better deal, new university, or new neighbourhood or city beckoned. Behind all this was a conscious pride in the growing ability to navigate and celebrate the aporia of urban centres.

In Vancouver's notoriously tight rental market, I found an apartment in a 72 hour stopover on the way to a conference. It had a bedroom, my partner could cycle to school and I to the archives, rent was within our budget. Though in awe of the natural setting of the city, with little in the way of local social network or experience of neighbourhoods, this choice centred on economic and spatial consideration rather than place.

As I look back through letters and other writings from the time, it is hard to pinpoint when or why my partner and I stopped this movement, but the evidence of neighbourhood associations joined, community gardens attended, Critical Mass rides enjoyed, and the neighbours' doors we could walk to and enter with ease, suggests a sudden shift in momentum, a hunkering down, an emplacement. We joined with others to address the growing stream of auto traffic in our neighbourhood, we signed up for a community-garden plot, my partner, struggling with the deaths of her parents, started walking neighbourhood dogs. While our network of close friends remained relatively constant, we found ourselves more entangled in a parallel network of intimate strangers in our neighbourhood.

One consequence of all this that I do recall is a shift in the experience of Vancouver and my neighbourhood. Dinners on the beach or during winter months smuggled into the eating area of a nearby public market—always something of a necessity given the cramped quarters of our apartment—were experienced less as giddy tourist and more as someone who belonged in and to the city. At about this point in time my partner and I started to call Vancouver home. Our home feelings had expanded beyond the confines of domestic space to the neighbourhood and larger city. When after two more moves I found myself in a new neighbourhood, commuting long hours across the Strait of Georgia, and a call went out for volunteers to bring a car-free street festival to my new East Vancouver neighbourhood, I couldn't resist. It was, alongside gardening on the boulevard, raising chickens for the family down the street, or sharing drinks in the alleyway, part of our repertoire of homemaking practices.

CAR FREE VANCOUVER DAY

To outsiders fed on a diet of Tourism Board press releases and the visitor's experience of the walkable downtown peninsula and rapid transit to the airport, Vancouver appears to be the city most likely to slay the beast of North

American sprawl. For many residents, however, especially the service workers slinging caffeine and the blue-collar workers building a city that seems under constant construction, the reality is somewhat different. For these folk, the "city of glass" is a mirage that constantly retreats from the Fraser Valley suburbs that are home to the majority of the area's population growth and its continued auto-dependency.

Though select areas of the nearest suburbs are served by automated Skytrain technology and Vancouver proper has a bus network that is relatively comprehensive, Metro Vancouver lags behind other major Canadian centres, such as Toronto, Montreal, and Calgary, in access to and use of rapid transit (Burda & Singer, 2014). Investments in a new, light metro system to Richmond and the airport (fast-tracked for the Winter Olympics), the addition of rapid bus lines, and an increase in cycling infrastructure pale in comparison to the continued expansion of road infrastructure in the region.

A particularly egregious example of this incongruity came with the announcement by the provincial government in 2005 of the Gateway Program, a three-billion-dollar "transportation" project (the bill later ballooned to 22 billion) that included the construction of a ten-lane bridge and road-widening projects. Defended by the province and trucking industry as necessary to allow for the expansion of container traffic through the Port of Vancouver, critics decried Gateway as a pavement project that would push asphalt through neighbourhoods and over farmland. The announcement of Gateway was met with mobilization by environmental organizations, alternative transportation groups, neighbourhood associations, and urban planners and activists. The Greater Vancouver Regional District and the City of Burnaby officially opposed parts of the project. Later on, a plant-in was held and an encampment occupied in an attempt to block the construction of the South Perimeter Road. While these protests are in the main largely forgotten, one legacy—beyond the tarmac, that is—of Gateway lives on: Car Free Vancouver Day.

Car Free Vancouver Day began in the Commercial Drive neighbourhood—a chaotic hotbed of progressive politics, alternative communities, and East Van pride that the pressures of Vancouver's gentrification industry have yet to tame convincingly. The neighbourhood is bounded and bisected by arterial roadways fed by Gateway. It is here that local activists decided to protest Gateway with a street hockey game. Word of mouth brought a few dozen people, including many children, into Commercial Drive on a Sunday afternoon. Traffic was shut down, a band played "O Canada" and the theme from Hockey Night in Canada, and passersby were urged to "score one for community." In much the same way that I and my friends yelled, "Car!" and stood aside for traffic when we played in the street, protesters yelled, "Bus!" and let transit through. When police arrived, confronted by a game of street hockey, they directed traffic.

The success of this street hockey protest was deftly seized upon by a larger group of activists, and by June organizers had created Commercial Drive

Fest, which in subsequent years was renamed Car Free Day and, upon expansion to neighbourhoods throughout the city, Car Free Vancouver Day. While its biography is rooted in more traditional protest, Car Free Days were, and remain, street festivals where local communities, businesses, non-profit and activist organizations, musicians, artists, artisans, and craftspeople are invited into streetscapes that are otherwise monopolized by automobiles. Strategically, there is plenty going on here—a subject to which I will return—but much of this is captured in the slogans "Fewer Cars = More Community = Fewer Cars," "No Boring Corporate Stuff," and "Fun for Free." Car Free Days are seen as a way of displacing vehicle traffic, building communities, and re-thinking the purpose of streets. The festival brings neighbours onto the street with the intention that sociability is strengthened, local/neighbourhood economies reinforced, and roads reconfigured as multi-use, public space.

There is debate in the literature about the political possibilities afforded by street festivals like Car Free Vancouver Day. At one end of the spectrum are those who see such festivals for their progressive, even revolutionary potential. Liberally quoting Baktin, Lefebvre, and Deleuze, these authors celebrate the disturbance of spatial routines of everyday life, the questioning of taken-for-granted interpretations embedded in everyday spatial practices, and the taking back of public time and space (Johansson & Kociatkiewicz, 2011). At the other end are those, often more empirical, studies of contemporary street festivals that question whether these have become tamed, controlled expressions of corporate interests. These pessimists—realists some might say—draw our attention to how festivals become commodified spectacles supported mainly for their usefulness as economic drivers, tools of gentrification, and civic boosterism (Jamieson, 2004).

It is safe to say that Car Free Day offers evidence for both such interpretations. Staging and growing a street festival in a neoliberal context, working with and against existing governance structures, and adapting to and challenging existing experiences and meanings of North American streetscapes engender a festival that reflects the tensions and contradictions of the city with which it engages.

To this day, Car Free Day re-enacts the transgressive power of that initial loosely scripted street hockey game. Once a year, across the city there is a dramatic repurposing of space. Corridors of pavement, generally off limits to anything but automized transit and the transport of commodities, are given over to people for a myriad of other purposes, many unexpected. Car Free remains an opportunity to disturb the expectations, rhythms, and meanings of the street, to deterritorialize space colonized by the automobile, and to give participants the physical and psychic space to play with alternatives. This side of Car Free is exemplified by the outset of the festival, when streets are barricaded long before any musicians, vendors, or even many volunteers are present. For some time, the rules of urban life go on undisturbed.

Well-trained pedestrians continue along, pressed up against the margins of the streetscape, unaware of or uncertain about how to navigate the reconfigured space. Almost inevitably it is a child with a skateboard or a bike who will wrest themselves from the sidewalk and sail right down the yellow line, yelling all the way. Thus begins a process of reclaiming space, a point I will expand upon shortly.

As it has emerged from unlawful protest to city-approved festival, Car Free has taken on a much more civilized demeanour. In Vancouver, shutting down a street to automobiles, by obtaining the proper permits, will cost you in time and money. Spontaneity is squashed by permitting processes, music falls prey to noise bylaws, attempts to share food, the most humane of experiences, are discouraged by food-safety regulations. Most disciplining of all, however, is the dull economic compulsion of paying for city and police services that have been downloaded. As a result, Car Free Vancouver has become a key player, alongside city staff and the police, in managing playfulness. What began as the free-flowing production of strangers has given way to a more choreographed experience—where visitors are guided purposely down a corridor of vendors to stages with musicians playing on set schedules. Strapped for cash, we enter into dubious arrangements with Business Improvement Associations (BIA) and clutter our festival with "noncorporate" trinket sellers, whittling away the freed space central to the reimagining of streetscapes.

This binary analysis has long shaped both my understanding of and participation in Car Free. As an organizer, I have cautioned against BIA ties, paid positions, interns, organizational hierarchy, and revenue generation schemes. As a sociologist, I have regarded Car Free with a Weberian fatalism and an expectation of bureaucratization. Mostly I have agreed with Jamieson's (2004) description of such festivals:

> Although spaces appear as though spontaneously formed by the company of strangers and the collective experience of performances, the city en fete is also the result of painstaking planning by a city administration that seeks to control the ways in which public spaces change. The city is nonetheless redefined by the altered energy and velocity of strategically planned festivalized spaces. (65)

Faint praise and a good distance from meaningful counterhegemonic practice.

The politics of home, however, allows for another more nuanced perspective. From this vantage, Car Free Day, like and alongside a host of other urban interventions, does more than disrupt expectations and inject the city with energy and velocity. In directing at least some of that energy towards creating the physical, social, and psychic conditions necessary for feeling at home at the community level and for making home in the community, Car Free, along with and alongside a myriad of other urban homemaking projects, not only disturbs existing geographies and social relations but helps build new (for us) ones. Later I will suggest that such altered geographies and relations are part of an emerging urban home front in a renewed ecopolitics, but for now I shall briefly sketch the immediate struggles of Car Free Day.

RECLAIMING STREETS AS PLACES FOR HOME FEELING AND HOMEMAKING IN PUBLIC SPACE

Homemaking in community requires a public space that is amenable to such homemaking, and in Vancouver, as in much of North America, this cannot be assumed—it must be struggled for. As Neal (2010) acknowledges, much scholarly and lay writing on public space is a lament for what has been, or perhaps is presumed to have been, lost. Critics have traced an urban world where there are fewer public spaces, and those that remain are more tightly controlled through policing, surveillance, architecture, and design. This loss of public space is mirrored by an increase in privatized space in shopping malls, privatized play spaces, and gated communities. Less directly acknowledged is the loss of streets themselves—not the sidewalks but the space between these sidewalks. As in the rest of North American cities and towns, most contemporary Canadian streets are not usable as public space, and the principal culprit here is our daily submission to a "postmetropolis" (Quinby, 2011, p. 15) infrastructure where roads become solely transportation corridors for automobile and truck traffic.

Some time ago, Sennett (1992) brought together these criticisms by arguing that the "erasure of lively public space" is directly attributable to "the making of space contingent on motion." Our architecture and our streetscapes have both become places of passing through, built with the specific purpose of first accommodating and then demanding ease of motion. The result, argues Sennett, is the re-creation of public space as "Dead Public Space," devoid of "any independent experiential meaning of its own" (14). While social historians remind us that this is an accomplished fact, one that was the result of legal, social, and cultural contest, most of us go about our urban lives "as if" there were no other way (Norton, 2008).

Car Free Day is at the most basic level an attempt to enliven the "dead public space" of streets, and herein is the first step in building public space available for home feeling. Early on, organizer Craig Olleneberger (2009) explained that "the festival offers a new view of our roadways as usable public space, available for many things beyond cars" and cofounder Carmen Mills adds, "These aren't street closures, they're street openings. Streets are public places. It's amazing how quickly things have changed" (Wood, 2009).

Opening up streets does not immediately confer alternative meanings or activities. In a revealing incident on Main Street, as the six lanes of asphalt (four of moving vehicles and two of parked cars) emptied and pedestrians trickled into the street, a woman with a small dog on a leash tried to do the same. The dog would have none of this; struggling against the pull of the leash, it was as confused as many humans when confronted with the option of playing in a space whose only previous meaning was "stay back."

Given a bit of time, though, people seem eager to experiment, and it is especially telling that the initial urge to move like a car, speedily and without concern, is replaced by the exact opposite—people plant themselves down firmly in place. Couches and overstuffed armchairs have become a trope of Car Free Days. Sometimes with an ironic wink they are on wheels and pushed or pulled around by bike. Most often, they are simply dragged into the street, parked in the middle of an intersection, and sat upon. A neighbour and former organizer for many years combined her duties by creating a side-street barricade with a couch and days' worth of knitting.

This lounging, it is important to note, was not a programmed phenomenon, at least at the outset. Indeed, on Main Street, my partner and I teamed up with the francophone owner of a local business to provide a French-language-themed space at an intersection. As Car Free Day coincided with a major francophone festival, the musicians never showed up, and after an hour or two of storytelling, all that was left of the "French Quarter" was a bunch of chairs and tables. We were red-faced and full of apologies. All day, however, the chairs were full, and many people later applauded us for the "great idea."

In a related phenomenon—and I have yet to pick apart all the symbolism here—children will run out into the middle of the street and lie down, sometimes having their outline drawn in chalk. This act seems at once transgressive and comforting. Sprawling out on the pavement can be viewed within the long tradition of nonviolent protest; these children put their bodies in the pathway of the automobiles that on most days threaten their lives on many levels. However, through the lens of a politics of home, I cannot help but see my own child sprawled out on a living-room floor. These children have reclaimed a formerly inhospitable space for home. It seems that when one is in constant motion or, as Hochschild (1997) reminds us, when one's home is a place of continual passing through, of timelines to be attended to and of rushing about, it becomes less home-like.

It needs to be acknowledged that critics have not always been warm to the idea of extending homemaking into public streets. Sennett (1992, p. 15) long ago bemoaned the loss of "ritual masks of sociability" presumed to sustain public life, foretelling backlash against mobile technologies that thrust the most intimate of conversations into public spheres. Referencing these same phone conversations and instant messages (IMs), Kumar and Makarova (2008, p. 336) speak of "the projection of private life into the public" in a manner that domesticates the public realm. For these critics, the extension of homemaking into the streets is destructive of public community.

But it is entirely possible to engage in homemaking in public and to feel at home in public spaces without domesticating these spaces, and this includes not only the churches for which Kumar and Makarova make exception but also streetscapes. Referencing Duyvendak's (2011) typology, streetscapes can feel familiar, offer physical and mental safety, and include places of retreat and relaxation while allowing for collective expressions of self as a member of a community. The fact that for many in Vancouver and elsewhere this is not the case—that streets are understood as places to be hurried through in the isolation of one's automobile, places of theme-park spectacle, or simply feared—says much about our streets and neighbourhoods but little about the possibility of feeling at home in the streets that one inhabits.

On Car Free Day, homemaking in public takes the form of building space for interaction, encouraging meandering in the streets with others, and in a plethora of ways setting the stage for sociability. Freed of cars, the streetscape encourages playful social interaction among friendly strangers that makes the street feel familiar. Games, food sharing, and interactive performance ensure that a walk down the street becomes a prolonged set of encounters, some with people one knows well, often with those one might have met for the first time. The intimacy of these interactions and their according emotional intensity vary from a passionate kiss, to the more frequent neighbourly chat, to the bracing confrontation with the bizarre.

For Car Free, the first step in feeling at home in the street is indeed a step. Walking streets to get one's groceries, to have a coffee, or to simply stroll breeds a type of familiarity necessary for home feeling and is, as noted, the most direct goal of the festival: getting folk onto the street so that they might come back tomorrow. But there is of course more going on here: in sharing food, couches, in playing games together, in simply walking together in the street, Car Free builds space for social connections, a familiarity with neighbours in addition to the built environment, that allows people to feel at home in their neighbourhood.

Such homemaking and home feeling in public spaces, in the community, and in a neighbourhood is not the same as feeling at home in a private space. In such intimate spaces, *others* are regularly excluded with little ethical or political consequence. At the scale of neighbourhood, city, or national level, such exclusion becomes much more problematic—which is one of the reasons progressive voices have shied away from the consideration of home.

Here the third element of Duyvendak's (2011) typology is essential: feeling at home in public spaces is at some level an engagement with community. For Car Free Day, community is both a goal and tactic in the struggle for social space. The slogan "Fewer Cars = More Community = Fewer Cars" bears repeating: automobile traffic fragments community, *and* rebuilding resilient communities is a necessary part of fighting traffic. Early on, Craig Ollenberger noted that the Commercial Drive neighbourhood that was the incubator for Car Free Day is bisected by arterials that fragment the community and that the festival "is a lot of things to a lot of people, but at the heart is a belief that a community becomes stronger through interaction" (Ollenberger, 2009).

As the festivals have grown, some questions have been raised about whether a party in the street, at least one of this scale, strengthens community ties. In 2006, founder Matt Hern, reflecting on the growth of Car Free Days, grappled with the conundrum: "The value of having a lot of people is that you can make a political push on something, but on another level it might be debilitating to a community," a reticence shared by planning professor Penny Gurstein, who argues, "When 50,000 people show up, it isn't really about building community. We need to think about more events where people can be engaged in creating communities" (Peters, 2006). Nonetheless, to this day community is invoked as both a goal and consequence of the festival. The Current Car Free Vancouver Society director, Matt Carrico, suggests, "It may be kind of random to throw a street festival and tie it to those things, but this has resonated with the citizens ... the sense of community on display on the streets of all the Car Free Days is really apparent" (Jackson, 2015).

Those who question the effectiveness of such events in building community fear that the sheer number and fluidity of the social contacts on Car Free Day cannot produce the sort of stability and commonality upon which people can feel at home in *their* community, a heavenly place, in Duyvendak's (2011) words, where one feels at home amid one's own people. However, maybe this is not the sort of home feeling being produced here. Carmen Mills, an inveterate defender of the power of a party, weighed into the debate saying, "We don't need to be afraid of different aspects that come into the neighbourhood as long as we're strong from the roots up. I mean do you resent it when people come to your party? I mean this is our party. It's for us" (Peters, 2006). Come on in, we are told—and it's okay to leave your shoes on.

I think Carmen is on to something here. Car Free Day is a house party of many rooms. There are spaces where one might retreat to the familiar, but the sound of others in their own familiar rooms always leaks through—and the hallways are a chaotic jumble of the familiar and the strange. On Car Free Day the streets are reclaimed not as quiet retreats from the public but as vibrant spaces where the expected and unexpected commingle. People create places for others like themselves, and they prance around announcing their difference. It is these acts and meanings that participants bring to and develop during the festival that announce Car Free Day as not only the liberation of space but also the reclaiming of that space as a place for homemaking and home feeling. However, this is a special sort of home: it is home in the street, in public, and out in the community. While home is related to and reflective of the emotive and material attributes of private homemaking, it is not the same thing—and this is for the best.

A Home of One's Own: Production of Home

Mary Douglas (1991, p. 289) famously observed that "home starts with bringing some space under control." But how is one to make home in Vancouver, where so many are so new to the city, to a neighbourhood, where gentrification and rapidly rising housing costs push the less advantaged from place to place and where others are pulled by the lure of home equity to move on.

As has been suggested earlier, Car Free festivals are run completely by volunteers. Early on, the slogan "Fun for Free" adorned posters and notices; however, over the years and due to much debate over such conundrums as whether to allow busking while musicians performed pro bono, and over the fact that vendors did vend while the selling of services such as art making or storytelling were disallowed, this slogan was quietly dropped. Such caveats aside, Car Free Day remains the product of many hands, most drawn from the immediate neighbourhood, through which no wages pass. This is true, of course, for the organizers and volunteers who spend months getting permits in order, appropriating space, recruiting day-of volunteers, and performing all the other tasks needed to get to the festival day. These folk self-organize in pods dedicated to specific tasks and report back to neighbourhood meetings in a decentralized, horizontal organizational structure that generally emphasizes the fact that anyone can put on a festival.

Sometimes things do not get done, and other times things get done that we never expected—but things do get done. On Main Street sometimes a good-sized skateboard ramp is constructed. I say "sometimes," as in certain years it just does not get made (we speculate that this has something to do with parties the night before). But that is okay. Others step in and find a creative use for the space; surprises remain. Radio-use protocol aside, I add to the chatter by holding down the talk button and laughing into the mic about the burlesque performance that has set up beside the children's bubble station. Others find this less than appropriate. Debate ensues.

Though merchants undoubtedly have economic motives and have (extra) hired staff on site, and some volunteers are compelled by resume padding, mostly it is students, college instructors, and mechanics rubbing shoulders as they pick up food waste from an overflowing bin at the end of the day because there is garbage on the street. Choir members raise their voices on this day, on this street, in part because it is their neighbourhood.

One consequence of Car Free, then, is that hundreds of people in each of the neighbourhoods see their own hand in transforming the streetscape into a more home-like place. On several occasions over the years, after the streets have been cleared of the material reminders of the festival, as the barricades are taken down and the first cars move through, tears have been shed by the volunteers who gather at the end of the day. While exhaustion is one explanation, this emotional response speaks also to loss and violation. The returning traffic speeds through a home space that volunteers and participants had created through hard work and conviviality; it feels like something has been stolen.

This consideration of streetscapes as home spaces is uncomfortable for many on many levels. Mostly this reflects the reactionary possibilities of home as haven of which we have spoken. That our home can quickly become not *their* home has led many to a strategy of containment. While acknowledging that homemaking means so much to so many, there is a real fear that such affective appropriation of space is necessarily a colonization of space. Private homes may be a safe place to allow rituals of homemaking, but this must not leak into public spaces and streetscapes.

Convenient to a range of political stances, and to those who both celebrate and fear enlivened public spaces, this strategy fails to reflect the affective appropriation of space that is part of lives lived through space. For all but the agoraphobic, the *hikikomori*, our home feelings messily extend across thresholds, onto porches, into hotels, and onto sidewalks. That such appropriation can be nasty and exclusionary, that it can replicate the insularity of homes that turn their back to chaotic and impersonal public realms cannot be denied. That it must be so is challenged by those whose street parties, and fraught politics, do not provide any one group the sort of control afforded to the private homemaker but nonetheless evoke a similar sense of meaningful and multiple commitments in contingent streetscapes.

CAR FREE DAY: BUILDING AN URBAN ENVIRONMENTAL POLITICS OF HOME

We are living in a time when unfettered capitalism is both thoroughly discredited and thoroughly triumphant. The veneer of paradox fades when one confronts the cold reality that triumph has come not simply through creatively destructive markets but through an equally creative disruption of movements posing viable alternatives. This situation is deftly captured by Mark Fisher's (2009) concept of "capitalist realism." That "there is no alternative" is no longer one side of a debate but is rather an attitude, a political resignation, shared by most—including those with powerful criticisms of precarious work, degraded natural and built environments, and commodified cultural and community life they confront every day. Viable alternatives to an ecologically and socially destructive capitalist system have sunk beneath the ideological horizon.

Key to the triumph of neoliberalism have been a widening and deepening of the dependency of people on capitalist markets, the strengthening of consumer identities, and the social fragmentation of daily lives. Late capitalism is marked by not only geographic expansion but also an expansion into every nook and cranny of contemporary life. As food, entertainment, and religion are commodified and social scarcities reproduced, envisioning life outside of commodity production and exchange becomes more difficult. While the personal, social, and ecological indignities that result from this are ever too apparent, exit strategies are contradiction ridden.

While many on the left have preoccupied themselves with this question, it is long-time activist and academic Alan Sears (2014) who has best captured the expression of this situation in Canada, its relation to global context, and the possibilities at hand. Sears, tracing periods of "mass insurgency" in the 1930s and 40s and the rise of the "new left" in the 1960s and 70s, draws attention to the "infrastructure of dissent"—"the means through which activists develop political communities capable of learning, communicating and mobilizing together ... ranging from informal neighbourhood and workplace networks to formal organizations and structured learning situations" (p. 2). Without robust infrastructures of dissent, the most meaningful outrage at unjust structures of power can dissipate into self-blame or scapegoating and be channelled into psychiatry, consumption, racism, and narcissism. When movements do gain traction—and both the anticorporate globalization movement at the turn of the century and more recently Occupy are emblematic—without an infrastructure of dissent to sustain and to fall back upon, they can wither at a dizzying pace.

Neighbourhood homemaking projects such as Car Free Day serve to both reveal and address a particular aspect of this atrophied infrastructure: the physical space and cultural aptitude to make and feel at home in neighbourhood spaces. In previous waves of dissent, such neighbourhood spaces have been crucial. Though the shop floor was a critical place of organizing for the labour movement, so too were the taverns and working-class neighbourhoods beyond the factory gates. Bookstores, coffee shops, and queer-friendly or gay neighbourhoods nurtured and supported lesbian and gay political challenges. Across communities, urban sprawl, gentrification, and urban renewal have weakened this neighbourhood infrastructure significantly. While many today, even those who otherwise lament the loss of such home spaces, suggests that virtual networks are the new union halls and public squares, the flurry of neighbourhood and urban homemaking projects I have discussed here suggests that urban neighbourhoods still have potential.

This potential rests partly on the scale of the neighbourhood. The neighbourhood is a meso-level social, physical, and political space whose inhabitants see themselves as having some hand in its production. While neoliberal conditions attempt to contain our home spaces to the commodified spaces of continually renovated kitchens and the cocoons of individualized automobile transport, our home feelings are not so easily contained. This is why urban politics often appear so absurd, lively, and nasty. People still feel they can and should have a say in what building gets built, what road goes where, and what type of house is built beside theirs. None of this is to ignore the apathy that has engulfed many such places, nor to overlook the pettiness, classism, and racism that animate these politics—only to say that it is at the level of the neighbourhood and the city that individuals seem to be able to faintly grasp themselves not simply as consumers but as producers of their lives.

Car Free Day and other such urban projects are building, if not an infrastructure of dissent to allow for the unlearning of these habits of thought and body, at least the scaffolding necessary to begin the task. These projects make explicit our role as Lefebvre's (1991) *citadin*, citizen and denizen of our neighbourhood; we are made aware of not only the possibility of remaking our streets but also the fact that everyday activities such as strolling, eating, cycling, and playing, when engaged in collectively and en masse, are central to the remaking of places we care about. What is re-created in Car Free Day, in community gardens, in Critical Mass rides, is public space, meaningful social relationships, and the awareness that the health of each of these depends upon our collective labour.

Unleashed from the strict confines of domestic spaces, such homemaking-in-public/community is not easily contained to the local level. Even a temporary reclaiming of space for public homemaking is an overtly political process, whereby the bureaucracy of the municipality, the interests of business owners, and the limits of public transit options are revealed. Dancing in the street, at least in the postmetropolitan neoliberal city, is contingent upon struggles at not only the neighbourhood but also the municipal, provincial, and federal levels. While the entry point of these politics is distinctly local, the success of the struggle invites us to make connections between global capital (big box stores), national politics (lack of infrastructure spending), and provincial priorities (roadways vs. transit).

For these reasons and many others, this street party, along with similar urban interventions, just might signal a future for environmental politics that until now, especially in North America, has exhibited much more light than heat. The structure of environmental politics and mobilization has become bifurcated, at once global and entirely personal, and climate change offers just the latest example of this. The movement has developed a sophisticated repertoire of—especially symbolic—protest to confront economic and political leaders in places across the planet. International networks and people's summits have underscored the linkage between profits and consumption in the Global North and the global hierarchy of victims of climate change. Meanwhile, back at home we are urged to drive less, change our light bulbs, and vote for *real action* on climate change.

This just may be the missing link in environmental politics—a politics that is rooted in everyday life while exposing the contingency of this life on political struggle on multiple scales. Car Free Day, urban gardening, Critical Mass, and other urban movements are all about finding ways to recognize and unveil, reassert and reinforce our role in the social reproduction of urban space. It is a politics more humane (and human) than wilderness struggles, less co-optive than appeals to individual-level consumption.

It may also be the missing link in progressive coalition building. Environmental and labour movements have both laid claim to being unifying, even universal movements. At the least, we can say that these meso-level, urban-based environmental movements may help recover, reveal, and reignite our passion for producing our own lives—and a counterhegemonic movement is inconceivable without subjects that understand their role as producers of their lives. Urban environmental movements, by celebrating public space as a commons and in centring our role as active producers of this space, suggest a meso-level, counterhegemonic strategy. This strategy may be useful not only in bridging the bifurcated levels of environmental movement struggle but also in intermovement bridging—the very sort of bridging necessary if we are to overcome the cultural and class fragmentation that underpins the triumph of discredited neoliberalism.

There are real reasons to be cautious here. Many, especially of the anarchist bent, have overextended the argument for "partying politics." Seen through the lens of a politics of home, however, urban homemaking defends public space, forges meaningful social relationships built around autonomous self-reproduction, and extends the realm of home feeling into diverse communities where our expression of self as members of a community need not deny others the same such claim to home. Such neighbourhoods, occupied by "grounded people living their home feelings 'lightly'" (Duyvendak, 2011, p. 124), might be just the place to hang our hope for a better future.

REFERENCES

Burda, C. & Singer, J. (2014). Fast cities: A comparison of rapid transit in major Canadian cities. Pembina Institute. Retrieved from http://www.pembina.org/pub/fast-cities

Douglas, M. (1991). The idea of home: A kind of space. *Social Research* 58(1), 287–307.

Duyvendak, J. W. (2011). *The Politics of Home: Belonging and Nostalgia in Western Europe and the United States.* New York: Palgrave Macmillan.

Fisher, M. (2009). *Capitalist Realism: Is There No Alternative?* Washington, DC: Zero Books.

Hamm, M. (2002, May). Reclaim the streets! Global protests and local space. Retrieved from www.republicart.net/disc/hybridresistance/hamm01_en.pdf

Hochschild, A. R. (1997). *The Time Bind: When Work Becomes Home and Home Becomes Work.* New York: Metropolitan Books.

Jackson, E. (2015, June 11). Vancouver's Car Free Day festivals growing stronger. *Metronews.* Retrieved from www.metronews.ca/news/vancouver/1394795/vancouvers-car-free-day-festivals-growing-stronger/

Jaleel, R. (n.d.). A queer home in the midst of a movement? Occupy homes, occupy home-making. Retrieved from www.what-democracy-looks-like.com/a-queer-home-in-the-midst-of-a-movement-occupy-homes-occupy-home-making/#sthash.uuye75Ha.0Py6m6OU.dpuf

Jamieson, K. (2004). Edinburgh: The festival gaze and its boundaries. *Space and Culture,* 7(1), 64–75.

Jasper, J. (2000). *Restless Nation: Starting Over in America.* Chicago: University of Chicago Press.

Johansson, M. & Kociatkiewicz, J. (2011). City festivals: Creativity and control in staged urban experiences. *European Urban and Regional Studies,* 18(4), 392–405.

Kumar, K. & Makarova, E. (2008). The portable home: The domestication of public space. *Sociological Theory*, 26(4), 324–343.

Lefebvre, H. (1991). *The Production of Space*. Oxford: Blackwell.

Neal, Z. (2010). Relocating public space. In Orum, A. & Neal, Z. (Eds.), *Common Ground? Readings and Reflections on Public Space* (pp. 201-207). New York: Routledge.

Norton, P. D. (2008). *Fighting Traffic: The Dawn of the Motor Age in the American City.* Cambridge, MA: MIT Press.

Ollenberger, C. (2009, July 6). Grandview-Woodland enjoys car-free streets. *The Georgia Straight*. Retrieved from www.straight.com/article-238312/craig-ollenberger-grand-viewwoodland-enjoys-carfree-streets

Peters, R. (2006, July 3). Vancouver: Street party central. *The Tyee*. Retrieved from www.thetyee.ca/Life/2006/07/03/StreetParty/

Quinby, R. (2011). *Time and the Suburbs: The Politics of Built Environments and the Future of Dissent*. Winnipeg: Arbeiter Ring Publishing.

Sears, A. (2014). *The Next New Left*. Halifax: Fernwood Publishing.

Sennett, R. (1992). *The Fall of Public Man*. New York: Norton.

Wood, D. (2009, March 24). Walk this way: Pedestrian streets on the rise. *BC Business*. Retrieved from www.bcbusiness.ca/tourism-culture/walk-this-way-pedestrian-streets-on-the-rise

CHAPTER 12

SEASONAL TINY HOUSE LIVING, SIMPLICITY, AND PERCEPTIONS OF AUTHENTICITY

Tracey Harris

> I shift gears, and I am not my best self in the city, in this big house that holds stuff and seems excessive … I'm a bit bitter about it really. To have to clean it and to maintain it and to have to, you know. I'm not my best self, but I'm coping, I'm okay. So I think that's the difference. I shift gears. (Angela, Interview Participant, 2015)

The Tiny House Movement has received a great deal of media exposure, and stories convey the transformational lifestyle as participants downsizing their stuff, paring back to the basic essentials, and moving into a tiny housing footprint. The media sometimes sensationalizes these accounts, leading the reader to believe that this is a solitary act that demonstrates individualism, as people "build their own homes" or transform their lifestyle to suit their personal desires and needs (Anson, 2014). But rather than acting in isolation, tiny house enthusiasts and eventual residents are firmly rooted in their communities, often utilizing communal resources to help realize their dreams (Anson, 2014). In my research on seasonal tiny house residents, I found that building community was also important for participants. Rather than wanting to be completely solitary in their tiny homes, these seasonal tiny residences gave participants the time and energy to focus on the people that matter to them, on hobbies or tasks that they found meaningful, and a community outside of their home, as well as time to spend in nature or with friends and neighbours.

For the purposes of this research, a seasonal tiny house is defined as a small second house used part time. All of the houses in this study were less than eight hundred square feet in size. In the literature on the Tiny House Movement, there is some debate on what constitutes a tiny house. Rather than putting a finite point on the actual size requirements, movement leaders prefer to advocate that a tiny house is one in which all space is being used well (Mitchell, 2014; Shafer, 2009). Mitchell (2014) [argues that "a key point that many don't understand about tiny houses is that: A tiny house is not just a home—it is a lifestyle"] (p. 15), as it brings into question societal values related to consumption and consumerism. He goes on to argue that square footage should be examined in relation to the size of the household, as "a single person living in 200 square feet and families of five living in 1,200 square feet are both living in tiny houses" (Mitchell, 2014, p. 15). My study found that small and simple seasonal residences helped participants create a more meaningful lifestyle within the confines of their existing lives. They gave people a sense that rather than getting away from real life, seasonal tiny house residents were getting back to activities and relationships that were important and meaningful for them. The participants in my study all have tiny homes that they utilize on a seasonal or part-time basis. They differ in terms of community location, housing style, and available amenities and utilities, but they share some important common characteristics. Participants indicated the importance of getting away from their daily routine and utilizing a simpler footprint while at their home-away-from-home. Most important, the smaller housing footprint seemingly allowed for feelings of authenticity and a sense of being their best selves while unencumbered by the complexities found in their regular lives and full-time residences. While on the surface seasonal tiny house and full-time tiny house residents do not seem to hold a great deal in common, I would contend that at a more fundamental level they actually do. Full-time tiny house residents are utilizing an alternative lifestyle as they closely examine their wants versus their needs (Mitchell, 2014). Seasonal tiny house residents are arguably doing the same. Some may contend that having two residences contravenes the spirit of the Tiny House Movement, but I believe that these seasonal properties may actually help facilitate a smaller footprint in the long term. Seasonal tiny house residents may begin to feel disconnected from their full-time residences and more connected to their part-time homes, which may facilitate important opportunities for contemplation and eventual change. Seasonal tiny homes may act as a stopgap between owning a conventionally sized house and transitioning to tiny house living fulltime. Several participants discussed the possibility of eventually moving fulltime to their seasonal property, and two participants were actively trying to sell their full-time homes at the time of the interviews. But even those who do not seek to downsize as a result of their part-time tiny house experience may begin to feel a sense of authenticity as a result of their smaller footprint. This authentic self may well emerge as a result of a simplified lifestyle that provides ample opportunities to strengthen important relationships, spend time in meaningful pursuits, build ties to community, and foster environmental stewardship. For participants, the seasonal tiny house facilitated feelings of being more connected to their true self, to others who are close to them, and to the outside world and nature.

THE SEASONAL TINY HOUSE DWELLER

In order to contextualize my analysis in this chapter, I will begin by providing some background on my interest in this topic, the study itself, and the literature related to the emerging themes of the Tiny House Movement: simplicity and authenticity. For each, I will intersperse respondents' voices with literature related to these broad themes. Within this chapter, I intend to use a "symbolic interactionist perspective ... to highlight how my participants understand their everyday lives and how they go about explaining them to me" (Van den Hoonaard, 2012, p. 114). From these narratives I have created a framework for understanding participants' conceptualizations of home, the connection to living more simply and deliberately, and what a small and simple home-away-from-home may help facilitate for participants.

I became interested in voluntary simplicity, small-cabin living, and off-grid technologies because my family bought a parcel of lakefront property and built a one-hundred-square-foot (plus sleeping loft) off-grid cabin. I know from my own experiences with an off-grid seasonal property that one of the most significant realizations for me was how present I feel when I am there. At home and at work I am in constant multi-tasking mode. Even when focusing on one task, I am perpetually one or two steps ahead in my mind. At home I will often perform routine tasks and have absolutely no recollection afterwards of what I just performed. For instance, I often check voice mail while loading or unloading the dishwasher and have dinner preparation going at the same time. The result is that nothing truly gets my full attention, and I have a blurry memory of any of the tasks that I have just performed. One of the biggest and most satisfying realizations for me was that the tasks completed at the cabin required more concentration, and with few distractions to impede me, I felt more satisfaction when the task was complete. Washing the dishes, for instance, is a multi-step process when you do not have running water; but such a task seems more satisfying when not crammed in with other chores. As a result of my experiences creating a seasonal retreat, I became interested in other people's motivations for attempting to live more simply. What factors shaped their motivations for a simpler life facilitated through the creation of a small, part-time home?

My original premise was that environmental concerns would be the driving force for these attitudinal and behavioural shifts, but in speaking with other small-cabin and cottage residents, I soon discovered that while all of the participants expressed the hope that they would not in any way harm the environment, only two named environmental concerns as a priority for the decisions they made regarding their tiny seasonal house. This research was an attempt to form a more complete picture of what motivates people to live more simply and how they then feel as a result.

Between the summer of 2013 and the spring of 2015, I completed in-depth interviews with six seasonal tiny house owners. Five respondents were interviewed face to face, and one took place via email due to the geographical distance between participant and interviewer. These seasonal residences varied in size between 200 and 800 square feet, with the average size being 372 square feet. The amount of property also varied from a quarter of an acre up to a little over three acres. Participants were asked their viewpoints on three areas of their experience with seasonal tiny house living: (1) background questions on acquiring or building their seasonal home; (2) rationales for the footprint of the home and utilities chosen; and (3) questions related to the feelings associated with their seasonal home and property. These six seasonal tiny home residents live in a variety of communities in Eastern Canada. Three participants were women, and three were men. They ranged in age from early thirties to early sixties. Three participants had young children, one had grown children, and two (a couple) had no children.

The Tiny House Movement

While there is little scholarly literature on the Tiny House Movement (with the notable exceptions of Anson, 2014 and Mutter, 2013), the media has embraced it, and news stories on the movement and its participants are published daily; as well, several television shows and documentaries examine the process of people acquiring tiny houses. In addition, many popular books on the topic focus on helping interested people transition to smaller housing footprints (e.g., Mitchell, 2014; Shafer, 2009; Walker, 1993; Williams, 2014; Zeiger, 2009). As mentioned in the introduction, there is no consensus in the movement or the literature as to what constitutes a tiny house. Anson (2014) argues that a tiny house can be anything less than 800 square feet (p. 292), and Mutter (2013) claims that they are usually between 65 and 400 square feet (p. 2).

Certainly these numbers stand in sharp contrast to the size of the average Canadian house. But historically speaking, small houses were actually the norm in Canada until only a short time ago. In 1945 the average house in Canada was 800 square feet, but by 1975 it grew to 1,075 square feet (Anderson, 2013, p. 189); the average jumps to 1,950 square feet by 2010 (Banerjee, 2012). At the same time the average house was growing in size, the average Canadian household size was shrinking. The average household in 1961 was 3.9 people, by 1981 it was 2.9 people, and by 2011 it declined to 2.5 people per household (Vanier Institute, 2013). Not only was the average house size increasing but so was the average household space available per person, as fewer people in a household means that each person has more room. Even though houses built today are better insulated and more efficient than in the past (Roberts, 2005, p. 152), each of these larger spaces requires more heating in the winter and cooling in the summer. Empty spaces are often filled with consumptive products. Larger homes cost more money to buy and are more expensive to maintain. They also require expensive monthly payments to pay down the interest and eventual principal on the mortgage. And it is not only the size of our houses that have grown: "Over-consumption is reflected ... in the sizes of our yards and streets as well. Oversized lots on vast roads, miles from any worthwhile destination, have made the ... suburb as inhospitable as it is vapid" (Shafer, 2009, p. 46). Clearly, connections between residents become more difficult as people drive to most activities and destinations, which also increases their environmental footprint along the way.

Rather than defining a tiny house in terms of square footage or what it appears to be missing, Shafer (2009) argues that "a small house is not merely as good as its larger correlate; it is better. A home that is designed to meet its occupants' domestic needs for contented living without exceeding those needs will invariably surpass the quality of a bigger one in terms of sustainability, economics and aesthetics" (p. 26). Mitchell's (2014) definition of tiny homes encompasses three related principles, and these help to facilitate a sense of well-being and comfort: "1. It focuses on effective use of space. 2. It relies on good design to meet the needs of the residents. 3. It serves as a vehicle to a lifestyle that the resident wishes to pursue" (p. 15). These values clearly relate to the experiences of my participants, as many worked hard to use their small spaces to the best of their abilities by finding key storage pieces to help stow their necessary stuff, some even implementing ruthless "one in, one out" rules to keep clutter to a minimum. As Jess indicated, "The cabin is like a boat. It is very small, so the efficiency of the space is important. It determines the amount of time relaxing or working on upgrades. Everything has a measured thought in terms of procedure, amount of time required to perform [the] task, and [the] ability to bring in materials."

For some, the smaller space facilitated a concern that everything they had was of good quality and made of environmentally friendly materials. Angela indicated: "So you either have to love it or use it, to be there. And another difference is everything in that house is good quality ... you know, the sheets are good quality, the cups are nice and sturdy and strong, and comfortable chairs, and the original art, right. So everything has a meaning, and it's either I love it or I use it."

For others, the seasonality of the space meant that they wanted the cheapest, least precious furnishings and finishes, as they did not want to have to worry about things being damaged or stolen during the off-season, and they wanted their family and visitors to feel a sense of casualness and fun while at the cottage. Tess discusses her family's conscious decision not to use valuable furnishings at their seasonal home:

> We didn't want the stress of what if, in the off-season, we're not here, somebody knows it's a cottage, they could break in and trash it or steal stuff or—so that's part of not having a leather couch sitting in it, that if somebody goes and takes the Klick Klack [an old sofa that came with the cottage], we'll be like, "We'll go get a new Klick Klack [laughter]. Whoa hoo!" But that things that are in it are—although we try to enjoy and treasure it and we wouldn't want anything to happen to [it], but it's not a stress in the off-season.

In both examples seasonal tiny house residents have made calculated decisions that assisted in the creation of a simple space that helped facilitate a sense of peacefulness and relaxation: one through the meaningfulness associated with all of the furnishings and finishes, and the other through the easy upkeep and potential ease of replacement if anything were to happen during the off-season.

Small spaces are said to help facilitate the lifestyle one wishes to pursue (Mitchell, 2014, p. 15). My participants discussed the smaller footprint being tied to increased time to spend in other pursuits, as they had less cleaning, maintenance, and distractions at their seasonal homes. In addition, the smaller footprint of the house itself provided the motivation or push to get outside and forge ties with others and nature. As Angela said, "I suppose having a small house does make you want to get out and have a little bit of space and air more often, so maybe there is a connection there." But even beyond the size facilitating out-of-doors activities, the joyfulness of the smaller footprint was discussed by participants in terms of ease of clean up, limited belongings and clutter facilitating less stress, and a ship-like feel to the space ensuring that everything had a place. In discussing simplicity, engagement, time in nature, and environmental stewardship, the seasonal tiny house dwellers were inadvertently espousing motivations of the Tiny House Movement.

Residents of tiny houses, whether full time or part time, are living in a countercultural footprint. In rich consumer cultures, we are encouraged to build big houses with all the latest bells and whistles. In reaction to this large-house trend, the Tiny House Movement questions the benefits of living large. Mitchell (2014) asks consumers to consider the fallout from overconsumption, clutter, credit-card debt, and the stress from buying, caring for, and working longer hours to pay for more and more stuff (pp. 16–19); as an alternative, he asks us to consider living in a smaller economic and environmental footprint. Even though the Tiny House Movement on its own is not sufficient to curb overconsumption, consumerism, and environmental degradation, "it is a politicized approach that transcends housing and gets us to look inward at our wants and needs, while firmly offering a different model of a socially responsible citizen" (Harris, 2015). Creating small spaces and utilizing a variety of off-grid and lower-impact utilities, such as rainwater catchment, composting toilets, and solar power, are not the norm. Yet some of the participants in this study noted that the off-grid elements they integrated, such as a composting toilet or a rainwater catchment system, added to the sense of ease associated with their seasonal property. Part of the comfort for seasonal tiny house residents may relate to "a lack of modern facilities as important to facilitate nature experience, the feeling of well-being at the cottage largely a function of being comfortable with simple means" (Williams & Kaltenborn, 1999, p. 221). When I asked what first attracted her to this property, Tess noted, "Small and simple and not complicated, no worry about [a] well and sewer in the off-season because you only use it for such a small period of time. That was a concern because that can be a big investment if it goes wrong. And when they are designed to be used year round and you don't." So, for several of my participants, the lack of what might be considered modern conveniences, such as a well or sewer system, actually helped facilitate less worry and lent a sense of simplicity to their seasonal property. But this is not to say that all participants were happy to have a composting toilet and lack of a reliable source of running water. Taylor, for instance, discussed how much he was looking forward to getting the septic system installed so they could stop using the composting toilet they had installed, and Lucy discussed wanting to get their well sorted out so that they could feel more relaxed about their water use while at their cottage.

Even though none of the participants resided full time at their cabin at the time of the interviews, they still felt an investment in the community and place. A second home can play an important role in creating family rituals and "often give[s] inhabitants or visitors a sense of belonging and meaning" (McIntyre, 2006, p. 19). More than tourists simply visiting a place, these seasonal tiny house residents are similar to other homeowners in their interest in building community. One participant mentioned wanting to go to the local community hall to participate in events, and another mentioned the importance of building community with other full-time area residents and seasonal neighbours. Angela also identified this connection when she said, "We love it when Sam's friends come to the door to see if he'll go fishing or go play board games, right—so there is a real very nice feeling of fun. There is always something going on." Not surprisingly, living part time in the same community year after year facilitates more of a connection than being a tourist. Svenson (2002) argues, "To be a tourist is to take a vacation from commitment; it is to be in a community without being responsible to it. But cottaging does involve a commitment. Cottagers return to the same place year after year, often with the same people" (p. 30). Building a sense of connectedness to home was facilitated in a variety of ways, such as fostering friendships with full-time and seasonal residents, participating in local events, taking an interest in the local community, and considering it a home-away-from-home.

Simplicity

Although the participants in this current study did not define their actions specifically in these terms, the literature on both downshifting and voluntary simplicity has relevance for their choices and experiences. Downshifting refers to people deciding to consume and work less in favour of creating the possibility of more time for other pursuits (Schor, 1998); and voluntary simplicity offers insight into the examined life—the act of being present and living deliberately (Luhrs, 1997, p. xiv). Living deliberately is often espoused as a means to live a more meaningful life through financial freedom, less stress, and increased time for meaningful pursuits, such as spending time with friends and family or taking part in creative pursuits. One participant, Jess, described how he measures getting away from it all: "Peacefulness. Solitude. Powering down. Me time. Simpleness." Others have argued that in a consumer-based society, voluntary simplicity requires learning and incorporating novel behaviours and values (Boujbel & D'Astous, 2012, p. 491). While the activities and interests of voluntary simplifiers cannot be reduced to only a few, they often seek to minimize the clutter in their homes, avoid overscheduling, work less and spend less, and seek community through alternative living arrangements such as co-housing (Huneke, 2005, pp. 531–532). Because of the small physical size of their seasonal homes, participants in this current study were forced to focus on issues related to clutter and storage solutions, were finding time outside of their regular lives for unscheduled leisure activities, and were seeking and discovering a sense of belonging in their seasonal communities. And because these pursuits made participants feel good about themselves and their relationships with others, they sought out such opportunities more habitually.

Satisfaction from completing tasks at the seasonal residence was mentioned by all participants but one. They seemed to believe that the work done there was more satisfying and genuine than the work at their full-time home or at their job. Most mentioned the fact that they felt present in their tasks at the cottage and not overwhelmed by multi-tasking, because most chores were done by choice, as they decided to go to the cottage and could pick and choose specific tasks that they wanted to complete on that visit. Since none of the participants had large seasonal residences or laundry facilities, everyday tasks were usually simple and sporadic. Lucy mentioned during our interview at her cottage that she had wanted her space to look nice for my visit, and within a few short minutes she had her four-hundred-square-foot cottage swept and dusted; she commented on the ease of summer living there. She also said that sometimes she looks around the space and thinks, "I could live here," and then she reiterated that she really could.

Three main factors related to simplicity emerged in the interviews: the importance of disconnecting, enhanced engagement with others as a result, and feeling present in routine activities. Only one of the participants I interviewed had Internet at their cabin, one had a telephone land line, and the others relied on spotty cell phone coverage. Angela stated, "Well, first of all, one of my favourite things is there isn't a telephone. So there is a sense of stillness there. I don't know—it's the unexpected idea that the phone is going to ring." She went on to say that her entire family was "much more relaxed and connected and authentic when we are in the little house." Only two of the six participants had a TV at the seasonal home, and none of the others wanted one. As Lucy mentioned in her interview, "We are thirty-five minutes from home and a million miles away." Four of the six participants mentioned that they worried that the things that they loved about their cabin or cottage and that made it special would be compromised if they were more technologically connected while there. As Tess, a mother of two young children, said when asked about how she measured getting away from it all: "The bungalow is relaxing and enjoyable, and you are forced ... it sounds terrible, but you are forced to focus on the people you are there with ... the distractions aren't there." She went so far as to say that at home there were always chores to be done and how a simple Internet search for the weather could become an hour away from her family and social interaction.

As a result of this part-time simplicity, seasonal tiny house residents are rewarded with a sense of peacefulness and relaxation. When I asked Tess what simple living means to her, she said, "Just taking what you need, not what you want ... kind of appreciating the natural things of just being outside and listening to the loons or watching the ducks." Probably the most charming answer relates clearly to claims that simple living for some is tied to less formality at the seasonal property. Taylor said, "Simple living? What? ... the word *simple* has so many meanings. Simple, simple is that—well, you know—I don't have to make a four-course meal? Simple, ah, I don't have too much cooking [so] I don't have a lot of cleaning up to do? Simple as in just sitting back and letting it happen?" He went on to argue that since eventually they were going to live in this house for half of the year, there really would be nothing abbreviated about it—there would still be beds to make and floors to clean because it will be a home. But, he argued, "It will be simple to the fact that you don't have to have your best clothes on all the time, you don't have to be dressed at all, all the time, because there is no one around to see it." While the phrase *simple living* does not mean the same thing to all participants, they all discussed some element of simplicity and how it translates at their part-time tiny house. Some discussed the ease of life at their tiny house; others advocated "less is more."

Authenticity

Relaxing, luxury, peaceful—these are the words used by participants to describe their seasonal homes. As a result of such associations, all participants, with the exception of one, noted feeling more genuine or true to themselves at their seasonal home. Vannini and Franzese (2008) "argue that authenticity is about being true to one's self" (p. 1621) and that "desires for authenticity may influence attitudinal views, beliefs and goals, and behavioral choices" (p. 1628). Williams and McIntyre (2001) discuss that "a sense of authenticity, involvement, and meaning in life may be constructed through individually managed outdoor recreation activities (e.g., camping, hiking, kayaking, etc.), the annual retreat to a second home, or regular visits to favorite places" (p. 398). Getting away from the daily demands of work and their full-time homes provided participants with the opportunity to foster connections with others, as well as opportunities to get out into nature, both of which seem to aid in the development of feelings of being closer to one's true self. A second home may elicit this sense in ways a full-time residence cannot (Hall & Müller, 2004, p. 12; White & White, 2007, p. 92), facilitating a "sense of place, rooted-ness, identity, and authenticity" (Williams & Kaltenborn, 1999, p. 227). For the following two participants, this certainly was true. Angela notes:

> I feel connected to people more there, like the community members there. Even though this is a tight street, I just feel—I just wish I could explain it—but I feel a real connection to my neighbours there and the young people who come to visit the house, like, a really big connection to them. They're always welcome, and they love to come, and they like to stay, right. But I just—the characters in the—my neighbourhood is amazing and so different from everybody else that I know here. Any-way, I think that's probably it … I just feel connected to the community and the people when I'm there. And it also makes me feel more creative there. And more awake. It's funny, I'm the opposite. Cities often make people feel more vibrant; I'm the opposite. Give me fog and the ocean and good-character people, and I'm ready to go. (Angela, Interview Participant, 2015)

And Tess shares: "We do enjoy having people around, and we enjoy the kids enjoying having people around. And the fact that it is a more casual setting, and I think when people get there and realize it is, I think it's kind of relaxing all the way around.… I like memories of different people, friends and family that have been around" (Tess, Interview Participant, 2013). Svenson (2002) argues that cottages can be "a place where extended family and friends gather together, where work is meaningful, where there is time for leisure and con-tact with nature, where community feels present" (p. 30); and I would argue that for my participants these were important opportunities that they highly valued and that made them feel good.

Participants varied in terms of the connectedness they felt to their full-time residences, with some discussing how overwhelmed they feel when they go home, while others argued that their full-time homes were also cozy and facilitated a reconnection with the larger world. But nonetheless the seasonal tiny house provided the possibility to get in touch with a part of themselves that was important and seems to have grown out of their opportunity to live more simply, disconnect, and engage with significant others, friends, and nature in meaningful ways unencumbered by the distractions of everyday life. In my original proposal for this study, I had expected that environmental stewardship would be the most significant rationale shaping my participants' motivation for simpler living, the size of their seasonal home, and the types of utilities used. While all the participants indicated that environmental concerns were important to them, it did not appear to be the most significant rationale for the choices made. Money, location, aesthetics, and time were all significant determinants in the decisions participants made related to the type of structure they built or bought, the type of materials used, and whether they incorporated off-grid technologies. I must acknowledge that there is an element of waste inherent in all of these properties, as all are second dwellings for participants. However, compared with many lavish cottages or retreats common in North America, these cottages, cabins, and bungalows are very small and do not make intensive use of fuel and/or water, and most rely fully or partially on off-grid utilities. The social construction of everyday life can sometimes make it difficult to maintain a consistency between our attitudes and behaviours (Bell, 2012, p. 38). Our lives are organized in particular ways, and this often makes it difficult to lead an environmentally friendly lifestyle easily. For instance, we may live in a cold climate with heavy snowfall that makes it impossible to use a bike for five months of the year, or we may live in a community with no public transit and therefore must rely on a car. As this demonstrates, there are limitations to consumer-driven environmental change, as environmentally friendly consumption, often referred to as green consumption, can only go so far: "Systemic change is the only way to engage with issues of production and social justice like reducing subsidies for oil companies or ensuring collective bargaining rights" (Lorenzen, 2014, p. 1072). Bell's (2012) concept of virtual environmentalism allows for the possibility of seeing environmental outcomes of participants as not strictly tied to individual motivation or rationale. Virtual environmentalism argues that if on a societal level environmentally friendly choices are made easy, accessible, and affordable, then people will utilize them without having to think about it. If public transit is cheaper and faster than using an individual vehicle, then the "choice" is simple. This concept relates to this study of seasonal tiny house residents because the participants can enjoy the simple pleasures associated with their properties, slowing down and eventually becoming more aware of their use of water, energy, and time; while doing environmental good, they do not have to place this at the forefront of their thought process. Bell (2012) argues that "virtual environmentalism is being environmentally good without having to be environmentally good"

(p. 284). Case in point, conventional black-water disposal can be costly and, if not done correctly and used year-round, largely ineffective and a potential environmental nightmare for a waterfront property. But the participants in my study who integrated off-grid technologies, such as composting toilets, did not cite environmental concerns as the primary rationale for their plumbing decisions. However, spending approximately two thousand dollars for a composting toilet was significantly more affordable than a full septic system; this system is also less environmentally taxing as it is a self-contained unit with little risk of contaminating groundwater or nearby lakes or rivers. Environmental considerations were not the only, or always primary, reasons for my participants' choices, as they instead cited concern for possible costly problems with a system only utilized for part of the year. As Bell (2012) says,

> "Virtual environmentalism is walking or taking your bicycle to work; buying food produced with sustainable production methods; replacing old appliances with energy-efficient ones; and using less heating, cooling, construction materials, and water … not because you've made a conscious decision to be environmentally good today, but because these were the cheapest, most convenient, and most enjoyable things to do" (Bell, 2012, pp. 283–284).

Participants in this study care about the environment; they all indicated that they did not want to do anything to hurt it, but other major motivating factors directing their actions and decisions at their seasonal homes were money, time, aesthetics, and location. Interestingly enough, these factors helped promote virtual environmentalism and an environmentally friendly lifestyle by keeping their seasonal residences small and simple, and their ecological footprint in terms of electricity and water consumption light. This simplicity also led to increased time spent outside in pursuits that participants found meaningful and that made them feel good about themselves and their relationships. To sum up those important connections to others and nature, Angela explains the big influence her little cottage has had on her entire family:

> I think back to what I mentioned before, that feeling of connection to the land, to the people, and to my best self. And I like what it has done for the family. So it's improved the family dynamic. Here, for instance, Sam, we noticed, one of … the reasons I was really looking for a place was Sam was getting into his technology so badly, and when we're there he goes … out playing outside like we used to when we were kids for hours, and, um, it's just a different feel altogether. So I think his childhood memories are going to be of that, of being outdoors and going fishing with his friends, and … if we were here in the city, there would be none of that, really, so I think that is the difference.

The participants in this study were able to create a more meaningful and sustainable existence within the confines of their existing lives by having a seasonal tiny house. Breaking away from distractions, such as technology, making time for important pursuits, spending time with friends and family, and getting out into nature all helped create a sense of a home-away-from-home at their cottage or cabin. These pursuits helped participants feel more contented, peaceful, complete, and authentic. These feelings are arguably good for the participants and their relationships with others, and they also help them facilitate stronger associations with community and the environment.

REFERENCES

Anderson, A. B. (2013). *Home in the City: Urban Aboriginal Housing and Living Conditions*. Retrieved from https://books.google.ca/books/

Anson, A. (2014). "The world is my backyard": Romanticization, Thoreauvian rhetoric, and constructive confrontation in the tiny house movement. *Research in Urban Sociology*, 14, 289–313.

Banerjee, P. (2012, January 18). Our love affair with home ownership might be doomed. *Globe and Mail*. Retrieved from www.theglobeandmail.com/real-estate/mortgages-and-rates/our-love-affair-with-home-ownership-might-be-doomed/article4179012/

Bell, M. M. (2012). *An Invitation to Environmental Sociology*. Thousand Oaks, CA: Pine Forge Press.

Boujbel, L., & D'Astous, A. (2012). Voluntary simplicity and life satisfaction: Exploring the mediating role of consumption desires. *Journal of Consumer Behaviour*, 11, 487–494.

Hall, C. M., & Müller, D. K. (Eds.). (2004). *Tourism, Mobility, and Second Homes: Between Elite Landscape and Common Ground*. Retrieved from https://books.google.ca/books

Harris, T. (2015, July 31). Living tiny: A richer and more sustainable future. *Counterpunch*. Retrieved from http://www.counterpunch.org/2015/07/31/living-tiny-a-richer-and-more-sustainable-future/

Huneke, M. E. (2005). The face of the un-consumer: An empirical examination of the practice of voluntary simplicity in the United States. *Psychology & Marketing*, 22(7), 527–550.

Lorenzen, J. A. (2014). Green consumption and social change: Debates over responsibility, private action, and access. *Sociology Compass*, 8(8), 1063–1081.

Luhrs, J. (1997). *The Simple Living Guide*. New York: Broadway Books.

McIntyre, N. (2006). Introduction. In N. McIntyre, D. R. Williams, & K. E. McHughs (Eds.), *Multiple Dwelling and Tourism: Negotiating Place, Home and Identity*. Retrieved from https://books.google.ca/books

Mitchell, R. (2014). *Tiny House Living: Ideas for Building & Living Well in Less than 400 Square Feet*. Blue Ash, OH: Betterway Home Books.

Mutter, A. (2013). *Growing Tiny Houses: Motivations and Opportunities for Expansion through Niche Markets* (Unpublished master of science thesis). Lund University, Lund, Sweden.

Roberts, P. (2005). *The End of Oil: On the Edge of a Perilous New World*. Retrieved from https://books.google.ca/books

Schor, J. B. (1998). *The Overspent American: Why We Want What We Don't Need*. New York: Harper Perennial.

Shafer, J. (2009). *The Small House Book*. Boyes Hot Springs, CA: Tumbleweed Tiny House Company.

Svenson, S. (2002). Cottaging: A tourist takes a vacation from responsibility; the cottager makes a commitment to place. *Alternatives Journal, 28*, 30–32.

Van den Hoonaard, D. K. (2012). *Qualitative Research in Action: A Canadian Primer*. Don Mills, ON: Oxford University Press.

Vanier Institute. (2013). *Then & Now: Trends in Canada*. Retrieved from www.vanierinstitute.ca/include/get.php?nodeid=2841

Vannini, P., & Franzese, A. (2008). The authenticity of self: Conceptualization, personal experience, and practice. *Sociology Compass, 2*(5), 1621–1637.

Walker, L. (1993). *The Tiny Book of Tiny Houses*. New York: The Overlook Press.

White, N. R., & White, P. B. (2007). Home and away: Tourists in a connected world. *Annals of Tourism Research, 34*(1), 88–104.

Williams, D. (2014). *The Big Tiny: A Built-It-Myself Memoir*. New York: Plume.

Williams, D. R., & Kaltenborn, B. P. (1999). Leisure places and modernity: The use and meaning of recreational cottages in Norway and the USA. In D. Crouch (Ed.), *Leisure/Tourism Geographies: Practices and Geographical Knowledge*. Retrieved from https://books.google.ca/books

Williams, D. R., & McIntyre, N. (2001). Where heart and home reside: Changing constructions of place and identity. In D. J. Stynes (Ed.), *Trends 2000: Shaping the Future: The 5th Outdoor Recreation and Tourism Trends Symposium*. Michigan State University, Department of Parks, Recreation and Tourism Resources, Lansing, Michigan. Retrieved from www.fs.fed.us/rm/value/docs/changing_home_identity.pdf

Zeiger, M. (2009). *Tiny Houses*. New York: Rizzoli International Publications, Inc.

CONCLUSIONS

HOMEMAKING AND A FUTURE FOR THE SOCIOLOGY OF HOME

Since the inception of this collection, we have had the occasion to speak to many people about the meaning of home. These conversations happened in spaces such as public transit, hospital rooms, and dinner tables. We have found that people welcome the opportunity to discuss home. If home has been rediscovered in academic literatures, Krishnan Kumar (1997) notes it has always been celebrated by most people, and indeed it has been generally held that "there is no place like home" (p. 205). As a very intimate and personalized part of living, many see home as a space that should be wholly defined by the person who occupies it. However, this collection demonstrates the classic sociological lesson that highly individualized notions of home will never capture the ways in which home animates the social relations and structures of our society. At its essence, this collection affirms that *home* is a fundamental concept for the sociological imagination.

Many people feel that they are quite capable of making home anywhere. For some it simply requires a suitcase with a few essential belongings; for others home is anywhere with friends and family. We have emphasized throughout this collection that material experiences of home matter. By speaking of actual, material homes, we do not seek to devalue articulations of home that locate its meanings in relationships or feelings. As Duyvendak (2011) has noted, home feelings, while complex, are fundamental to our understanding of home. Similarly, we do not seek to use the material as a predictor of the social. In reference to the term *suburban*, Rupa Huq (2013) argues that we should be wary of using geography to oversimplify or overdetermine the concept of suburbia, and remember that the "structuring structures like social class, educational attainment, ethnicity and gender are also predictors of life chances and cultures of the suburbs" (p. 192). While we have not advanced a particular theory of home, we join other scholars of home like Margarethe Kusenbach and Kristen Paulsen (2013) who embrace an interpretive lens that does not reduce the home to a house and seeks to explore home through the meanings that social actors attach to it. Still, as our collection is an explicitly sociological one, we felt it important to nudge the analysis squarely into the material and to make a strong claim for the importance of the material for the *sociological* analysis of home. Our contributors have explored how social relations and emotions are lived and experienced through the spaces and places that we call home. The invisible relational structures of home matter, but so too do the walls, the neighbourhoods, and the objects that decorate the room.

MURAL IN EAST VANCOUVER

Source: Joseph G. Moore; mural by Paul Antony Carr

In addition to arguing for a material analysis of home, this collection illustrates that the notion of *homemaking* should demand a prominent place in the sociological vocabulary. The concept of homemaking has a larger history in the analysis of gender and work. A sociology of home may re-engage feminist political economy in sociological thought, as it offers a rich theoretical tradition of analyzing the relationship between homemaking and social life. In dialoguing with this important history, we insist that the process of homemaking has a continued and wider relevance for sociological analysis. Exploring how, when, and why people make homes gives social actors agency and interrogates how they may draw on normative models of homemaking, as well as create new models of inhabiting (Lauster, 2013). Homemaking speaks well to the complex and dynamic enactment of contemporary social life in Canada. As our contributors have so well illustrated, as we homemake, we enact citizenship, gender relationships, and the life course; we constitute and reconstitute the line between public and private lives; we make claims about happiness and the good life; and we respond to (or against) the demands of late capitalism that see home as a marker of individual achievement. Homemaking is not only something that women do. Homemaking is a human experience.

The sociological analysis of home is clearly anchored in the familiar sociological analyses of class, gender, race, and ethnic inequalities. As several contributors have shown in this volume, it is important to explore how homelessness is tied to larger patterns of marginalization and displacement. In this way, sociologists of home will continue to contribute to the analysis of social inequality in ways that are fundamental to our discipline. However, in the tradition of Bourdieu and others, home also demands that we explore the experiences of the *housed* and look at how homes build middle-class and elite identities. So too will home demand a rich account of consumption. If home is a space of happiness and refuge, how is home consumed? How is the market implicated in the transformation of a house into a home? What are the ecological consequences of our homemaking practices? How do our homemaking practices harm others? As we write this conclusion, the home bloggers and design fanatics are discussing the *she-shed* as a response to the *man-cave*, and an air freshener commercial is claiming in a tongue-in-cheek fashion that you can make your home smell like you are in a "different tax bracket." If we are to take seriously an analysis of home, we will need to explore how home is consumed *across* the spectrum of social class.

Home space has strong cultural value in Canada, and houses are still the key asset for most Canadians. The recent recession in North America led many to criticize the way in which housing is leading many families to debt. Many American communities were devastated by foreclosures. In Canada, the mortgage insurance system was held up as saving Canadians from a similar fate. Still, Canadians have seen housing prices rise steadily, and more recently certain markets are now witnessing the effects of decreasing oil prices. Vancouver is always on international lists for the most unaffordable cities in the world, and given that most middle-class families are outpriced of detached homes, there is continued debate as to whether Vancouver is witnessing the death of the single-family home. The boom-and-bust economic patterns of late capitalism will continue to impact the home lives of Canadians, and in turn the connection between house and home will continue to be an uncertain one for many.

Readers will note that this collection does not cover the entire landscape of the Canadian experience of home. We have not, for example, addressed how technology has contributed to a mediated or virtual or networked experience of home and community. Nor have we offered a comparative regional approach. Clearly the Canadian experience of home is a vast one, and there are fundamental differences between living in rural Saskatchewan and living in Quebec City. We have only scratched the surface of this diversity. Like many other countries, Canada has mobile citizens who move between different countries that they call home. Some are mobile elites, and others, like the Florida "snowbirds," move to avoid the Canadian winter; and still others are immigrants who value a plurality of homes. None of these phenomena are unique to Canada, but in combination they carve out the narrative of Canadian home.

The sociology of home requires continued attention to the relationship between public and private. Whether we describe the division between the private and public acts as a kind of "threshold," as Shelley Ikebushi discusses in her piece in this volume, or whether we embrace other understandings of this division, it is clear that important debates are played out when we identify a space as home. As home is so intimately tied to family and processes of individualization, changing patterns in these social relationships will clearly play out in home as a threshold. While the home is defended as a space of intimacy, privacy, and autonomy, Krishan Kumar (2008) warns against the privileging of the home and sees the relationship between the public and private as a "fragile compact": "It is not the public that overwhelms the private but the private that threatens to overwhelm the public" (p. 336). He sees problems in a home-centred movement that takes over public spaces and that is not able to cope with novelty and strangeness. In this vein, all the world should not be a home. The question remains, however, about the balance between the private and the public, and how home is negotiated in this balance. Home speaks to the divisions between the individual and the community, leisure and work, and the strange and the familiar. For us, this reaffirms the importance of an interpretive approach that can speak to how home gives lived meaning to these divisions.

What will a progressive, engaged, and inclusive sociology of home look like? As we approach this question, we might think of the demands that we have come to place upon our homes. Home is a space on which we write our hopes and dreams, and a vehicle of strong normative and moral claims. We may discover that home could never be all these things for all people, and that it should play a more minor role in our lives. However, we may also discover that the reason that home occupies such a huge role in the minds and hearts of people is because there is no place like home. A politics of home may find itself engaged in some of the most important debates about the nature of the public good. In our minds, this is exactly where a sociology of home should be located.

REFERENCES

Duyvendak, J. W. (2011). *The Politics of Home: Belonging and Nostalgia in Western Europe and the United States*. New York: Palgrave Macmillan.

Huq, R. (2013). *Making Sense of Suburbia through Popular Culture*. London: Bloomsbury.

Kumar, K. (1997). Home: The promise and predicament of private life at the end of the twentieth century. In J. Weintraub and K. Kumar (Eds.), *Public and Private Thought and Practice: Perspectives on a Grand Dichotomy* (pp. 204–236). Chicago: University of Chicago Press.

Kumar, K. (2008). The portable home: The domestication of public space. *Sociological Theory*, 26(4), 324–343.

Kusenbach, M. & Paulsen, K. E. (2013). *Home: International Perspectives on Culture, Identity and Belonging*. New York and Frankfurt: Peter Lang.

Lauster, N. (2013). "Kinda just a home I guess": Towards theorizing the making of home in Vancouver. In M. Kusenback and K. E. Paulsen (Eds.), *Home: International Perspectives on Culture, Identity and Belonging* (pp. 15–194). New York and Frankfurt: Peter Lang.

Contributor Biographies

Gillian Anderson is a mother, feminist, cat lover, and professor in the Department of Sociology, Vancouver Island University (VIU), Nanaimo, British Columbia. She received her PhD from McMaster University, and her research and teaching interests include the sociology of home, families and gender relations, motherhood and motherwork, and women's organizing for social change. Her current work focuses on feminist activism in neoliberal times and gender, work, and mompreneurship.

Kate Butler's research examines how youth-in-care practise citizenship. She is interested in the intersections of vulnerability and resilience for young people on the margins. She received her PhD in sociology from the University of Victoria in 2013. She is currently employed as lead, Policy and Research at Maytree, a private foundation in Toronto, Ontario, that focuses on using a rights-based approach to poverty reduction.

Amber Gazso is an associate professor of sociology at York University. She received her PhD from the University of Alberta, and her main areas of research interest include citizenship, family and gender relations, research methods, poverty, and the welfare state. Much of her research explores family members' relationships with social policies of the neoliberal welfare state and has been published in such journals as the *Canadian Journal of Sociology, Citizenship Studies, Journal of Family Relations, Journal of Family Issues,* and the *International Journal of Sociology and Social Policy.*

Renaud Goyer is a PhD candidate in sociology at the Université de Montréal. His research interests include the sociology of housing, particularly tenants' experiences, social movements, community organizing, and the sociology of inequality. He currently teaches courses on qualitative methodology and the sociology of deviance at the Université de Montréal.

Tracey Harris is an assistant professor of sociology at Cape Breton University in Nova Scotia, Canada. She teaches courses in environmental sociology, consumption and consumerism, and critical animal studies. Her current research is on the Tiny House Movement.

Shelly Ikebuchi received her PhD in sociology from the University of British Columbia and currently teaches at Okanagan College in Kelowna, British Columbia. Her research takes a postcolonial/poststructural approach to examining the social, legal, and historical intersections of gender, race, and religion in a Canadian context. Her book, *From Slave Girls to Salvation: Gender, Race, and Victoria's Chinese Rescue Home, 1886–1923* (UBC Press, 2015), uncovers practices and discourses around moral regulation and the ways in which they play out in particularly racialized and gendered ways. Ikebuchi is especially interested in the convergence of race, gender, and religion with discourses of domesticity.

Christine Knott is a doctoral student in sociology at Memorial University. Her current research focus is investigating employment change over time in the seafood processing industry in rural communities in New Brunswick, including the more recent need for temporary foreign workers in this industry.

Kathy Mezei is professor emerita in the Humanities Department at Simon Fraser University, and life member, Clare Hall, Cambridge. Her research and writing focus on translation studies, domestic space, modern British women writers, and Canadian and Quebec literature. Recent publications include *Translation Effects: The Shaping of Modern Canadian Culture* (2014), edited with Sherry Simon and Luise von Flotow; *The Domestic Space Reader* (2012), co-edited with Chiara Briganti; and *Domestic Modernism, the Interwar Novel and E. H. Young* (2006), coauthored with Chiara Briganti. She was a founding editor of the feminist journal *Tessera*.

Joseph (Joey) Moore is an instructor of sociology at Douglas College in New Westminster, British Columbia, and makes home in an East Vancouver neighbourhood. He received his PhD from McMaster University, and his interests, both research and otherwise, include struggles over urban space, homemaking in public space, labour and environmental movements, cycling, and chickens.

Alan O'Connor teaches media studies at Trent University Durham in Oshawa, Ontario. His most recent book is *Punk Record Labels and the Struggle for Autonomy* (2008). He is currently writing a book on the underground arts scene in a small Ontario city.

Ondine Park's research considers the ways in which the ordinary and everyday are imagined, represented, and reproduced, as well as how and with what consequences their seeming obviousness and necessity are constituted, re-enforced, challenged, and reinterpreted. She is particularly interested in what liberatory possibilities can be discovered hidden within oppressive and alienating modes of ordinary life. Ondine's most recent book, *Ecologies of Affect: Placing Nostalgia, Desire, and Hope* (WLUP, 2011), co-edited with Rob Shields and Tonya Davidson, explores the flickering syncresis between affect and places. She is currently employed as a sessional sociology instructor at MacEwan University in Edmonton, Alberta.

John Phyne is a professor in the Department of Sociology at St. Francis Xavier University. From 1991 to 2010, he researched and published on the social, economic, and environmental dimensions of the global salmon aquaculture industry, with a focus on Ireland, Chile, and Norway. From 2009 to 2013, he researched (with Lynda Harling Stalker) the social impact of out-migration on the Strait Region of Nova Scotia. His current research with Christine Knott (funded by the Social Sciences and Humanities Research Council) deals with the last decades (1945 to 1966) of the "old city centre" of St. John's.

Jennifer L. Robinson, PhD, currently holds the positions of professor and program coordinator in the Bachelor of Community and Criminal Justice program at Conestoga College in Kitchener, Ontario. Her current research interests are broadly based around social justice, focusing on community development and social inclusion.

Laura Suski is a professor in the Departments of Sociology and Liberal Studies and in the Global Studies Program at Vancouver Island University, Nanaimo, British Columbia. She received her PhD from York University's Social and Political Thought Program. In addition to a research interest in the sociology of home, she researches the ethics of consumption, the sociology of emotion, and global humanitarianism.

Lisa-Jo K. van den Scott is an assistant professor at Memorial University of Newfoundland. She specializes in the sociology of walls and qualitative research, using symbolic interactionism, cultural studies, urban sociology, and science and technology studies as theoretical lenses. Her publications include articles in *The Journal of Contemporary Ethnography*, *Sociology Compass*, and *American Behavioral Scientist*. She has authored several book chapters ranging in topic from airplane travel in the Arctic, to ethics boards, to the methodological leverage of ethnography in science and technology studies. Her current work involves a book project on the Inuit experiences of housing.